THE NEW GROVE®
GOSPEL, BLUES AND JAZZ

The Composer Biography Series

THE NEW GROVE®

Gospel, Blues and Jazz

with
SPIRITUALS and RAGTIME

Paul Oliver
Max Harrison
William Bolcom

W. W. NORTON & COMPANY
NEW YORK   LONDON

Parts of this material were first published in
The New Grove Dictionary of Music and Musicians,®
edited by Stanley Sadie, 1980

The New Grove and *The New Grove Dictionary of Music and Musicians*
are registered trademarks of Macmillan Publishers Limited, London

First published in UK in paperback with additions 1986 by
PAPERMAC
a division of Macmillan Publishers Limited
London and Basingstoke

First published in UK in hardback with additions 1986 by
MACMILLAN LONDON LIMITED
4 Little Essex Street London WC2R 3LF
and Basingstoke

British Library Cataloguing in Publication Data

Oliver, Paul
    The New Grove gospel, blues and jazz.
    1. Gospel music—History   2. Jazz music—
    History   3. Blues (songs, etc.)—History
    and criticism.
    I. Title   II. Harrison, Max   III. Bolcom,
    William
    783.7'09   ML3187

        ISBN 0-333-40785-7 (hardback)
        ISBM 0-333-40784-9 (paperback)

First edition in book form with additions 1986 by
W. W. NORTON & COMPANY
500 Fifth Avenue, New York NY 10110

ISBN 0-393-01696-X

ISBN 0-393-30100-1 (PBK.)

Printed in Hong Kong

3 4 5 6 7 8 9 0

Contents

List of illustrations

Illustration acknowledgments

We are grateful to those listed below who supplied and/or gave permission to reproduce illustrative material: Paul Oliver Collection, Woodstock, Oxford (pll.1, 4–14; pll.5, 8, 10: photo Paul Oliver; pl.9: photo David Gahr, New York); John Edward Hasse Collection, Alexandria, Virginia (pll.2, 3); Arhoolie Records, El Cerrito, Calif./ photo Craig Street (pl.11); Jazz Music Books, Middleton-on-Sea, West Sussex (pll.15, 24); David Redfern Photography, London (photo William Gottlieb: pll.18, 19, 21; photo David Redfern: pll.25, 28, 29).

Cover: Jazz Music Books, Middleton-on-Sea, West Sussex

Music example acknowledgments

We are grateful to the following for permission to reproduce copyrighted material: Consolidated Music Publishers, New York (ex.5, from H. Traum: *The Blues Bag*, 1968); Doubleday and Co., Inc., New York, and J. de Spoelberch Associates, Inc., Belmont, Mass. (ex.6, from C. Sawyer: *The Arrival of B. B. King*, 1980); Blues Unlimited, London (ex.8, from *Blues Unlimited*, no.117 (1976), 22); Paul Oliver, Oxford (ex.9, from P. Oliver: *Screening the Blues: Aspects of the Blues Tradition*, 1968).

General and bibliographical abbreviations

AACM	Association for the Advancement of Creative Musicians
ABC	American Broadcasting Company
b	born
c	circa [about]
d	died
diss.	dissertation
EM	*Ethnomusicology*
Grove 5	*Grove's Dictionary of Music and Musicians* [5th edn., ed. E. Blom]
JEMF Quarterly	*J[ohn] E[dwards] M[emorial] F[oundation] Quarterly*
JIFMC	*Journal of the International Folk Music Council*
L. of C.	Library of Congress [recording label]
MELUS	*Journal of the Society for the Study of the Multi-Ethnic Literature of the United States*
MJQ	Modern Jazz Quartet
n	note
n.d.	no date (of publication)
ODJB	Original Dixieland Jazz Band
orig.	original(ly)
PRMA	*Proceedings of the Royal Musical Association*
pubd	published
R	(photographically) reprinted
repr.	reprinted
suppl.	supplement
trans.	translation, translated by
transcr.	transcribed by
U.	University

Discographical abbreviations

Details are given for selected recordings of works cited as representative of a performer's or composer's output. Original issues are cited in preference to reissues or collections of works. Citations normally consist of the following information: the title of the work/song, and, in parentheses, the name of the record label, country of issue, issue number and date of recording. The record label is given in full (with the exception of historical recordings issued by the Library of Congress on the label Archive of American Folk Song – AAFS – or Archive of Folk Song – AFS), but abbreviations that are commonly used in discographies to indicate the country of issue have been adopted here (they are listed below). The names of a number of record labels consist of a series of capital letters; although these may be abbreviated forms of company names they are taken to constitute the full names of the labels concerned.

Recordings were issued in the USA unless otherwise stated.

Ar	Argentina	G	Germany
Cz	Czechoslovakia	H	The Netherlands
D	Denmark	I	Italy
E	United Kingdom	J	Japan
Eu	Europe	Sd	Sweden
F	France		

A note on the capitalization of song titles

Generally, song titles that are derived from the text (normally the incipit) of a song are set with lower-case initials (except for proper nouns), and true titles that are not so derived are set with upper-case initials.

Publishers' note

This book is one of a series of volumes derived from *The New Grove Dictionary of Music and Musicians* (1980). Much of the material it contains was initially written for that work; this has now been substantially revised and supplemented. The new material contains additional information on individual artists, while the authors have also recast several sections to make the material suitable for publication as a separate book.

Introduction

A vast literature on jazz has accumulated since the second decade of this century, and, in the last 25 years, on blues. Ragtime attracted attention during the last two decades, and black American religious music, somewhat neglected since the spate of books on spirituals in the 1920s, has regained attention. Each of these types of music has undegone its own, far-reaching processes of change and development. The substantial body of literature has risen from the need to explore both new and old modes of expression and to relate them; it is a feature of these types of music that innovation does not cancel out earlier practice and many styles co-exist. Thus the patterns of activity tend to become more complex.

It was customary to regard spirituals, blues and ragtime as tributaries of jazz; this view, taken by earlier writers, has been influential. Swing, long recognized as a vital phase in the growth of jazz resources, was formerly considered to be a commercialized dilution of 'real' jazz. Similarly bop, a decade later (in the 1940s), was initially thought to be the negation of all that jazz stood for, whereas it has since become clear that it was simply another phase in its development. Again, the 'coon' songs of the ragtime era and the ragtime song genre itself have only recently been admitted to study on the same level as ragtime piano solos; and it seems likely that a reappraisal of rhythm-and-blues forms, including the big band blues groups of the 1950s, may change the emphases of future blues histories. Similarly, the significance of the early jubilee ensembles of the Reconstruction period has been re-examined, their

concert approach to spirituals being seen not as a dilution of the idiom but their role acknowledged as important catalysts in the formation of the harmonizing
groups in the development of gospel music.

These shifting perceptions of musical links and iden-
tities within the broad spectrum of blues, jazz and
related music raise problems of definition and limitation,
especially in such a book as this, which for the first time
in many years brings them together in a single volume.
Is what is usually called 'European free music', a col-
lectively improvised form that has developed since the
1960s and that took jazz as its starting-point, still to be
considered part of jazz? Are the gospel quartets of the
white churches to be considered along with those of the
black? If rhythm-and-blues is an aspect of blues, do the
jump bands and vocal groups that were part of it have a
place in the discussion? Is rock-and-roll a part of
rhythm-and-blues, which profoundly influenced it? –
and, if so, is white country rock also to be included?

This book has been shaped by consideration of these
and many other fundamental questions affecting inclu-
sion and exclusion, reflecting the changing status of jazz
and blues within music as a whole. It attempts to clarify
a complicated, sometimes confusing scene, to demonstrate relationships between genres while indicating the
character of each and identifying the styles and the work
of the outstanding artists that fall within them. In keeping with the policy of *The New Grove*, the authors have
emphasized factual data. However, whereas in that large
work separate entries were made for individual artists
and many sub-genres, in the present volume they are
subsumed within the main subject areas. This is part of an
extensive revision and expansion of these texts for their
new context. Because much of their history lies within

the era of recording, most points are illustrated by citations of recorded examples (added as notes in Chapter
Two because, in ragtime, alone of the types of music
discussed, recordings are less important as sources than
sheet music). As reissues have a limited period of availability, original record labels, catalogue numbers and
years of recording are given for identification.

Recordings are, indeed, a prime resource for the study
and enjoyment of these genres. It has to be admitted
that their limitations of length, sound-quality and
coverage, particularly in the years before tape recording
and the long-playing disc, restrict knowledge and
understanding. Thus black improvising string bands
were widely distributed in the South but only a couple
were recorded. Many of the earliest pioneers of jazz in
New Orleans were also missed. Yet a vast quantity of
music was recorded. Recordings are, after all, the only
ways of preserving music characterized by sponteneity
and improvisation.

The aim of this volume is to focus on the main
currents of these idioms, indicating the uncertainty of
the boundaries between them. To assist readers in
penetrating more deeply into the subject, not least with
regard to the numerous artists who could not be
mentioned separately, substantial bibliographies are
included.

Help from Vic Bellery, Charles Fox and Anthony
Wood in revising the jazz section is gratefully acknowledged.

Paul Oliver, Max Harrison
May 1986

CHAPTER ONE

Spirituals

I Origins

Of all the bodies of folksong that have survived in
America to the present century spirituals are
probably the most extensive; they are certainly, in
one form or another, the best known. As 'negro
spirituals' they have entered church and concert
hall, have influenced composers from Dvořák to
Virgil Thomson and have been sung in schools and
by choirs throughout the English-speaking world.
Yet, in spite of their widespread popularity through
publication and performance, their origins are
obscure and the ways in which they were first sung
are probably unknown. Even the term 'spirituals' was
not widely used by Blacks (though it was common
in the Sea Islands), the word 'Anthems' being much
more widespread and surviving to the 1950s in rural
areas.

St Paul the Apostle's advice to the Colossian church
to 'let the word of Christ dwell in you richly in all
wisdom; teaching and admonishing one another in
psalms and hymns and spiritual songs, singing with
grace in your hearts to the Lord' appeared to differ-
entiate between three forms of religious song. Apart
from psalms and hymns, which were published, there
were spiritual songs which were outside traditional

church usage. Spiritual songs were common to Whites and Blacks and were one outcome of the Great Awakening, the religious revival movement that swept through the colonies in the early 18th century. John and Charles Wesley, the founders of Methodism, visited Georgia in the 1730s. In the next decade, under the inspiration of such preachers as the English evangelist George Whitefield and the immensely talented Jonathan Edwards, the revival movement spread with great rapidity.

After the War of Independence the teachings of the Methodist churches and of the Separatist Baptists, in modified form, were used for the instruction of slaves in the southern Plantation states. Slaves brought from Africa were expected both to learn to speak English and to adopt the professed religion of their owners. Biblical authority was quoted to endorse slavery and instil obedience. Slaves embraced the new religion, many believing that their sufferings would be rewarded in the next life 'in heaven above'. The recollections of former slaves indicate that few plantations had separate churches for Blacks, but many had segregated sections for slaves within white churches. Thus they learnt many of the hymns and spiritual songs of the Whites, in particular those of the English composer Isaac Watts (1674–1748) whose new hymns were to be popular with Blacks for well over two centuries.

In some parts of the south there was considerable opposition to slaves being given any kind of religious instruction or permission to worship. In many instances services were conducted in secret at clandestine bush gatherings. However, there is much evidence that slaves became committed to Christianity with a degree of involvement that is now difficult to comprehend. In 1937 there were still over 100,000 ex-slaves living in the USA; interviews with 2000 of them, conducted under the auspices of the Works Project (Progress) Administration Writers' Program, were eventually published, together with many others. Though they are not very informative on spirituals as such, they clarify attitudes to religious song and worship by both Whites and Blacks before Emancipation. With the learning of English, biblical teaching and participation in church services, black slaves learnt much of the formal structure of white hymnody and were able to use the imagery and concepts expressed in sermons. The non-conformist belief in the importance of being 'called' to preach was shared by many local and illiterate preachers on plantations, and some black preachers gained considerable renown even among white congregations.

The cycles of the weekly sabbath, the festivals of the church year and those marking the phases of the Christian life – baptisms, weddings and funerals especially – broke up the monotony of work but the slave's essential function was to provide labour for the cotton, rice and other southern industries. The majority of slaves working under the overseer's lash were employed in cultivation that required unified effort; singing work songs provided a means of coordinating activities. Often taking a leader-and-chorus form, sometimes overlapping anti-phonally, many of these songs were clearly related in form and function to traditional African work songs:

> Dere's no rain to wet you,
>   O' yes, I want to go home,
> Dere's no sun to burn you,
>   O' yes, I want to go home,
> Dere's no whips a-crackin'
>   O' yes, I want to go home.

Slaves in the fields had every opportunity to invent new songs and devise new tunes. A great many spirituals appear to have been created in this way and sung with inflections, extended syllables and quarter-tones that were the wonder and despair of the few people who tried to notate them. Although Afro-American singing, whether in fields or churches, was remarked on by many writers in the 18th and early 19th centuries, few commented on the songs in detail. The English actress Fanny Kemble, wife of a slave-owner, noted in her diary in 1839 'how they all sing in unison, having never, it appears, attempted or heard anything like part-singing' (p.159). She described how at a funeral 'the whole congregation uplifted their voices in a hymn, the first high wailing notes of which – sung all in unison ... sent a thrill through my nerves' (p.140). She did not, however, note the words she heard. In the early 1860s Colonel Thomas Wentworth Higginson, in command of a black regiment, wrote down the texts of songs he heard his men sing. Some of these were later included in his published memoirs (1870), for example (p.209):

> I know moon-rise, I know star-rise,
>   Lay dis body down.
> I walk in de moonlight, I walk in de starlight,
>   To lay dis body down.
> I'll walk in de graveyard, I'll walk through de graveyard,
>   To lay dis body down.
> I'll lie in de grave and stretch out my arms,
>   Lay dis body down.

This form was typical of many spirituals: an alternating line and refrain which permitted endless extemporization. To the soldiers such songs, Higginson wrote, were 'more than a source of relaxation; they were a stimulus to courage and a tie to heaven' (p.221). In 1867, William Francis Allen, Charles Pickard Ware and Lucy McKim Garrison published their *Slave Songs of the United States*, a collection that included some of the best-known and still-surviving spirituals, among them *Old ship of Zion, Lay this body down, Michael, row the boat ashore* and *We will march through the valley*, as well as many lesser-known songs. The authors confirmed the absence of part-singing but added, 'yet no two appear to be singing the same thing'. The leader, who would frequently improvise, was generally supported by 'basers' who provided a vocal background and interpolations. The singing they heard abounded in 'slides from one note to another, and turns and cadences not in articulated notes'. In presenting their collection the authors regretted their inability to convey in notation 'the odd turns made in the throat, and the curious rhythmic effect produced by single voices chiming in at different irregular intervals ... the best that we can do ... with paper and types ... will convey but a faint shadow of the original'.

II African and European sources

Among early commentators on black spirituals there was much speculation on possible African elements in the songs. Allen and others considered them 'to have become imbued with the mode and spirit of European music – often, nevertheless, retaining a distinct tinge of their native Africa' (1867). Wallaschek, who examined a number of transcribed examples, asserted in *Primitive Music* (1893) that the songs had no African elements; but he had never been in the USA and had never heard black spirituals sung by Blacks. After analysing some 500 collected spirituals, H. E. Krehbiel contended that they were essentially Afro-American in character and origin, but Erich von Hornbostel was the first scholar to hear the music in both Africa and America. In 1926 he made an important distinction between transcriptions of spirituals and their performance by American Blacks: 'In short, the American Negro songs are European in style and pattern, they are American folk songs as far as they have originated amidst American folk and culture, and they are African when sung by Negroes'. Whatever view musicologists hold in this debate, few have questioned the African nature of the plantation 'walk-around' or 'ring-shout', a shuffling circular dance to chanting and hand-clapping which accompanied the more joyous jubilees (see p.11). Often viewed with alarm by southern Whites, such ring-shouts were still being performed in the 1930s.

Their ecstatic and trance-inducing nature had evident links with African custom. Other elements that might be evidence of African retention in this type of spiritual, such as improvised antiphonal singing, shouting, chanting, stamping and the involuntary spasms of 'possessed' members of the congregations, have also been observed in fundamentalist white churches and may be related to the highly emotional forms of religious expression developed in the Great Awakening.

The large number of hymns published by Isaac Watts and others during this period were learnt by the old Scottish custom of 'lining out': the singing of a line by a precentor and its repetition by the congregation. The 1820 edition of Watts's hymns had wide circulation throughout the southern USA and 'Dr Watts songs' were popular among Blacks. The closeness of lining out to the traditional African work song form of leader-and-chorus antiphonal singing undoubtedly contributed to the popularity of this style. And many of the hymn texts were used, in whole or in part, as the basis for spirituals.

Doubts have been raised about the origin of the black spiritual as a genre. Lovell (1972) contended, as had Krehbiel, that spirituals were the innovations of black slaves, but Newman White (1928), Guy B. Johnson (1930), and George Pullen Jackson (in several publications) produced evidence that supported the view that a common source for both the black and white spiritual lay in camp meetings and white southern rural churches. Jackson, in particular,

Ex.1

(a) *Roll Jordan*, white camp-meeting spiritual (Jackson, 1933/*R*1964)

He comes, he comes, The Judge se – vere,
The sev – enth trum – pet speaks him near,

Roll Jor-dan roll; I want to go to
Roll Jor-dan roll.

heav'n, I do; Hal – le – lu – jah, Lord; We'll

praise the Lord in heav'n a – bove, Roll Jor-dan roll.

(b) *Roll Jordan*, black spiritual; transcr. G. P. Jackson

O brothers, you ought t'ave been there, Yes, my— Lord, A-

- sit-ting in the king-dom To hear Jor-dan roll.

Roll Jor-dan roll, roll Jor-dan roll, I want to go to

hea-ven when I die To hear Jor – dan roll.

argued for white origins, suggesting that many black spirituals were variants of songs published earlier in white tunebooks, especially those in the shape-note tradition. Ex.1*a* and *b* shows the same spiritual, *Roll Jordan*, first as a white camp-meeting song, and second as transcribed from black singing. But priority in publication is hardly proof of origin where folk music is concerned, especially when one body of the music in question is that of a group both obliged to be illiterate and denied access to publication. It seems certain that there was considerable mutual exchange between black and white traditions. As early as 1819, J. F. Watson warned his white readership against the 'Methodist error' of imitating the camp-meeting music of Blacks, who for hours sang 'short scraps of disjointed affirmations, pledges, or prayers . . . with repetition choruses. These are all sung in the merry chorus-manner of the southern harvest-field, or husking-frolic method, of the slave blacks'. Whites heard slaves singing at corn-huskings, candy pulls and log-rollings on the plantations; some heard them on the levees, on riverboats and in work gangs. Though many of the songs were secular and some have survived in fragments, it is clear that work songs were frequently of a religious nature and were, in effect, spirituals.

Many spirituals were suffused with melancholy and were frequently termed 'sorrow songs'. Intensely moving slow spirituals such as *Sometimes I feel like a motherless child, He never said a mumblin' word, Were you there when they crucified my Lord?* or *Nobody knows the trouble I've had* (ex.2) reveal the singers'

9

Ex.2 *Nobody knows the trouble I've had* (Allen, Ware and McKim
    Garrison 1867/*R*1971)

2 I pick de berry and I suck de juice,
       O yes Lord!
     Just as sweet as de honey in de comb,
       O yes Lord!

3 Sometimes I'm up, sometimes I'm down,
       O yes Lord!
     Sometimes I'm almost on de groun',
       O yes Lord!

own trials and identification with the suffering of Jesus Christ. The theme of death ran through many spirituals; some, like *Toll the bell, angel, I jus' got over*, suggest a spirit that has already left this earth. Others, however, were quick, highly rhythmic and often syncopated, performed in a call-and-response manner, and were settings of positive, and optimistic texts. Among them are *Didn't my Lord deliver Daniel?*, *I an' Satan had a race*, *Blow your trumpet, Gabriel*, *Git on board, chillun* and *Little David, play on your harp* (ex.3). On the day of atonement the Lord told Moses 'ye shall . . . proclaim liberty throughout the land unto all the inhabitants thereof; it shall be a jubilee unto you; and ye shall return every man unto his possession, and ye shall return every man unto his family' (*Leviticus* XXV.10). For the slaves, the year of jubilee was to be the year of freedom, and the songs that rejoiced in the prospect came to be called jubilees, though when the term was first used is unknown.

Some writers (e.g. Fisher, 1953) maintain that virtually all spirituals were codified songs of protest. The runaway ex-slave and black leader Frederick Douglass (c1817–95) wrote of singing spirituals when a slave: 'A keen observer might have detected in our

11

Ex.3 *Little David, play on your harp* (Fenner, rev. 4/1909)

repeated singing of "O Canaan, sweet Canaan, I am bound for the land of Canaan" something more than a hope of reaching heaven. We meant to reach the *North* and the North was our Canaan' (p.157). Such spirituals as *Steal away, Didn't my Lord deliver Daniel?* and *Children, we all shall be free* must have been seen as incitements to escape from bondage, while *We'll stand the storm* and *We shall walk through the valley in peace* were reassuring to faltering spirits. Often the imagery of spirituals included vivid juxtapositions of phrases and literal interpretations of metaphoric biblical texts. The *Revelation of St John* provided an important source of images for songs. But to quote spirituals out of context tends to emphasize their naivety; it is while they are being sung that their beauty and freshness are most apparent.

In their performance, black spirituals differed from those of Whites in a number of ways. Significant was the use of microtonally flattened notes. Sometimes identified as lowered thirds, fifths and sevenths, they were frequently arrived at by progressive shading, particularly in the singing of the extended syllables of 'long-metre' spirituals. Syncopation was commonly introduced by individuals or small groups of singers within a congregation who shifted accents by anticipation or delay of the expected note. Counter-rhythms were marked by hand-clapping and, in those denominations that permitted it, by 'holy dancing' without crossing the feet. Frequently members of the congregations 'got happy', entering an ecstatic, trance-like state induced by the singing and rhythms of faster spirituals, some also 'speaking with tongues' or uttering meaningless syllables.

Structurally, black spirituals frequently start with the chorus preceding the first verse; others alternate

13

refrain lines sung by the whole congregation. Responsorial singing was common, either in reply to a line or stanza sung by the leader, or by collective singing of the second half of a line that was opened solo. Qualities of vocal timbre, including the use of the rasp and shrill falsettos, enriched the sound, and the shouts and interpolated cries of 'Glory!' and other words or phrases of encouragement or affirmation made the spiritual in performance, whether 'sorrow song' or 'jubilee', far more varied than some collections suggest.

III Early collections and popularization

The publication of collections in the 1860s increased interest in black spirituals. But they were brought to an international audience through the appearances from 1871 of the Jubilee Singers from Fisk University, Nashville, Tennessee. The group's purpose was to raise funds for the university, which was intended for black students, but they were unsuccessful until they included a number of spirituals in their programmes. Thereafter they performed concert arrangements of spirituals both in the USA and in Europe, and awakened an abiding interest in this form. The Jubilee Singers and later the Hampton Singers from the Hampton Institute in Virginia were the inspiration for Frederick J. Work, R. Nathaniel Dett, T. P. Fenner and Clarence Cameron White (who all conducted both groups) to arrange and publish their songs.

Many collectors were aware that spirituals in their pre-war form were already disappearing. 'One reason

14

for publishing this slave music is that it is rapidly passing away', Thomas Fenner wrote in 1874, introducing a collection of Hampton Institute songs. 'The freedmen have an unfortunate inclination to despise it as a vestige of slavery; those who learned it in the old time, when it was the natural out-pouring of their sorrows and longings, are dying off.' Yet, after 35 years, in a later edition, Robert Moton noted that 'many more melodies, striking and beautiful, have been brought in by students from various parts of the South. The field seems inexhaustible'.

Early collections indicate that spirituals were sung in minor keys, or slaves sang in major scales but used the shading or flattening of certain notes, especially sevenths, which added to the melancholy of the 'sorrow songs'. However, as compilers of such collections admitted, the notation could not convey accurately the styles of spiritual singing before the Civil War.

From the 1870s a number of troupes and stage productions used plantation scenes with black singers acting as slaves and singing spirituals. These helped bring spirituals to a wide public but they fixed stereotypes of the genre and its origin. From a folk form spirituals rapidly became a part of the repertory of concert artists, cathedral choirs and even symphony orchestras. Many of the performers and composers who popularized them in concerts all over the world were black, among them Roland Hayes (1887–1976), Paul Robeson (1898–1976), William Grant Still (1895–1978) and James Weldon Johnson (1871–1938).

Publication ensured lasting respect for spirituals and conservation of their words and melodies, but transcription for voice and piano, orchestral arrangements and the use of art-music singing techniques destroyed the spontaneity and unpredictable quality of the spiritual as a folk form.

IV Spirituals on record

Although the popularity of spirituals on the concert platform increased during the 20th century, their appeal had already waned in black churches. By the late 19th century, gospel song began to replace the spiritual. The popular jubilee groups, mainly quartets, which recorded extensively in the 1920s and 1930s often included spirituals among their songs. Their approach was already that of the gospel quartet, and though there are detectable differences between earlier and later recordings, their relatively sophisticated arrangements removed spiritual singing from the traditional forms. Surviving examples of earlier styles were to be found in the recordings of preachers and their congregations, of which many hundreds were issued, principally in the late 1920s. Among them are many examples of 'lining out', such as Reverend E. D. Campbell's *Come let us eat together* (Victor 35824, 1927) or *I heard the voice of Jesus say* on Reverend P. E. Edmunds's *There's a hole in the wall* (Paramount 12876, 1929). 'Long-metre' singing of a 'Dr Watts song' is to be heard on Reverend J. C. Burnett's *Amazing Grace* (Decca 7494, 1938), while alternating responses to a chanted vocal is well represented on Reverend Gipson's *John done saw that holy number*

(Paramount 12555, 1927). An excellent example of overlapping singing against syncopated hand-clapping is to be found in a version of *Trouble don't last always* on Reverend J. M. Milton's Atlanta recording with his congregation, *A Four Day Ramble* (Columbia 14501, 1929).

The adoption of the jubilee songs by the sanctified churches is vigorously demonstrated in the singing of *All God's chillen got wings* on Reverend F. W. McGee's *The Holy City* (Victor 21205, 1927). Later recordings by preachers and congregations were frequently of this kind. Mention should also be made of black 'sacred harp' singing from shape-note books. Though seldom recorded, early examples include *Rejoicing on the way* by the Fa Sol La Singers, recorded in Atlanta (Columbia 14656, 1931), and *Bells of Love*, sung virtually as a round, by the Middle Georgia Singing Convention No.1 (Okeh 8883, 1930).

Recordings of preachers and their congregations were relatively few after 1930, and when they resumed, in the 1950s, gospel songs substantially replaced spirituals. However, older forms of the spiritual survived in the remoter backwaters of black culture and particularly in the more conservative churches of the South. Many hundreds of recordings of these rural spirituals were made between 1933 and 1942 for the Archive of Folksong of the Library of Congress. By far the most important pockets for conservation of the early spiritual and the ring-shout were in the Sea Islands of Georgia and South Carolina, as demonstrated by Lydia Parrish in 1942.

17

Recordings made 20 years later from this region and from elsewhere in the South such as Georgia and Alabama emphasize the persistence of the tradition in isolated communities unassailed by outside influences. In *Run old Jeremiah* recorded by J. W. Brown and A. Coleman, L. of C. AFS L3, 1934; correct title, *Good Lord*), a ring-shout from Jennings, Alabama, there is a train-like accompaniment of stamping feet. Another shout, *Eli you can't stand*, was performed with hand-clapping accompaniment to chanted lead-singing by Willis Proctor and others on St Simon's Islands (Prestige International 25002, 1959). Two singers who recorded spirituals extensively for the Library of Congress during the 1930s and early 1940s were Vera Hall and Dock Reed. Field recordings of these two a decade later included two examples of the simplest form of additive spiritual, *Dead and gone* and *Free at last* (recorded 1950, reissued on Folkways FE 4418, 1960), the latter dating from the mid-1860s. The complexity of the early shouting spirituals is suggested in *Rock chair, tol' you to rock* (*Rock Chariot*, 1950), performed by Rich Amerson, Earthy Ann Coleman and Price Coleman at Livingston, Alabama, which includes a counter-chant sung against the main theme (Folkways FE4418, 1960).

Re-creations of the Sea Islands spiritual songs with drum, fife and banjo accompaniment were made by Bessie Jones and a mixed group, including fine versions of *Before this time another year* and *Beulah Land* (Prestige International 25001, 1959). An outstanding example of the early form with unison singing and moaning is *Father I stretch my hands to thee* (Folkways 2656, 1956), performed by Jake Field, Eastman Brand and Arthur Holifield. This is one of the many recordings that show the relationship between black spirituals and white hymns, since the text is by Charles Wesley (1707–88). Several spirituals with texts by Watts were sung by John and Lovie Griffin of Perry County, Alabama, including *When I can read my title clear* (Folkways 2656, 1956).

Early recordings were made of the Fisk Jubilee Singers, such as *Roll Jordan roll* (recorded c1913, reissued on RBF5, 1962), showing the concert-style spiritual. Some of the better-known of these arrangements, including those published by the Fisk Jubilee Singers themselves in 1872, have remained favourites in black churches where gospel song has otherwise replaced the older traditions. Versions of concert spirituals also appear among recordings by many leading gospel singers and groups.

Thus, although the spiritual as a folk form has declined in popularity among Blacks because of its association with slavery, extensive collecting, recording and scholarly study have ensured that the tradition will not be lost even though knowledge of how spirituals were originally sung is limited.

V **Bibliography**

LITERATURE

F. A. Kemble: *Journal of a Residence on a Georgian Plantation in 1838–1839* (New York and London, 1863, rev. 1961)

T. W. Higginson: 'Negro Spirituals', *Army Life in a Black Regiment* (Boston, 1870), 197ff

J. B. T. Marsh: *The Story of the Jubilee Singers with their Songs* (London, 1876)

F. Douglass: *Life and Times of Frederick Douglass* (Hartford, Conn., 1882), 157

R. Wallaschek: *Primitive Music* (London, 1893)

H. E. Krehbiel: *Afro-American Folksongs: a Study in Racial and National Music* (New York and London, 1914)

N. I. White: *American Negro Folk-songs* (Cambridge, Mass., 1928)

G. B. Johnson: *Folk Culture on St. Helena Island, South Carolina* (Chapel Hill, North Carolina, 1930), 117f

G. P. Jackson: 'Tunes of the White Man's Spirituals Preserved in the Negro's Religious Songs', 'White Man's and Negro's Spiritual Texts Compared', *White Spirituals in the Southern Uplands* (Chapel Hill, North Carolina, 1933/*R*1964), 242–302

M. J. Herskovits: 'The Contemporary Scene: Africanisms in Religious Life', *The Myth of the Negro Past* (New York and London, 1941), 207–60

M. M. Fisher: *Negro Slave Songs in the United States* (Ithaca, NY, 1953)

G. P. Jackson: 'Spirituals', *Grove 5*

F. Ramsey jr: 'Music from the South, vi–vii: Elder Songsters', Folkways FP 2655–6 [disc notes]

A. Lomax: 'Georgia Sea Islands', INT 25001–2 [disc notes]

W. H. Tallmadge: 'Dr. Watts and Mahalia Jackson: the Development, Decline and Survival of a Folk Style in America', *EM*, v (1961), 95

H. Courlander: 'Anthems and Spirituals as Oral Literature', *Negro Folk Music, U.S.A.* (New York and London, 1963), 35–79

J. C. Downey: *The Music of American Revivalism, 1740–1800* (diss., Tulane U., New Orleans, 1968)

P. Oliver: 'Gospel Songs and Spirituals', *Jazz on Record*, ed. A. McCarthy and others (London, 1968), 325ff

J. Lovell jr: *Black Song: the Forge and the Flame* (New York, 1972)

Bibliography

G. P. Rawick: *The American Slave* (Westport, Conn., 1972–8)

E. Southern: 'An origin for the Negro spiritual', *Black Scholar*, iii (1972), 8

D. D. Bruce jr: *And They All Sang Hallelujah: Plain-folk Camp-meeting Religion 1800–1845* (Knoxville, Tenn., 1974)

P. K. Maultsby: *Afro-American Religious Music: 1619–1861* (diss., U. of Wisconsin, 1974)

I. V. Jackson-Brown: 'Afro-American Sacred Song in the Nineteenth Century: a Neglected Source', *Black Perspective in Music*, iv (1976), 22

P. K. Maultsby: 'Black Spirituals', *Black Perspective in Music*, iv (1976), 54

D. Epstein: *Sinful Tunes and Spirituals* (Urbana, 1977)

A. J. Raboteau: *Slave Religion* (New York, 1978)

J. W. Blassingame: *The Slave Community* (New York, 2/1979)

W. Tallmadge: 'The Black in Jackson's White Spirituals', *Black Perspective in Music*, ix (1981), 139

——: 'Jubilee to Gospel: Commercially recorded Black Religious Music 1921–1953', JEMF–108 (1981) [disc notes]

D. Epstein: 'A White Origin for the Black Spiritual? An Invalid Theory and how it Grew', *American Music*, i (1983), 53

E. Southern: *The Music of Black Americans* (New York, 2/1983)

P. Oliver: *Songsters and Saints: Vocal Traditions on Race Records* (London and New York, 1984)

COLLECTIONS

S. Occom: *A Choice Collection of Hymns and Spiritual Songs Intended for the Sincere Christians of all Denominations* (New London, Conn., 1774)

J. Smith: *Divine Hymns or Spiritual Songs for the Use of Religious Assemblies and Private Christians* (Norwich, Conn., 2/1794, 9/1799)

B. F. White and E. J. King: *The Sacred Harp* (Philadelphia, 1847)

W. F. Allen, C. P. Ware and L. McKim Garrison: *Slave Songs of the United States* (New York, 1867/R1971)

T. F. Seward: *Jubilee Songs by the Jubilee Singers of Fisk University* (Nashville, 1872)

T. P. Fenner: *Cabin and Plantantion Songs of the Negro* (Hampton, Virginia, 1874, rev. 4/1909 by R. R. Moton as *Religious Folk Songs of the Negro*)

21

T. F. Seward and G. L. White: *Jubilee Songs* (New York, 1884)

J. W. and J. R. Johnson: *The Book of American Negro Spirituals* (New York and London, 1925–7)

H. W. Odum and G. B. Johnson: *The Negro and his Songs* (Chapel Hill, North Carolina, 1925)

D. Scarborough: *On the Trail of Negro Folk Songs* (Cambridge, Mass., 1925)

R. N. Dett: *The Dett Collection of Negro Spirituals* (Chicago, 1936)

G. P. Jackson: *Down East Spirituals, and Others* (New York, 1939)

J. W. Work: *American Negro Songs* (New York, 1940)

L. A. Parrish: *Slave Songs of the Georgia Sea Islands* (New York, 1942)

G. P. Jackson: *White and Negro Spirituals* (New York, 1943)

CHAPTER TWO

Ragtime

I Origins and characteristics

The term is probably of black origin. In its broadest
sense, 'ragtime' is the effect generated by an internally
syncopated melodic line pitted against a rhythmically
straightforward bass. This phenomenon can, of
course, be found in music before the ragtime craze,
as its early detractors were quick to point out. But
ragtime's importance lies less in what it originated
than in what it emphasized: the constant collision
between internal melodic and underlying rhythms was
its raison d'être, not just a stylistic feature. Ragtime,
especially in the so-called 'Missouri style' (particularly
the music of Scott Joplin, James Scott and Joseph
Lamb), is primarily a written style, whereas jazz is
primarily improvised; even though rag tunes were
often used in jazz improvisations it is inaccurate to
call ragtime an early form of jazz. Such figures as
Jelly Roll Morton bridge the two, and in the 1920s
ragtime led directly to popular song (Irving Berlin's
'rag songs' are not true ragtime). While 'ragtime' may
be a vague term, 'rag' is not, as that dance form
became as definite as (and quite similar to) that of a
Sousa march. Composers like Louis Moreau Gottschalk, Dan Emmett and Stephen Foster may have
evoked ragtime, but they did not write rags; yet the

23

fact that Gottschalk approached the style as early as 1847 (*La bamboula*) indicates an aural history of ragtime reaching back perhaps to a time when black slaves fused European harmony with African rhythm.

Ragtime's huge popularity was abetted by its wide dissemination in print (Scott Joplin's *Maple Leaf Rag*[1] of 1899 quickly sold a million copies). In 1897 – the year of the first published piano rag (*Mississippi Rag*,[2] by the white bandmaster William H. Krell) – print was still the chief mass medium for music, and the piano was the instrument of musically literate amateurs; thus, although ragtime banjo players (perhaps the style's originators), ad hoc ragtime bands (made up perhaps of flute, cornet, violin, piano and drums) and ragtime singers like Ben Harney abounded, the style spread – in the white community, at least – mainly on living-room pianos, where simplified sheet music guided the amateur pianist through its rhythmic intricacies. Ragtime's real spawning-ground was undoubtedly the parlours of bordellos, partly because its foremost practitioners, the predominantly black 'jig-pianists', could not find work elsewhere. Most of the great rag pianists and composers – Scott Joplin, Eubie Blake, Jelly Roll Morton – started there, and hence the style was frowned on by the more prudish American music critics. It is surprising that music springing from such a 'disreputable' source (and composed mainly by Blacks) should have achieved print at all in those times, but it did, owing to immense popular demand, and thus the publication of *Mississippi Rag* marked the beginning of a rapid worldwide dissemination of the style.

24

Krell's rag is rather loosely constructed compared with later examples; however, with Harney's early rag songs (*You've been a good old wagon but you've done broke down*, 1895;[3] *Mr Johnson turn me loose*, 1896[4]) it shares the repeated 16-bar period, or 'strain', that was to endure throughout ragtime's hegemony. This was usually divided into four clear phrases with standard cadences, betraying the rag's debt to 'set dances', quadrilles and marches ('Tempo di marcia' is a common Joplin heading). With Joplin's 1899 *Maple Leaf Rag* the form was codified into four strains, sometimes with a four-bar introduction and similar transitions. Common strain patterns were *AAB BACCDD* (the *Maple Leaf Rag* form), *AABBCCDD* and *AABBCCA*. As in a march, the trio or *C* strain was often in the subdominant; few rags were in the minor mode, and those that were often finished their strains in the relative major. This unremarkable format was to house a fusion of black American folk melody with fairly complex syncopation, and its simplicity may have helped make these 'innovations' accessible to a wide public. Many rag melodies are strongly pentatonic, and characteristic rhythmic cells, rarely found in white imitations of the form, abound in black ragtime (see ex.4). Ragtime waltzes do exist, especially in Joplin, but until about 1915 most rags were written in 2/4, and afterwards in common or cut time.

The special magic of the rag form, then, lies in the richness of imagination that can be poured into such an inflexible mould, and with its best composers the rag enjoys a sonnet-like tension between form and

Ex.4 Joplin: *Maple Leaf Rag*

material. With lesser musicians, 'rags' meant the mere stringing-together of catchy tunes; these commercial 'junk rags' comprised the bulk of the early mechanically cut player-piano rolls. At first they were made, sometimes at home (with a small machine resembling a breadbox) but usually by piano-roll manufacturing companies, by direct transference from printed sheet music without benefit of a player; later pianists recorded with a device that left markings on a roll which were then 'translated' and cut. In both types an 'editor' usually added octave doublings and counter-melodies to the original, which resulted in a thick quasi-orchestral texture. 'Penny arcades' and the like sported mechanical pianos that churned out ever faster and more hectic ragtime well into the 1930s, and the impression still remains that ragtime is a welter of notes at breakneck speed, jingling over the keyboard.

II Joplin and 'classic' or Missouri ragtime
To this level of activity the figure of Scott Joplin stands in striking contrast. Solidly trained by a German music teacher (probably sent south by Reconstruction policy), Joplin distinguished his scores

26

from most popular music by a more correct orthography, a use of dynamics and phrasing, and a sophistication of musical content. In Sedalia, Missouri, and later in St Louis he became the leader of a style of ragtime notable less for its technical brilliance than for its folklike, danceable character. At Tom Turpin's Rosebud Café in St Louis Joplin often met such rag composers as Arthur Marshall, Scott Hayden and Louis Chauvin. (Turpin was himself a composer, whose 1897 *Harlem Rag* [5] was the first published black rag.) Joplin took down strains from Marshall, Hayden and Chauvin, adding one or two of his own to complete a rag, and this may account for the stylistic consistency of the Missouri school; apart from its simplicity on the page, the Missouri style is characterized by lyrical melodies and relatively slow tempos.

The white New Jersey composer Joseph F. Lamb (1887–1960) [6] is usually included with the Missouri group because of Joplin's strong influence; his style seems almost a fusion of Joplin and Ethelbert Nevin. James Scott (1886–1938) [7] is considered the third in the Joplin–Lamb–Scott triumvirate of 'classic' ragtime composers. Scott, based in Kansas City, Missouri, shared the same publisher with Joplin and Lamb, John Stark, who espoused classic ragtime with evangelical zeal. One of hundreds of music store owners who also published music, Stark was enabled by the earnings from *Maple Leaf Rag* to move his small publishing house from Sedalia to St Louis and finally to New York (where it eventually foundered). Stark and Joplin, who had also moved to New York,

27

fell out about 1908, but Stark continued to publish rags by Lamb, Scott, Artie Matthews and other 'classic' rag composers until about 1922, several years after the vogue had passed.

III **Eastern ragtime**

Apart from a few rag songs and the 'Red Back Book' ragtime band arrangements of about 1912, Stark's catalogue was almost exclusively for solo piano. Considerably less 'good-quality' ragtime from composers in New York, Baltimore, New Orleans or Atlantic City was published in that period, so it is hard to ascertain whether eastern ragtime shared the orientation towards the piano of its Missouri counterpart; songs, band transcriptions and piano solos are equally plentiful. 16-bar strains were still the rule in these rags though it was common to have only three strains, with the second and trio often extended to twice their normal length. Otherwise eastern ragtime betrays a diversity of style that obscures clearcut distinctions between ragtime, 'stride piano' and early jazz. The tendency was towards a fast, brilliant piano style (rarely reflected in the drastically simplified published scores); whereas one danced a stately slow drag or cakewalk to a 'classic' rag, only the frenetic 'animal dances' such as the turkey trot or chicken scratch were suitable for the more urban tempo of eastern ragtime. Music publishers in the large cities, far more intent on profit than Stark, brought out a stream of 'junk rags', usually imitation black ragtime (with titles like *Bunch o' Blackberries*) by white composers. Courses advertising 'ragtime in ten easy lessons' flourished, with predictable results; for the more professional players, 'cutting contests' (with as many as 30 competing pianists) generated a style remarkable more for surface brilliance than for content. But this is the most familiar form of ragtime, from *Hello ma baby* (Howard and Emerson, 1899)[8] to *12th Street Rag* (Euday Bowman, 1914)[9] and there is no denying its exuberance. This was the ragtime that would inspire Irving Berlin's *Alexander's Ragtime Band* (1911) which (if not a true rag) is a landmark in that it heralded the incorporation of a raglike liveliness into American popular music.

If Joplin and his school evince a stylistic unity, three eastern pianists and composers – Luckey Roberts, James P. Johnson and Eubie Blake – show a similar consanguinity.[10] Each adopted a form of ragtime known variously as 'Harlem stride' or 'stride piano', in which a broken octave is interposed between the on- and off-beats in the left-hand part. Their published rags appeared in the 1910s in simplified form, but all three achieved greater notoriety as composers during the renaissance of the black musical theatre in the 1920s. Roberts is remembered not only for his *Junk Man Rag* and *Pork and Beans* (both 1913)[11] but for his 1941 song *Moonlight Cocktail*.[12] More successful than Roberts's musicals were those of James P. Johnson, but, like Joplin, he later attempted serious opera, to public failure. Blake's earliest rag publications correspond in date with those of his friend Roberts, but his highly successful musical *Shuffle Along* (1921), written with Noble Sissle, instilled the chief characteristic of ragtime, internal melodic syncopation, indelibly into the American musical comedy and popular song.

IV Decline and revival

The demise of ragtime can perhaps be traced to the moment recordings superseded piano rolls as the principal home entertainment, and to its suppression by jazz about 1915 as the most obviously black-derived musical style. By then it had worked an effect on European composers such as Satie, Stravinsky, Milhaud and Hindemith; but these and other composers seemed primarily attracted by its exoticism rather than its specific manner of syncopation, and in any case took their impressions from printed editions of east-coast junk rags and the misnamed rag pieces of Irving Berlin; an example is the 'American Girl' section of Satie's ballet *Parade* (1916), the shape and rhythmic content of which is taken directly from Berlin's *That Mysterious Rag* (1911). (Stravinsky is reported as saying that he had never heard ragtime at the time of his famous rag pieces.) Ragtime's 16-bar strain expanded to the 32-bar chorus of the 1920s and 1930s popular song, which thus retained something of the squareness of the original march form. But more important, ragtime's particular brand of syncopation survived in nearly all forms of American popular music.

The preservation of ragtime as a specific style can largely be credited to Blesh and Janis's book *They All Played Ragtime* (1950), Max Morath's various new editions of rags, and to a few surviving performers. In the late 1960s players and composers such as

Notes on recordings

William Albright, Joshua Rifkin and William Bolcom discovered in classic ragtime an important kind of American serious piano music, a link, as it were, between the native popular and imported classical traditions of American music. Many new rags owing much to the style of Scott Joplin have been written by these and other musicians, less in the spirit of nostalgia than in homage to this recently rediscovered master, and ragtime now appears widely in concert programmes, film scores and elsewhere in America's musical life. This revival virtually took the form of a craze in the late 1960s and early 1970s and, before subsiding, had established ragtime in the view of music historians as the first clear fusion, and perhaps the most successful, of America's salient musical features.

V Notes on recordings

[1] Recorded on a piano roll by Joplin himself, probably in 1916, and reissued on *Scott Joplin: Ragtime Pioneer* (Riverside (Eu) RLP8815) in 1970; it has been recorded by others including Joshua Rifkin and Dick Hyman (the latter's version is on *Scott Joplin: the Complete Works for Piano*, RCA CRL5-1106, 1975).

[2] Recorded by Eubie Blake on *The Wizard of the Ragtime Piano* in 1960 (20th Century-Fox 3003).

[3] Recorded by Carrie Smith and Dick Hyman on *Satchmo Remembered: the Music of Louis Armstrong at Carnegie Hall* (Atlantic SD1671, 1975).

[4] Recorded by Max Morath on *Jonah Man and other songs of the Bert Williams era* (Vanguard VSD79378, 1976); a version for

31

banjo and piano, recorded in New York in 1896 by Vess Ossman (originally issued on a 5-inch cylinder by Columbia and reissued on L. of C. LBC14), was probably the first ragtime recording made.

[5] Recorded by Trebor Tichenor on *The King of Folk Ragtime* (Dirty Shame 2001, 1973).

[6] Lamb recorded a number of his own works which were issued on an LP entitled *Joseph Lamb: a Study in Classic Ragtime* (Folkways FG3562, 1959); another recording of works by him was made by Milton Kaye (*The Classic Rags of Joe Lamb*, Golden Crest CR4127, 1974).

[7] A representative selection of Scott's works, with pieces by Artie Matthews as well, has been recorded by William Bolcom (*Pastimes and Piano Rags*, Nonesuch H71299, 1973).

[8] Recorded by Joseph Howard in 1926 and reissued on *And then we wrote . . .* (New World NW272) in 1977.

[9] Recorded by Richard M. Jones (Gennett 5174, 1923).

[10] Representative recordings by Johnson and Blake are (respectively) *Carolina Shout* (Okeh 4495, 1921) and *Baltimore Buzz* (Emerson 10434, 1921).

[11] Recorded by Roberts himself (*Junk Man Rag*, Circle 1026, 1946; *Pork and Beans*, Circle 1027, 1946).

[12] Recorded by Roberts himself; the hit recording under the title *Moonlight Cocktail* made by Glenn Miller in 1942 (Bluebird B11401) is an adaptation by one of his arrangers of the principal theme of Roberts's original *Ripples of the Nile* (Circle 1028, 1946).

VI Bibliography

LITERATURE

I. Schwerke: *Kings David and Jazz* (Paris, 1927), 31ff

I. Goldberg: *Tin Pan Alley* (New York, 1930), 139–77

H. Kaufman: *From Jehovah to Jazz* (New York, 1937), 240ff

J. Moynahan: 'Ragtime to Swing', *Saturday Evening Post*, ccix (13 Feb 1937), 14

Bibliography

W. Sargeant: *Jazz: Hot and Hybrid* (New York, 1938, rev. and enlarged 3/1964/*R*1975), 131ff

W. Cook: 'The Origin of the Cake-walk', *Theatre Arts*, xxxi (1947), Sept, 61

C. Wilford: 'Ragtime: an Excavation', *Jazzbook 1947*, ed. A. McCarthy (London, 1947), 18

S. Campbell: 'Ragtime Begins', *Record Changer*, vii (1948), March, 8

R. Carew: 'Ragtime', *Playback*, ii (1949), July, 6

R. Blesh and H. Janis: *They All Played Ragtime* (New York, 1950, rev. 4/1971)

E. Shapiro: 'Ragtime', *Notes*, viii (1950–51), 457

G. Chase: *America's Music* (New York, 1955, rev. 2/1966)

M. Stearns: *The Story of Jazz* (New York, 1956), 140ff

G. Waterman: 'Ragtime Piano Rolls', *Jazz Review*, i (1958), Dec, 42

C. Wilford: 'Elite Syncopations', *Decca Book of Jazz*, ed. P. Gammond (London, 1958), 29

T. Davin: 'Conversations with James P. Johnson', *Jazz Review*, ii (1959), June, 14; July, 10; Aug, 13; Sept, 26; iii (1960), March–April, 11

G. Waterman: 'A Survey of Ragtime', *The Art of Jazz*, ed. M. Williams (New York, 1959), 11

——: 'Ragtime', *Jazz: New Perspectives*, ed. A. McCarthy and N. Hentoff (New York, 1959/*R*1975), 45

A. R. D. Charters: 'Negro Folk Elements in Classic Ragtime', *EM*, v (1961), 174; repr. in *Ragtime Review*, iv/3 (1965), 7

S. Charters and L. Kunstadt: *Jazz: a History of the New York Scene* (Garden City, NY, 1962), 42ff

Ragtimer (1962–)

Ragtime Review (Jan 1963– April 1966)

W. Mellers: *Music in a New Found Land* (London, 1964), 276ff

B. Rust: 'Ragtime su dischi', *Musica Jazz*, xx (1964), Aug–Sept, 28

Anon: 'Sedalia, Mo., Stakes Claim as Birthplace of Ragtime', *Variety* (10 Nov 1965), 1

A. Charters, ed.: *The Ragtime Songbook* (New York, 1965)

S. Grossman: *Ragtime Blues Guitarists* (New York, 1965)

H. Lange: *Jazz in Deutschland 1900–60* (Berlin, 1966), 7ff

S. Brown: 'Negro Producers of Ragtime', *Negro Music and Art*, ed. L. Patterson (New York, 1967), 49

F. Gillis: 'Hot Rhythm in Ragtime', *Music in the Americas*, ed. G. List (Bloomington, Ind., 1967), 91

Rag Times (1967–)

H. P. Hofmann and P. Czerny: *Der Schlager, ein Panorama der leichten Musik*, i (Berlin, 1968), 227ff

M. Harrison: 'Early European Ragtime and Jazz Recordings', *Jazz Monthly*, xvi (1970), June, 24

E. Walker: *English Ragtime: a Discography* (Woodthorpe, Chesterfield, 1971)

D. A. Jasen: *Recorded Ragtime 1897–1958* (Hampden, Conn., 1973) [discography]

E. Thacker: 'Gottschalk and a Prelude to Jazz', *Jazz Monthly*, xix (1973), March, 10, 17

R. Kimball and W. Bolcom: *Reminiscing with Sissle and Blake* (New York, 1973)

A. W. Reed: *The Life and Works of Scott Joplin* (diss., U. of North Carolina, Chapel Hill, 1973)

W. J. Schafer and J. Riedel: *The Art of Ragtime* (Baton Rouge, Louisiana, 1973/*R*1977)

E. Thacker: 'Ragtime Roots', *Jazz Monthly*, xix (1973), Nov, 6; Dec, 4

P. Gammond: *Scott Joplin and the Ragtime Era* (London, 1975)

R. Blesh: *The Ragtime Current* (New York, 1976)

T. Waldo: *This is Ragtime* (New York, 1976)

E. A. Berlin: 'Ragtime and Improvised Piano: Another View', *Journal of Jazz Studies*, iv/2 (1977), 4

W. Morath: *Songs of the Early 20th Century Entertainer* (New York, 1977)

J. Haskins and K. Benson: *Scott Joplin* (Garden City, NY, 1978)

D. A. Jasen and T. J. Tichenor: *Rags and Ragtime: a Musical History* (New York, 1978)

P. Dickinson: 'The Achievement of Ragtime', *PRMA*, cv (1978–9), 63

A. Rose: *Eubie Blake* (New York, 1979)

T. J. Tichenor: *Ragtime Rediscoveries* (New York, 1979)

E. A. Berlin: *Ragtime: a Musical and Cultural History* (Berkeley, Calif., 1980/*R*1984 with addenda)

L. Cerchiari: 'Il ragtime', *Musica jazz*, xxxviii (1982), March, 35

C. Hamm: *Music in the New World* (New York, 1983), 390ff

E. Southern: *The Music of Black Americans* (New York, 2/1983), 310ff

M. Harrison: 'Beyond Ragtime: the "Novelty" Pianists', *The Wire* (1985), Jan, 41

J. E. Hasse, ed.: *Ragtime: its History, Composers and Music* (New York, 1985)

Bibliography

COLLECTIONS

J. P. Johnson: Piano Solos, transcr. D. Meares and D. LeWinter (New York, 1945)

M. Morath, ed.: *100 Ragtime Classics* (Denver, 1963)

J. F. Lamb: Ragtime Treasures (New York, 1964)

M. Morath, ed.: *Ragtime Guide: a Collection of Ragtime Songs and Piano Solos* (New York, 1964)

S. Joplin: The Complete Works, ed V. B. Lawrence, i: *Works for Piano* (New York, 1971, rev. 2/1981)

R. Blesh, ed.: *Classic Piano Rags: Complete Original Music for 81 Rags* (New York, 1973)

M. Morath, ed.: *Giants of Ragtime* (New York, 1973)

Golden Encyclopaedia of Ragtime, 1900–74 (New York, 1974)

E. Blake: Sincerely Eubie Blake: Original Compositions for Solo Piano, transcr. T. Waldo (New York, 1975)

T. Tichenor, ed.: *Ragtime Rarities: Complete Original Music for 63 Piano Rags* (New York, 1975)

——: *Ragtime Rediscoveries: 64 Works from the Golden Age of Rag* (New York, 1979)

J. R. Morton: The Collected Piano Music of Ferdinand 'Jelly Roll' Morton, ed. J. Dapogny (Washington, DC, 1982)

CHAPTER THREE

Blues

I Introduction

In most histories of jazz 'the blues' is considered one of the tributaries that fed the mainstream; a significant, formative one, but secondary to jazz itself. From this perspective blues is also frequently regarded as a primitive precursor of jazz rather than its contemporary, and its exponents are viewed as survivors of an older tradition. Only since the late 1950s has this perception been seriously challenged, when blues became recognized as a music in its own right, with an origin, development and history largely independent of that of jazz. Scholarship and critical appraisal of the blues developed more than 20 years after jazz history and criticism were established, so that even today, to the non-specialist, the two are confused and even inseparable.

Blues is a secular, Afro-American music of the 20th century with a history sometimes related to that of jazz. It has taken many forms and, as an expressive folk and popular music, has a short but complex history. This development and some of its implications are discussed here, but it may be useful before examining the blues as an independent music to consider some of the associated meanings of the term 'blues'. Of its extra-musical meanings, the most important is of the blues as a state of mind. Since the 16th century, 'the Blue Devils' has meant a condition of melancholy or depression, but 'having a fit of the blues' did not enter popular American usage to any extent until after the Civil War. As a term applied by black people to a song expressing such a mental state, it may not have gained currency until after 1900. The two meanings are closely related in the history of the blues as music. It is often understood that a person will 'sing the blues' or 'play the blues' in order to rid himself of 'the blues'. This is so important to blues singers and musicians that many maintain that one cannot play the music unless one has a 'blue feeling' or 'feels blue'.

It follows that blues is also a way of performing. To many it is the essence of the art; a singer or performer who cannot, or does not, express blues feeling through his performance is not a 'bluesman'. Certain qualities of timbre involving rasp or growl vocal techniques are associated with this manner of expression and flattened and shaded notes that produce sad and mournful sounds are recognized as part of its musical vocabulary. Thus blues performance can be imitated but, many of its exponents contend, blues feeling cannot.

As blues was created largely by illiterate musicians, scarcely any of whom could read music, it is in their terms primarily 'ear music' (aurally learnt). Performers place some importance on being able to 'rhyme up a song' and improvisation is an essential part of blues, though not to the extent that it is in jazz. To facilitate improvisation, whether in verse making or on instruments, a number of patterns evolved of which the most familiar is the 12-bar blues. It appears that this form crystallized in the first decade of the 20th century as a three-line stanza in which the first line was repeated. Theoretically, this permitted the blues singer to improvise a third, rhyming line, while singing the repeat of the first. The sequence of accompanying chords is known to all blues performers and played almost automatically.

Blues songs take many forms, some of which express common sentiments and attitudes. Sung and performed with blues expression and intonation, they do not always accord to standard blues structures and are not improvised. To these might be added the blues dances, of which there are a great many in all periods. These may have a standard 16-bar or 32-bar structure but may also be played or sung on a 12-bar framework, though not necessarily in three-line stanzas. Such blues dances form the basis of blues as entertainment, often having their roots in earlier dance routines; in later stages of blues development they were performed to guitar or piano boogie-woogie accompaniment (see p.75 below). However, the standard form is so widely known that 'playing the blues' generally implies that the 12-bar structure is being used. It has had a history of at least 80 years and has been so influential on modern rock music that its all-pervasive use now passes almost unnoticed. Blues has had a considerable influence on recent popular music, not only among American Blacks but in general and internationally. Until the mid-1950s and the emergence of blues-influenced rock-and-roll, blues was essentially a black idiom with the characteristics of a folk music.

Deeply rooted in the black experience in the USA, the blues as a perpetual presence in the lives of Afro-Americans is frequently personified in song as 'Mister Blues'. As a song form, the blues has been recognized as expressing much of the complex social and emotional stresses which a large, but under-privileged minority has endured. Symbolically, at least, the blues represents the struggle of black people to regain their sense of pride and identity after the humiliations and sufferings of the African diaspora and 200 years of slavery.

II Origins

It is widely assumed that blues existed in the slave period and this belief is shared by blues singers. As one explained, 'the blues have been goin' on for centuries and centuries, and the blues was written years and centuries ago – they was always here'. But there is no surviving evidence to confirm that blues existed before the Civil War in the 1860s or even in the second half of the 19th century. Within the slave tradition were song types that may well have been influential on its formation. These included the collective, unaccompanied work songs of the plantation culture, which can be traced not only to pre-war origins but to African sources. In a 'leader-and-chorus' pattern, these group work songs generally died out after the breakup of the plantations, though they persisted under plantation conditions in the southern penitentiary farms until the 1950s. After the Re-

39

construction era black workers were either engaged in seasonal collective labour in the south (cane cutting or cotton picking) or tended smallholdings leased to them by the system of debt-serfdom known as share-cropping. Work songs increasingly took the form of solo calls or 'hollers', which were comparatively free in form. Calls of this type have been recorded in the savannah regions of West Africa, for example Senegal, where cultivation in open fields rather than forests is common.

Early observers noted that a holler or 'cry' might be echoed by many other workers or passed from one to another. Although it was commonly associated with cotton cultivation, the holler was also to be heard among levee workers, mule-skinners and field hands in rice and sugar plantations. According to Frederick Law Olmsted (1853) it was a 'long, loud, musical shout, rising and falling and breaking into falsetto'. This description also fitted examples recorded a century later, some of which are wordless, like the *Field Call* by Annie Grace Horn Dodson (Folkways P417, 1950). Others combine improvised lines expressing the singer's thoughts with elaborated syllables and use of melisma, such as the long example by 'Bama' of a *Levee Camp Holler* (Tradition 1020, 1947) recorded at Parchman Farm (penitentiary), Mississippi. An unidentified singer of a *Camp Holler* was urged on with shouts and comments by his friends, suggesting that the holler could also have a social role (L. of C. AFS L59, 1941). Some street cries might also be considered an urban form of holler though they serve a different function;

an example is the call of 'The Blackberry Woman', Dora Bliggen, in New Orleans (Folkways FA2659, 1954). Similar in feeling and expression, the holler may have been the antecedent of the blues. No recordings of hollers exist from before the mid-1930s, but some blues recordings, such as *Mistreatin' Mama* (Black Patti 8052, 1927) by the harmonica player Jaybird Coleman, may be associated with that tradition.

Vocal traditions have their roots in African practice but it is open to question whether there are African elements in all black American instrumental music. During the slavery period the use of drums was forbidden in a number of states and repressed in others. West African practice among a number of peoples, including the Ashanti of Ghana, was to use 'talking' drums as a form of communication. Their potential in insurrections led to their widespread prohibition, though they were apparently permitted in New Orleans.

Many drum and whistle or fife bands have been identified and recorded in Tennessee and northern Mississippi since 1960 and there is evidence of their continual existence from earlier in the century. Though recordings of them sound superficially 'African' it seems likely that these ensembles are derived from the instrumentation of military bands. The drum rhythms and percussive use of the flute may have their origins in the 'pats' or 'patting juba', rhythms played on the hard and soft parts of the body with the palms of the hands, and in the 'quills', or cane panpipes common in rural areas. Drumming was proscribed, but the playing of string instruments was often permitted and even encouraged. Africans from the savannah regions, with their strong traditions of string playing, predominated. Their *jelli*, or *griots*, professional musicians who also acted as tribal historians and social commentators, performed roles not unlike those of the later blues singers. One-string instruments, or 'diddley bows', have been common in the south while the banjo, or 'banjar', was a direct descendant of the *bania* or *khalam* of the *griot*. Banjo and fiddle music from the plantations was parodied in 19th-century blackface minstrel troupes. Reels, dances and jigs of Anglo-Scottish-Irish origin were adapted to African timing and intonation before the end of the Civil War, and after Emancipation the meeting of African and British elements was evident in the exchange of songs between Blacks and Whites.

In the late 19th century, the post-Reconstruction bitterness of southern Whites towards Blacks hardened into segregation laws. In a sense this forced the black communities to recognize their own identity, resulting in a flowering of black sacred and secular music. It was the period when the old spirituals began to give way to the gospel songs of the Pentecostal churches of God in Christ, when the parade music of New Orleans blossomed into jazz and when the plantation dances and walk-arounds were transferred to the piano to become ragtime.

Yet it was also a period of stereotypical songs in the ragtime genre which fixed images of Blacks as comic, ostentatious, childlike and licentious. Several hundred 'coon' songs were composed that purported to be in black idioms or that used Blacks as subjects of ridicule and contempt. Tom Logan's song *The Coon's Trade Mark: a Watermelon, Razor, Chicken and a Coon* (1897) typified this genre, but it was one to which some black composers contributed, among them Ben Harney, Bert Logan, Chris Smith, Bert Williams and Irving Jones. Some used authentic black idioms and others, notably Jones, used subtle artifice to mock the stereotypes while profiting from the entertainment. Many of the phrases and musical elements of these songs both fed on black folk traditions and contributed to them, persisting in the blues for several decades.

Traditional Anglo-Scottish ballads were adopted by Blacks to extol the exploits of black heroes. The earliest may have been the *Ballad of John Henry*, which told of the heroic contest between a railroad worker and a steam drill, believed to have taken place in the 1870s. But the majority, including *Duncan and Brady*, *Stack O'Lee*, *John Hardy* and *Po' Lazarus*, appear to date from the turn of the century.

It seems likely that the consolidation of blues form was the outcome of the convergence of the work song and holler tradition with the instrumental music of the plantation and post-plantation eras and the European-influenced song structures widely adopted by Blacks in the 19th century. Some of the ballads popular among black singers, for example *Railroad Bill* and *Frankie and Albert*, had a couplet with a rhyming third line as a refrain. It is this pattern that seems to have given hollers the discipline of the blues structure, the couplet coming to be replaced with a repeat line:

See, see rider, see what you have done,
See, see rider, see what you have done,
You've made me love you, now my man done come.

See, see rider, Joe Turner Blues and *Fare thee well Blues* were among the earliest songs of this type.

The loose form of the holler, without instrumental or other constraints, became more structured in the blues. Eight-bar, two-line blues were common and four- or five-line repeats may be found. But when the blues form crystallized, the three-line, 12-bar stanza became the preferred structure. Within it a number of rhyme schemes, including *aaa, abb, abc,* were used. Also common was a form that followed the 12-bar sequence but that consisted of a repeated couplet, the first sung within four bars, the second over eight. However, by the time blues came to be recorded the conventional *aab* form predominated. In the key of E, it consisted of four bars on the tonic, of which two might be accompanied vocal, the fourth bar falling to the dominant 7th; two bars on the subdominant, possibly accompanying a vocal, followed by two bars on the tonic; two bars in the dominant 7th, accompanying the rhyming line of the vocal, concluding with two bars in the tonic. Such a sequence was followed in other keys, though blues guitarists favoured E or A and jazz musicians favoured B♭. There are many variants but this pattern is so widely known that to 'play the blues' generally presupposes the use of this sequence.

At first the blues were probably sung as a new song form, the titles covering a loose arrangement of verses related to a theme. Early collected examples were given titles like *Florida Blues*, *Atlanta Blues* or *Railroad Blues*, which often referred to migration, or at least the declared intention to leave home. Among other early examples, *Make me a pallet on the floor* or *See, see rider* had the directness of expression for which the blues became well known. But the majority of early blues, though known by a title phrase, may have been nodal rather than narrative, consisting of a cluster of verses rather than a sequence of ideas. As such they lent themselves to rapid adoption and dissemination, a process in which songsters played an important part.

III From songsters to blues singers

Songsters, a class of black American musicians of the post-Reconstruction era, performed a wide variety of ballads, dance tunes, reels, minstrel, coon and ragtime songs, a repertory that overlapped that of white rural singers. Sometimes they were supported by 'musicianers', or non-singing instrumentalists, who played strings. By favouring the guitar instead of the earlier banjo and fiddle, the second-generation songsters form a link between older song traditions and blues. A number of them made recordings, probably the oldest being Henry Thomas of Texas (1874–*c*1959); his *John Henry* (Vocalion 1094, 1927), sung and played on both guitar and reed pipes, was one of the first recorded versions of this earliest of black ballads. Of much the same generation was the Memphis blacksmith Frank Stokes (*b* Tutwiler, Mississippi, 1883; *d* 1954) whose *You shall* (Paramount 12576,

45

1927) may date from before the Civil War. Younger than Stokes, Jim Jackson (*b* Hernando, Mississippi, *c*1880; *d* Hernando, *c*1938) played the guitar simply but was extremely popular with such songs as *He's in the jailhouse now* (Vocalion 1146, 1928) and *Traveling Man* (Victor 38517, 1928). Songs like these were in the repertory of every songster and the tradition was extremely widespread.

Earliest of the songsters on record was Papa Charlie Jackson (*b* New Orleans, *c*1885; *d* ?Chicago, 1935) a banjo player who, according to the Paramount publicity, was a 'witty, cheerful, kindhearted man'. Jackson worked at fairs, racecourses and on travelling shows and he recorded bowdlerized versions of the more earthy songs of the black folk tradition, including *Shave 'em dry* (Paramount 12264, 1925). He came from Louisiana, but the high-voiced Luke Jordan, a brilliant instrumentalist, came from North Carolina; his *Pick poor robin clean* (Victor 20957, 1927) was outstanding.

The breadth of the songster's repertory is demonstrated by the recordings of singers like 'Mississippi' John Hurt and Blind Blake. Living in Avalon, Mississippi, as a farmer and railroad labourer, Hurt (*b* Teoc, March 1894; *d* 3 Nov 1966) never played professionally; thus, apart from its intrinsic merit, his work is important in that it preserves an old tradition. When he made his earliest recordings, including *Frankie* (Okeh 8560, 1928), *Stack O' Lee Blues* (Okeh 8654, 1928) and *Spike Driver Blues* (Okeh 8692, 1928) on the *John Henry* theme, these were already 'old time tunes'. Typified by a light beat and rapid fingerwork, his guitar playing was a perfect foil to his gentle voice and often almost whispered vocals. Hurt performed only for local functions, but other songsters travelled extensively. Arthur Blake ('Blind Blake') (*b* ?Jacksonville, Florida, *c*1895; *d c*1935) was a well-known songster and guitarist in Florida, Georgia and the eastern states. He toured widely, entertaining in Tennessee and eventually Detroit. Between 1926 and 1932 he recorded some 80 items, including a number of instrumental ones, of which *Blind Arthur's Breakdown* (Paramount 12892, 1929) demonstrated his unparalleled technique. In common with eastern guitarists he showed a strong ragtime influence in his playing, which was light and flowing. Many of his songs were ideal for dancing, like *Come on boys let's do that messin' around* (Paramount 12413, 1926); others, such as *He's in the jailhouse now* (Paramount 12565, 1927), derived from the medicine-show repertory. Blake had a melancholy voice peculiarly suited to blues and heard to advantage on *Search Warrant Blues* (Paramount 12737, 1928) or *Cold Hearted Mama Blues* (Paramount 12710, 1928) with its delicate accompaniment and solo.

Many songsters and early blues singers in the south worked in 'medicine shows', street entertainments promoted by vendors of patent medicines to attract purchasers. Similar to the 19th-century minstrel show and often performed in blackface, these shows featured blues as well as old songs. Wandering singers who, by necessity through physical handicap or by inclination, sang and played for a living, also helped spread the blues. They followed the example of the

47

street evangelists who, at much the same time, were popularizing gospel songs. The blues singer, who sang and played only blues, began to replace the songster.

Songsters performed versions of composed songs or, in their ballads, concentrated on the exploits of legendary black heroes, but blues singers invented their songs and sang of themselves and those who shared their experiences. Many stanzas rapidly became traditional and certain images or lines entered the stock-in-trade of every blues singer. But the inventive singer expressed his anxieties, frustrations, hopes or resignation through his songs. Some blues describe disasters or personal incidents; crime, prostitution, gambling, alcohol and imprisonment have always been prominent themes. Some blues are tender but few reveal a response to nature; far more express a desire to move or to escape by train or road to an imagined better land. Many are aggressively sexual, and there is much in blues that is consciously and subconsciously symbolic of the black singer's perception of his relationship with society.

IV Publication and recording

By 1910 blues had been noted by white collectors of black folksong in many parts of the south. E. C. Perrow in Mississippi, Howard Odum in Mississippi and the Carolinas, John A. Lomax and Willard Gates Thomas in Texas had all found examples. A number were specifically termed 'blues' by the singers but generally they were collected with other black song types. The new idiom attracted song composers, notably W. C. Handy, a black bandleader who had heard blues sung by a folk guitarist in Mississippi as early as 1903. Handy's *The Memphis Blues* was published in 1915, but Leroy 'Lasses' White, a blackface entertainer, who composed *Nigger Blues*, 1912 (published 1913) was one of the first to write in the 12-bar form. It was recorded in 1916 by the white singer George O'Connor (Columbia A2064), one of several entertainers who used the new idiom though seldom the blues form. *Baby Seals Blues* by Baby F. Seals and the ragtime pianist Artie Matthews (1912), Euday Bowman's *Kansas City Blues* (1914) and Douglas Williams's *Hooking Cow Blues* (1917), though using a chorus and verse structure, helped popularize blues among white audiences.

Published blues were intended to be played largely as written. They included compositions that sometimes used elements of blues tonality or structure, including *Dallas Blues* by Hart Wand and Lloyd Garrett (1912), which was the first published 12-bar blues, and W. C. Handy's *St Louis Blues* (1914). Although they brought blues sounds to a larger audience, many published songs bore the name but had little connection with blues. They were suitable vehicles for jazz improvisation, however, and this connection with jazz has contributed to the confusion about blues as music with a separate identity.

It is still unclear how important published sheet music was in disseminating blues among Blacks. Few blues singers could read music and published blues may have circulated more among jazz musicians and singers. Nevertheless, the idiomatic use of blues language suggests an awareness of the folk blues tradition or of earlier song types from which both folk blues and composed blues may partly have derived. Few rural blues singers sang composed blues: the rare exceptions included Jim Jackson's recordings of *St Louis Blues* and *Hesitation Blues* (Vocalion 1477, 1930). Of blues copyrighted by publishing companies, only an insignificant number have appeared in sheet music form, so it is unlikely that sheet music played much part in spreading blues in the south. More important were the recordings of cabaret and stage performers: black women singers whose 'blues' were often songs written by composers of black music. Among these were Perry Bradford's *Crazy Blues* (1920), *Arkansas Blues* (1921) by Anton Lada and Spencer Williams, *Down Home Blues* (1922) by Alberta Hunter and Lovie Austin, and Clarence Williams's *Gulf Coast Blues* (1923). Similar blues songs probably influenced rural singers in providing images and phrases that they reworked into their own songs, though even the immensely popular *Crazy Blues*, recorded by Mamie Smith in 1920, was never recorded by a southern blues singer or collected in the field.

Mamie Smith was not the first black singer to record, but she was the first whose records were sold to black purchasers. In her early teens Mamie Smith (*b* Cincinnati, 26 May 1883; *d* New York, *c*16 Sept 1946) toured as a dancer with Tutt-Whitney's Smart Set Company and she was a featured singer in Harlem clubs and theatres before World War I. *Crazy Blues* (Okeh 4169, 1920) was a tremendous success that made a fortune for Smith and her promoter Perry

Bradford and opened the way for the recording of black singers. Smith was extremely attractive, with a lively stage personality and a strong voice. Many of her best records were with her 'Jazz Hounds' which included Johnny Dunn and sometimes Bubber Miley playing cornets, as on *I ain't gonna give nobody none o' this jelly roll* (Okeh 4752, 1922), or *The Darktown Flapper's Ball* (Okeh 4767, 1922). But *Jenny's Ball* (Okeh 8915, 1931), being well recorded, gives a better impression of her appeal as a singer. Smith was a vaudeville–jazz performer rather than a blues singer and she seldom used blues form or inflection.

Other record companies were quick to respond to the success of Mamie Smith and Okeh and with such singers as Edith Wilson, Rosa Henderson, Lucille Hegamin and Viola McCoy, they began to issue phonograph records made specially for black consumers. These, called 'race records' (a term coined by Ralph Peer of Okeh), were grouped in numbered series. Okeh began its 8000 series in 1921; other race series included the Paramount 12000s (from 1922), Columbia 14000s (from 1923), Vocalion's 1000s (from 1926) and the Victor 21000s and 38000s (from 1927). Many smaller companies had race series and by 1927 some 500 race records were being issued each year. Sales declined with the Depression and many concerns closed. But in 1933 Victor's Bluebird subsidiary started issuing them to compete with those of the American Record Corporation labels and in 1934 the English Decca company started its successful American Decca 7000 race series.

Although jazz records were issued in the race series,

vocalists with instrumental accompaniment predominated. Between 1921 and 1925 these were mainly
of spiritual and gospel quartets and women 'classic'
blues singers. Most of these women were professional
entertainers working with touring shows on the circuit
of TOBA (Theater Owners' Booking Association),
which managed black artists.

V Classic blues

Many of the women who made race records in the
1920s were professional performers, and some (like
Fae Barnes, Ethel Waters, Alberta Hunter and
Gertrude Saunders) played on Broadway and toured
in Europe on the wave of popularity for all-black
shows. Some used hints of blues phrasing and
intonation in their singing though many never
attempted to compose their own blues or even to sing
in the blues form: their songs were blues in name only.
But there were a number of singers who mixed blues
and blues songs with their performances, like the
extensively recorded Sara Martin, whose *Blind Man
Blues* (Okeh 8090, 1923) featured Clarence Williams's
Blues Five with the young Sidney Bechet playing the
soprano saxophone. More important was Beulah
'Sippie' Wallace, whose warm voice was effectively
accompanied by Louis Armstrong on *Special Delivery
Blues* (Okeh 8328, 1926). She was the sister of George
W. Thomas, a composer from Houston who promoted other members of his family, including his
daughter Hociel Thomas, who was accompanied by
the teenage Hersal, George's much younger brother,
in the splendid tune *Fish Tail Dance* (Okeh 8222,

1925). Louis Armstrong played for a number of these classic blues singers, most brilliantly on Bertha 'Chippie' Hill's version of a Richard M. Jones composition *Trouble in Mind* (Okeh 8312, 1926), which passed into the tradition.

'Classic' blues is an imprecise term (probably first used in print by John Jacob Niles in 1930) that has been loosely applied to the songs of the urban women singers based in New York and Chicago. More accurately, it describes the bigger-voiced contraltos who featured blues prominently among their records, which were seldom recorded self-accompanied and were usually backed by jazz musicians. Some were comparatively little known, like 'Kansas City Butterball', Lottie Beamon, whose *Red River Blues* (Paramount 12201, 1924) was made to a guitar accompaniment by the Pruitt Twins. Another strong singer was Lillian Glinn from Texas, whose powerful *Shake it down* (Columbia 14315, 1928) was made in New Orleans. Atlanta, Georgia, may have been the home of Cleo Gibson, who made only one record, *I've got Ford engine movements in my hips* (Okeh 8700, 1929), deservedly called 'classic'.

Of the outstanding singers, Gertrude 'Ma' Rainey (*b* Columbus, Georgia, 26 April 1886; *d* Rome, Georgia, 22 Dec 1939), who first heard blues sung in 1902, was the closest to the folk tradition. Born Gertrude Pridgett, she began her career at a talent show, the 'Bunch of Blackberries' when she was 12. She married Will 'Pa' Rainey in 1904 and toured with him in F. S. Wolcott's Rabbit Foot Minstrels and other shows; in 1916 they formed their own company.

By the time she started recording she was famous throughout the south. Her Paramount recordings scarcely did justice to her vocal power but her majestic phrasing is evident in her first record *Bo-Weavil Blues* (Paramount 12080, 1923) and *Moonshine Blues* (Paramount 12083, 1923), her most celebrated compositions. She made over 100 records in five years, her moaning intonation investing *Jelly Bean Blues* (Paramount 12238, 1924), made with Louis Armstrong, or *Yonder come the blues* (Paramount 12357, 1926), made with her Georgia Jazz Band, with a tragic quality. She toured with her Georgia band throughout the south and into Mexico during the 1920s, playing to large audiences. Though rumbustious in disposition, that is rarely evident in her records: *'Ma' Rainey's Black Bottom* (Paramount 12590, 1927) is one of the few showing her lighter side. In 1935 Ma Rainey retired to Columbus and in her last years was active in the Friendship Baptist Church.

Though they may have worked together, it is not certain that Ma Rainey was Bessie Smith's mentor. There was probably respect and rivalry between them but black entertainment was large enough to accommodate both the 'Mother of the Blues', as Ma Rainey was affectionately known, and Bessie Smith (*b* Chattanooga, 15 April 1894; *d* Clarksdale, Mississippi, 26 Sept 1937), the 'Empress of the Blues', who began her professional career in 1912 with Moses Stokes's show, which included Gertrude and Will Rainey. She toured with minstrel shows and, sought by Clarence Williams, began recording with *Down Hearted Blues*

(Columbia A3844, 1923) which established her as the most successful black artist of her time. She recorded regularly until 1928, accompanied by members of the Fletcher Henderson Band, including the trumpeters Louis Armstrong, Tommy Ladnier and Joe Smith. Touring extensively, leading a tempestuous life with her ex-policeman husband Jack Gee, she was addicted to gin. In 1929 she appeared and sang in a short film, *St Louis Blues*. Her last recording session was in 1933 but in 1936 she was planning to make a comeback when she died after a car accident.

Bessie Smith was the greatest of the vaudeville blues singers, bringing emotional intensity and personal involvement to the jazz repertory with unexcelled artistry. *After you've gone* (Columbia 14197, 1927), made with Joe Smith, and *Nobody knows you when you're down and out* (Columbia 14451, 1929), with Ed Allen playing the cornet, illustrate her capacity to take popular songs and give them new meaning through her sensitive interpretations. Her broad phrasing, fine intonation and blue-note inflections made hers the measure of jazz-blues singing in the 1920s. She made nearly 200 recordings of which her remarkable duets with Louis Armstrong, including *St Louis Blues* (Columbia 14064, 1925) and *You've Been a Good Old Wagon* (Columbia 14079, 1925), are among the best. Though she excelled in slow blues she also performed vigorous versions of jazz standards, including the exhilarating *Cake walking babies (from home)* (Columbia 35673, 1925) and *Alexander's Ragtime Band* (Columbia 14219, 1927), both made with a group from Fletcher Henderson's

Orchestra. Joe Smith, the cornet player on these recordings, was her preferred accompanist, but possibly
her finest record, the best known in its day, was *Back
Water Blues* (Columbia 14195, 1927) with James P.
Johnson playing the piano. Her voice had coarsened
when she made *Gimme a pigfoot* (Okeh 8949, 1933) at
her last session, but few jazz artists have been as
consistently outstanding.

For many blues enthusiasts Bessie Smith's approach was too jazz-inflected. Some prefer the harder,
less elaborate technique of Ida Cox (*b* Toccoa,
Georgia, 25 Feb 1896; *d* Knoxville, Tenn., 10 Nov.
1967). Although she joined a minstrel show as a child
and was singing in theatres at the age of 14, she
depended less on vaudeville songs, and nearly all her
records were in traditional blues vein. Her first, *Any
Woman's Blues* (Paramount 12053, 1923), shows her
characteristic resonant, rather nasal quality. With
appropriate material, particularly her own blues
compositions, she was among the finest women
singers. *Ida Cox's Lawdy Lawdy Blues* (Paramount
12064, 1923) and *I've got the blues for Rampart Street*
(Paramount 12063, 1923), both with excellent
accompaniments by Tommy Ladnier playing the
cornet, have strong yet relaxed vocals. For several
years Cox was accompanied by the pianist Jesse
Crump, who is heard playing a sombre organ setting
for *Coffin Blues* (Paramount 12318, 1925), in which
the singer hums a chorus and wrings the meaning
from the funereal words.

There were few good male classic blues singers:

Willie Jackson and George Williams from New Orleans were mediocre. Few blues singers could work in a jazz context; one who did, having known jazz in childhood, was Alonzo 'Lonnie' Johnson (*b* New Orleans, 8 Feb 1889; *d* Toronto, 16 June 1970). He started playing the guitar and the violin professionally in his teens in Storyville, New Orleans. By 1917 he was working with Charlie Creath's Jazz-O-Maniacs on the *St Paul* riverboat, later joining Fate Marable's riverboat band. It was as a guitarist that he became famous, playing brilliantly in solos like *Stomping 'em Along Slow* (Okeh 8558, 1928) or in duets with Eddie Lang (Salvatore Massaro) like *A Handful of Riffs* (Okeh 8695, 1929). Johnson played with Duke Ellington in his Orchestra's *Move Over* (Okeh 8638, 1928), with Louis Armstrong in the celebrated *Mahogany Hall Stomp* (Okeh 8680, 1929) and with King Oliver (as Blind Willie Dunn's Gin Bottle Four) on *Jet Black Blues* (Okeh 8689, 1929). He began his long career as a recording blues singer with *Mr Johnson's Blues* (Okeh 8253, 1925) in which he played the violin. Johnson had a reedy, somewhat insinuating voice but his lyrics were generally interesting. *Low Land Moan* (Okeh 8677, 1927) was typical in this and also in its use of a melody that he employed too frequently. He liked sentimental themes, such as *Baby please don't leave home no more* (Okeh 8754, 1929), in which, however, he still played with flair. As an accompanist he was sensitive, providing a sympathetic support to the irregular singing of Alger 'Texas' Alexander on *Bell Cow Blues* (Okeh 8563, 1928) and with

57

Victoria Spivey he made a number of amusing, suggestive duets, like *Furniture Man Blues* (Okeh 8652, 1928).

Daughter of the leader of a string band, Victoria Spivey (*b* Houston, 15 Oct 1906; *d* New York, 3 Oct 1976) was performing at the Lincoln Theatre in Dallas when she was 12. She began recording in St Louis, where she made *Black Snake Blues* (Okeh 8338, 1926) to her own piano accompaniment. Her voice was lean and nasal and she made much use of moaned syllables. Her partnership with Lonnie Johnson produced many notable recordings, including *T. B. Blues* (Okeh 8494, 1927) and *Murder in the First Degree* (Okeh 8581, 1927). In 1929 she appeared in *Hallelujah!*, an all-black film directed by King Vidor, and she made several recordings with Henry Allen's New York Orchestra, including the *double-entendre* song *Funny Feathers Blues* (Victor 38088, 1929) and a characteristic *Moaning the Blues* (Victor 38546, 1929).

As one of the youngest classic singers Spivey was able to pursue her career through the 1930s and 1940s but the majority stopped performing professionally as the popularity of vaudeville, in which their acts were largely heard, declined in the 1930s. So too did vaudeville duettists like Butterbeans and Susie, and 'Coot' Grant and 'Kid Sox' Wesley Wilson who used blues vocal techniques in their comedy routines. Only in the tent shows and the travelling companies like the Rabbit Foot Minstrels and Silas Green's minstrel show from New Orleans did these acts have a lingering audience during the Depression.

VI **Southern folk blues**

Many of the classic blues singers came from the south or the border states and had heard folksingers whose blues they borrowed. The early development of blues may be reconstructed but there is little evidence to explain its rapid distribution or where the form originated. Blues verses were collected in the Carolinas, Georgia, Mississippi and Texas – a vast area – in the first years of the century. But, in spite of the popularity of women singers, it was not until the beginning of the second quarter of the century that the folk idiom was recorded commercially, by which time its form was firmly established and vocal and instrumental techniques well developed, with regional styles and approaches already discernible. Called 'country blues', 'rural blues' or 'downhome blues', the blues sung and played by local community performers had the characteristics of a folk music: performed mostly by illiterate or only partially literate singers and developing traditions of phrase and stanza almost independent of professional entertainers. However, songsters played a part in spreading blues lyrics and techniques, while lines or verses from commercial records of classic blues singers were to be heard in the first recorded examples of folk blues.

Although the majority of folk blues singers were born in rural areas and worked on farms many gravitated to the black sectors of the nearest cities, to sing in the streets and to benefit from the free spending of the 'sporting life'. Blues was as much an urban phenomenon as a country one, and 'southern folk blues' may be a more accurate collective term.

The record industry began to make known country blues with Papa Charlie Jackson's *Papa's Lawdy Lawdy Blues* (Paramount 12219, 1924), recorded with banjo accompaniment. Jackson's style was simple and much of his repertory characteristic of songsters, but it was *Long Lonesome Blues* (Paramount 12354, 1926) by Blind Lemon Jefferson that brought the authentic sound of rural blues to thousands of black homes.

Within the folk blues idiom no singer has been more influential than Blind Lemon Jefferson (*b* Couchman, Texas, *c*1897; *d* Chicago, *c*1930). His sight deteriorated in early childhood and he made a living by singing in the streets of Dallas and other Texas towns, sometimes in the company of Leadbelly (see p.118 below). His voice was high, piercing the traffic noise, but it could also have a low, moaning quality extended by 'bending' the notes on his guitar to produce crying sounds or imitative passages on the strings, characteristically in *Match Box Blues* (Okeh 8455, 1927), his best recorded song. Jefferson's compositions, which often implied at least partial sight, were frequently autobiographical, like *Pneumonia Blues* (Paramount 12880, 1928); others, like *Blind Lemon's Penitentiary Blues* (Paramount 12666, 1928) or *Hangman's Blues* (Paramount 12679, 1928), showed concern for the fate of prison inmates. Jefferson's imaginative blues were recorded in many versions by other singers long after his death.

High-voiced, lean-toned singing exemplified the Texas approach to blues. Willard 'Rambling' Thomas followed this style and the use of the guitar as an expressive second voice, answering the vocal material, but 'Texas' Alexander was so close to the holler tradition that he did not even play an instrument. One of the most popular recording blues singers, Alger Alexander (*b* Jewett, 12 Sept 1900; *d* Richards, 18 April 1954) was raised and spent most of his life in east Texas. He worked as a farm hand and as a store-man in Dallas and was imprisoned for at least two offences. His earliest records, including *Levee Camp Moan* (Okeh 8498, 1927), are strongly influenced by work song. In his well-known *West Texas Blues* (Okeh 8603, 1928), among others, he was supported by the guitarist Lonnie Johnson, who was able to complement his irregular timing and verse structure. Alexander had a low, moaning singing style and used hummed choruses to good effect, as in his two-part *Awful Moaning Blues* (Okeh 8731, 1929) with Dennis 'Little Hat' Jones playing the guitar. His lyrics were often unusual and poetic but he favoured a limited number of tunes and sang almost exclusively in the three-line blues form. Other Texan singers who displayed fluency in their guitar playing, lightness of expression and poetry in their imagery were 'Little Hat' Jones, 'Funny Paper' Smith and Gene Campbell.

The approach to blues in Mississippi was quite different. The Mississippi delta is often regarded as the birthplace of blues. Hundreds of miles north of the river delta proper, it is a wedge of low-lying fertile land between the Mississippi and the Yazoo rivers, due south of Memphis and the northern Mississippi hill country. Many blues singers came from this area, where the black population equalled, and in many townships far outnumbered, Whites. The cotton fields

61

of the delta plantations may well have spawned the blues, but the proximity to Memphis and the relative ease with which record executives could reach the area by rail from Chicago also meant that it was well placed for location recording. Similarly, many Mississippi blues singers were able to migrate to Chicago. Many of the earthiest, least sophisticated recordings came from Mississippi. Most of the singers were guitarists who played a heavily accented rhythmic accompaniment to their frequently guttural, expressive singing.

The most influential blues singer was Charley Patton (*b* ?Bolton, Mississippi, *c*1887; *d* Indianola, Mississippi, 28 April 1934), who generated a school of singer-guitarists near Clarksdale, before World War I; his role in Mississippi blues was comparable with that of Jefferson in Texas. Light-skinned and of slight build he had, nevertheless, a rasping voice of the 'heavy' kind admired by many blues singers. In 1912 he moved to the Dockery plantation where he worked with Tommy Johnson, Willie Brown and other Mississippi blues singers who exchanged songs and techniques. Patton was noted for his clowning but his recordings present a serious musician. *Pony Blues* (Paramount 12792, 1929) was his most celebrated, but *Moon Going Down* (Paramount 13014, 1930), with Willie Brown playing flat-pick guitar accompaniment, is one of his best-remembered records. The themes of his blues were often autobiographical, though sometimes the stanzas were confused, but *High Sheriff Blues* (Vocalion 02680, 1934) is a consistent narrative. On record Patton's blues are sombre, often with a percussive accompaniment from a guitar in open G tuning. As his repertory included ballads, ragtime songs and spirituals, like *Frankie and Albert* (Paramount 13110, 1929), *Hang it on the wall* (Vocalion 02931, 1934) or *Oh Death* (Vocalion 02904, 1934) he could be classed as a songster, but it was his blues that influenced younger singers like Son House, Bukka White and Chester Burnett.

Often regarded as the quintessential blues singer, Eddie 'Son' House (*b* Riverton, Mississippi, 21 March 1902) did not begin to perform until his mid-20s. As a child he sang in church and later preached, which may have helped shape his forceful style. After working on a farm and in a steel plant in St Louis, he returned to Mississippi and became associated with Charley Patton and his companion Willie Brown. In 1930 he recorded three two-part blues of remarkable strength, including the influential *Preachin' the Blues* (Paramount 13013, 1930) and an account of a farming crisis in Mississippi, *Dry Spell Blues* (Paramount 12990, 1930), characterized by bellowed vocals against repetitive phrases played with a bottleneck slide on the guitar strings.

It is sometimes assumed that the deep, 'heavy' voices of Charley Patton or Son House were typical of the Mississippi approach; they had many local imitators. But there were also high-voiced performers like 'Crying' Sam Collins, Bo Weevil Jackson and Nehemiah 'Skip' James. James, from Bentonia, Mississippi, had an uncanny, shrill voice and a dazzling rapid guitar technique; his *I'm so glad*

63

(Paramount 13098, 1931) displayed his skill, while the lyrics of *Cypress Grove Blues* (Paramount 13065, 1931) matched those of any Texan for poetic expression. Though he has been regarded as a singular musician, research has revealed that he represented a local tradition centred on an unrecorded singer, Henry Stuckey; this underlines the fact that recordings alone may not give an accurate picture of the spread, evolution or styles of blues.

Tommy Johnson (*b* Terry, Mississippi, *c*1896; *d* Crystal Springs, Mississippi, 1 Nov 1956) was arguably the finest of the Mississippi bluesmen. He worked as a field hand and farmer in Crystal Springs, playing at local functions and occasionally in touring shows. Influenced by Patton and others in Drew, he developed a beautiful and moving style, exemplified on *Cool Drink of Water Blues* (Victor 21279, 1928). His blues was slow with falsetto phrases, accompanied by the guitarist Charlie McCoy, who played a complementary line in mandolin style. In *Big Road Blues* (Victor 21279, 1928) traditional verses are forcefully sung against a compelling accompaniment of ascending steps. In *Canned Heat Blues* (Victor 38535, 1928) he sang about his addiction to alcohol, a performance of great beauty with elements related to the former songs.

Sharing the sessions with Johnson was his companion Ishman Bracey (1901–70) whose voice was nasal and harder but whose records, like *Saturday Blues* (Victor 21349, 1928), were scarcely less remarkable. Both men continued to perform during the 1930s and 1940s but they did not record. While

Johnson was noted for his humour (not evident on his records), Bracey joined the church, following Reverend Rubin Lacy, whose sole record only hinted at the fame he enjoyed as a blues singer in the 1920s.

Mobile units, notably those of Columbia, Victor and Okeh, made field recordings of many blues singers who would otherwise have remained unknown. But vast areas of the south were unrepresented: hardly any recordings were made in the 1920s in the Carolinas, Alabama, Florida or Arkansas. In Atlanta, Georgia, a school of 12-string guitar players with rich voices was recorded. Several used a knife, bottleneck or other tool to slide against the strings to produce whining, mournful sounds in keeping with blues feeling. Some turned to an open chord (e.g. *D–a–d–f–a′–d′*), producing a 'cross-note' tuning that enabled them to press the slide against all the strings while playing a blues sequence. By pressing strings across the frets, wailing sounds could be made; thus the guitar's adaptability made it favoured among blues singers.

Barbecue Bob (Robert Hicks) (*b* Walnut Grove, Georgia, 11 Sept 1902; *d* Lithonia, Georgia, 21 Oct 1931) was the central figure of the group of blues singers working in and around Atlanta, which included his elder brother Charlie and Curley Weaver. He worked on a farm before moving to Atlanta, where he was a cook in Tidwell's Barbecue Place. His first record, *Barbecue Blues* (Columbia 14205, 1927), was a best seller, showing his characteristic vocal range and the ringing notes of his 12-string guitar played with a slide. He experimented with blues

65

form, was continually inventive in his themes, as in *We sure got hard times now* (Columbia 14558, 1930), and occasionally played dances or comic songs. With his brother 'Laughing Charlie' Hicks (who also recorded solo under the name of Charlie Lincoln) he made *Darktown Gamblin'* (Columbia 14531, 1930), its simulated crap and skin games typical of their vocal exchanges. After his early death, his brother became an alcoholic and ceased performing. Their former companion, Curley Weaver, and the youthful Buddy Moss continued to play, Weaver sometimes teaming up with another gifted 12-string guitarist, 'Blind' Willie McTell.

McTell (*b* Thomson, Georgia, *c*1898; *d* Milledgeville, Georgia, 19 Aug 1959) enjoyed considerable fame. He was trained at schools for the blind in Georgia, New York and Michigan and travelled as far as South America as a popular singer and musician. He was a versatile guitarist and his recordings are instrumentally varied. His voice, though lighter than that of many Georgia singers, was ideally suited to the blues, as in *Death Cell Blues* (Vocalion 02577, 1933) with its excellent lyrics. *Mama 'tain't long fo' day* (Victor 21124, 1927), from his first session (made on location in Atlanta), revealed his effortless bottleneck slide style of playing; *Atlanta Strut* (Columbia 14657, 1929) has a ragtime dance theme with imitative, impressionistic guitar breaks and spoken narrative. McTell was really a songster whose recordings were mainly blues. He was one of the best known of the 'Piedmont' bluesmen, as the singers of the hill country of north Georgia, South and North

Carolina and even southern Virginia have been termed. Blind Willie Walker was also one of the most famous in the 1920s but he made only one record. He led a string band that included Blind Gary Davis, then a blues singer but later to be known as an evangelical gospel singer and guitarist. That Walker's string band was not recorded was a great loss to the documentation of black music.

VII String, jug and washboard bands

Joshua Barnes 'Peg Leg' Howell (*b* Eatonton, Georgia, 5 March 1888; *d* Atlanta, 11 Aug 1966) gave some indication of the rougher songster tradition of Georgia and a hint of its string bands. With a rasping and dolorous voice, he recorded a wide range of country and southern urban songs, from *Rolling Mill Blues* (Columbia 14438, 1929) which evoked the white ballad *900 Miles*, to a gambling song, *Skin Game Blues* (Columbia 14473, 1927), as well as many sombre slow blues. But with his 'Gang', which included the fiddle player Eddie Anthony and the guitarists Henry Williams, Jim Hill or Ollie Griffin, he recorded rowdy country dances like *Beaver Slide Rag* (Columbia 14210, 1927) or *Peg Leg Stomp* (Columbia 14298, 1927) on which Anthony's 'alley fiddle' sawing and scraping contributed a raw but swinging movement.

String bands are known to have been widespread throughout the south, but they seem not to have attracted record companies. One of the few to make recordings was the Texas-based Dallas String Band led by Coley Jones. Its *Dallas Rag* (Columbia 14290,

67

1927), with ringing mandolins, guitar and bass fiddle, is an exceptional example of string ragtime, while *Shine* (Columbia 14574, 1929) demonstrates the range of popular music that such bands played for black and white audiences.

In Mississippi, Sid Hemphill's string band, like the Texas string group led by the Wright Brothers, remained unrecorded. But the Mississippi Sheiks, in reduced form, made many records. It was a family band with as many as 11 members playing a variety of instruments, including the clarinet and the piano as well as guitars and fiddles. Bo Carter (Armenter Chatmon) (*b* Bolton, Mississippi, 21 March 1893; *d* Memphis, 21 Sept 1964) was the best known. During World War I the Mississippi Sheiks worked for country dances and played for white functions. Later, three or four members, including Bo Carter and his brother Sam Chatmon, made some lively recordings like *The Jazz Fiddler* (Okeh 45436, 1930), *Loose like that* (Okeh 8820, 1930) and *Sales Tax* (Bluebird 5453, 1934). Some had comic elements but gave a good impression of southern string band music. Bo Carter went on to make a career as a solo blues singer and was one of the most extensively recorded in the 1930s, his work being noted for its clear, fluent guitar picking and somewhat wistful vocals.

Popular for their novelty at medicine shows and rural picnics were jug bands, in which a jug, blown across the top, was played as a bass instrument. Generally only one jug was used in such a band, which otherwise comprised strings and a melody instrument like a harmonica or kazoo. However, one of the earliest groups to record, the Dixieland Jug Blowers from Louisville, Kentucky, occasionally used two jugs, as in *Skip skat doodle do* (Victor 20649, 1926), and as many as three horns, as in *Southern Shout* (Victor 20954, 1927). The jazz clarinettist Johnny Dodds performed with them on some recordings and the jazz pianist Clarence Williams also favoured the jug, playing it himself on *Chizzlin' Sam* (Columbia 2829, 1933). Will Shade's Memphis Jug Band and Gus Cannon's Jug Stompers, both based in Memphis, were pre-eminent among early jug bands. The former's *K. C. Moan* (Victor 38558, 1929) features an interplay of harmonica or kazoo against strings and jug, making it a masterpiece in the genre.

Jug bands played blues and songster material, as shown by the recordings of Gus Cannon or 'Banjo Joe' (*b* Red Banks, Mississippi, 12 Sept 1883; *d* Memphis, 15 Oct 1979). Cannon was raised on a Mississippi plantation where, as a child, he made a banjo from a frying pan. In his early teens he played at labour camps in the south while working on the railway. Playing with the harmonica player Noah Lewis from about 1910, he performed for country dances and travelling medicine shows. His first recordings, under the name Banjo Joe, included a satirical song about Booker T. Washington, *Can you blame the coloured man?* (Paramount 12571, 1927). The first recordings by Cannon's Jug Stompers, in which Cannon himself played the bass line on the jug, were made in 1928. Cannon's vocals had curious diphthong vowels, as in *Heart Breakin' Blues* (Victor 38523, 1928) or the fast *Feather Bed* (Victor 38515,

69

1928). *Minglewood Blues* (Victor 21267, 1928) was distinguished by Noah Lewis's sensitive harmonica playing, while Hosea Woods's kazoo imparted a 'country' quality to the band's sound; their performances, however, were carefully integrated and considered, as a comparison of two 'takes' of *Viola Lee Blues* reveals (Victor 38523, Victor RCX202, 1928). For the last 40 years of his life, Cannon worked as a street cleaner in Memphis.

Jack Kelly's South Memphis Jug Band was more primitive than Cannon's groups, as *Highway No.61 Blues* (Melotone 12773, 1933) shows, but members of this loosely formed group were still performing in the 1960s. Jug bands existed in other states, including the Birmingham Jug Band from Alabama who recorded a fine *Gettin' Ready for Trial* (Okeh 8856, 1930), and the Cincinnati Jug Band led by the guitarist Bob Coleman in *Newport Blues* (Paramount 12743, 1929).

Similar to the jug band, the washboard band was an instrumental group that included a scrubbing board as a rhythm instrument, played by drawing a nail, fork or thimbles over the corrugations to produce a loud, staccato sound. Early washboard bands included string instruments and were frequently augmented by other improvised instruments such as a wash-tub bass (perhaps distantly related to the African earth bow), comb and paper, or kazoo, as well as a harmonica. They are closely related to the children's 'spasm bands' of New Orleans; the white band led by Stalebread Lacoume in 1897 was the best documented, though it may not have included a washboard player. Typical performances by folk washboard bands are *Diamond Ring* (Gennett 7157, 1930) by Walter Taylor and the Washboard Trio and Chasey Collins's *Atlanta Town* (Bluebird 6187, 1935). Washboards were frequently used to accompany blues vocalists, and at least one singer, Washboard Sam (Robert Brown), played a washboard while singing, as on the rasping *Rack 'em back* (Bluebird 8044, 1938) or *Levee Camp Blues* (Bluebird 8909, 1941).

As novelty bands, jug and washboard groups sometimes featured women singers, like Jennie Clayton or Hattie Hart; Laura Dukes played the ukulele with Will Batts, Jack Kelly and the South Memphis Jug Band. Although women folk blues singers made records, they were much in the minority compared with men. Exceptions were Bessie Tucker, a powerful-voiced singer from Texas whose songs were largely about prison, and Lucille Bogan (Bessie Jackson) from Birmingham, Alabama, who sang robust blues about prostitution and lesbianism.

Memphis Minnie McCoy (née Douglas) (*b* Algiers, Louisiana, 3 June 1896; *d* Memphis, 6 Aug 1973) stands in relation to the women country blues singers as Bessie Smith did to those in vaudeville; no other woman singer attained her stature. She was the only significant woman instrumentalist, playing the guitar with the forceful, swinging rhythm characteristic of many Memphis-based musicians. As Kid Douglas, she earned her living in the streets of Memphis at the age of eight. Her voice was strong, with breadth in the middle range, and her guitar playing was ex-

71

tremely well phrased, as in her best-selling *Bumble Bee* (Vocalion 1476, 1930). Many of her blues were topical or autobiographical: *Memphis Minnie-jitis Blues* (Vocalion 1588, 1930) referred to her illness. Among her finest recordings were the guitar duets with her first husband, the Mississippi blues guitarist and mandolin player Joe McCoy, including the exceptional *Let's go to town* (Vocalion 1660, 1931). Later she married the guitarist 'Casey Bill' Weldon, with whom she made a rousing *Joe Louis Strut* (Vocalion 3046, 1935). Her third husband, Ernest 'Lil Son' Lawler, was also a blues guitarist who supported her in *Me and my Chauffeur Blues* (Okeh 06288, 1941). For nearly 30 years she lived in Chicago, where her 'Blues Monday parties' for singers were celebrated.

These women folk blues singers were admired for the masculinity of their approach; femininity was replaced by a bragging sexuality. Black women were expected to raise children and keep the home together; black males often had to migrate to obtain work, at any rate seasonally, and male blues singers were acknowledged as footloose. They took blues to the urban north.

VIII Piano blues and the northern migration

Though blues is strongly associated with guitar playing, there were many southern blues pianists. Some, like Skip James, played both instruments: his *Little Cow and Calf is Gonna Die Blues* (Paramount 13085, 1931) is typically idiosyncratic with its broken rhythms and unusual phrasing. Many southern blues singers worked naturally with the piano, Whistling Alex Moore (*b* Dallas, 22 Nov 1899) being among the more original. He earned a living as a junk man in Dallas and augmented it by playing in bars and saloons. His blues are notable for their unusual lyrics, which have the poetic cast characteristic of Texas; they include *West Texas Woman* (Columbia 14496, 1929) and the mildly erotic *Blue Bloomer Blues* (Columbia 14596, 1929). Moore's blues tended to be contemplative; those of Charles 'Cow Cow' Davenport (*b* Anniston, Alabama, 23 April 1894; *d* Cleveland, 3 Dec 1955) were more robust. Davenport played at cabarets and clubs in Atlanta and toured with travelling shows before World War I. With its strong, percussive technique, his playing showed the influence of ragtime on *Atlanta Rag* (Gennett 6869, 1929) and of the backroom style known as 'barrel-house' in *Back in the Alley* (Vocalion 1282, 1929). His reputation and his nickname came from *Cow Cow Blues* (Vocalion 1198, 1928), a powerful, medium-tempo train imitation with impressive climbing phrases and studied discords.

The shadings and inflections of blues are achieved relatively simply on a guitar, but the blues pianist can only produce the grace notes and glissandos of blues by 'crushing' the keys (striking them not quite simultaneously) and create blues rhythm by syncopation and strongly accented rhythmic phrases. Blues piano style may have derived partly from ragtime; the type played in 'barrelhouses', bars and makeshift saloons of lumber camps and towns in the south, has affinities with improvised rags. *Chain 'em Down* (Paramount

73

12879, 1929) by Blind Leroy Garnett or *Barrel House Man* (Paramount 12549, 1927) by the Texas pianist Will Ezell demonstrate the link. 'Barrelhouse' was used as a term for 'rough' or 'crude', as in 'Mooch' Richardson's *Low Down Barrel House Blues* (Okeh 8554, 1928), and as a nickname for several blues singers, among them Nolan Welch, Buck McFarland and Bukka White.

As a piano style, barrelhouse was generally played in regular 4/4 metre with ragtime bass figures or the heavy left-hand vamp known as 'stomping' used to provide bass variations. Characteristic recorded examples are *The Dirty Dozen* by Speckled Red (Rufus Perryman) (Brunswick 7116, 1929); and *Soon this morning* by Charlie Spand (Paramount 12790, 1929); both Perryman and Spand worked in Detroit after leaving the south. Washboard Sam's *Diggin' my potatoes* (Bluebird 8211, 1939) with Joshua Altheimer (piano) and *Shack Bully Stomp* (Decca 7479, 1938) by Peetie Wheatstraw (William Bunch) are examples of the persistence of the style. Many barrelhouse themes became 'standards' and were played by blues pianists after later styles had been adopted.

Bass figures were important in the development of piano blues; the 'walking bass' of broken or spread octaves repeated through the blues progression provided the ground for countless improvisations. They are reported to have been used by 19th-century ragtime pianists and the first in print appears to be in Boone's *Rag Medley no.11* (1909). The bass figures are used by Artie Matthews in his *Pastime Rag no.1* (published 1913) and his *Weary Blues* (1915). George

Thomas (Sippie Wallace's father) composed *New Orleans Hop Scop Blues* (1911, published 1916) which included a walking bass and (under the pseudonym Clay Custer) made the first recorded example of the idiom, *The Rocks* (Okeh 4809, 1923).

The 'Rocks', the 'Chains', the 'Fives' and other bass figures were loosely identified and used even quavers, dotted quavers and semiquavers, and triplets. The right-hand configurations were both rhythmic and melodic, with sharp ostinato passages and sequences in 3rds and 6ths. There are some unusual, virtuoso performances on record, like Wesley Wallace's train imitation *No.29* (Paramount 12958, 1930) which used 6/4 time in the bass and 4/4 in the treble. Such a feat is made possible by the independence of the right-hand improvisations from the left hand's steady, rolling rhythm, which may also give rise to startling dissonances and frequent cross-rhythms. Discords and rapid 'crushed' or 'press' notes were obtained by striking adjacent notes in rapid succession, for example in Meade 'Lux' Lewis's *Honky Tonk Train Blues* (Paramount 12896, 1927), one of the first recordings to feature the fast piano blues style known as 'boogie-woogie'.

Boogie-woogie probably originated in the south, being favoured by bar-room pianists for its volume and momentum. It is characterized by the use of blues chord progressions as a forceful, repetitive left-hand figure. There are many such bass patterns but the most familiar are the 'doubling' of the simple blues bass and the 'walking bass' in broken octaves. Clarence 'Pine Top' Smith (*b* Troy, Alabama, 11 Jan

75

1904; *d* Chicago, 15 March 1929) was the first to popularize the style and the original issue of *Pine Top's Boogie Woogie* (Vocalion 1245, 1928) was probably the most influential and widely imitated of all blues records. It is a piano solo with spoken comments, suggesting that it was the accompaniment to a dance. Smith was an entertainer and tap-dancer as well as a musician, and this is evident in the monologue style of *Now I ain't got nothin' at all* (Vocalion 1298, 1929). Only his *Pine Top's Blues* (Vocalion 1245, 1928) is in traditional blues vein and he sings it in a high, even petulant and childlike voice. Though Smith influenced Albert Ammons, a pianist who used the 'powerhouse' rhythm of left-hand walking-bass figures later popularized in jazz, his playing was characterized by a more mellow, lightly rolling quality. He was accidentally shot when he was 25 during a fracas in the masonic lodge where he was performing.

The first generation of 'boogie-woogie' pianists, who prominently featured walking bass and eight-to-the-bar rhythms, recorded some notable examples, among them Romeo Nelson's *Head Rag Hop* (Vocalion 1447, 1929), Arthur 'Montana' Taylor's *Indiana Avenue Stomp* (Vocalion 1419, 1929) and Charles Avery's *Dearborn Street Breakdown* (Paramount 12896, 1929). A few were recorded some years later, among them 'Cripple' Clarence Lofton (*b* Kingsport, Tennessee, 28 March 1887; *d* Chicago, 9 Jan 1957) who was one of the earliest blues and boogie-woogie pianists. He moved to Chicago in 1917 and became celebrated as a 'rent-party' pianist, later playing in his own saloon in State Street. In spite of having a club foot, he was a dynamic performer, dancing, whistling, singing and tapping rhythms while he played the piano. His earliest recordings included *Brown Skin Girls* (Melotone 6-11-66, 1935) with the guitarist Big Bill Broonzy and (with an unknown washboard player) *Strut that thing* (Vocalion 02951, 1935), one of the most vigorous examples of boogie–barrelhouse on record, enriched by his character-istically gritty vocal. Lofton also accompanied Red Nelson (Nelson Wilborn, *b* 1907) in whose *Streamline Train* (Decca 7171, 1936) he played a rolling version of the *Cow Cow Blues* with strong walking-bass figures.

Nearly 20 years younger than Lofton, Roosevelt Sykes (*b* Elmar, Arkansas, 31 Jan 1906; *d* New Orleans, 11 July 1983) was one of a remarkable generation of blues pianists. He ran away from home at the age of 15 to play in barrelhouses in Louisiana and Mississippi, often with Lee 'Porkchops' Green, who taught him to play the *44 Blues* (Okeh 8702, 1929). The climbing bass figures of this distinctive blues theme, first recorded by Sykes, became a 'standard'. A strong, if generally uncomplicated pianist, Sykes was the innovator of other popular blues, including *32–20 Blues* (Victor 38619, 1930), made under his pseudonym of Willie Kelly, and *Highway 61 Blues* (Champion 16586, 1932). His records sold well and he was one of the most frequently recorded blues pianists of the 1930s, often accompanying other singers, including Mary Johnson, Edith Johnson and 'St Louis Jimmy' Oden.

Although he settled in St Louis, Sykes often stayed in Chicago, which he reached before his lifelong friend and rival, Eurreal Wilford 'Little Brother' Montgomery (*b* Kentwood, Louisiana, 18 April 1906; *d* Chicago, 6 September 1985). Montgomery was the son of a honky-tonk owner so he heard many blues pianists. He had a remarkable aural memory. Besides blues, he played ragtime, jazz and novelty pieces, sat in with Sam Morgan's Jazz Band in New Orleans and toured with jazz groups, including Clarence Desdune's Joyland Revelers, arriving in Chicago in 1928. *Vicksburg Blues* (Paramount 13006, 1930), his first record, was his version of the *44 Blues* (already recorded by Sykes). He showed his mastery of bass figures and subtle right-hand work on a train imitation, *Frisco Hi-ball Blues* (Vocalion 02706, 1931). Later, on a visit to the south in October 1936, Montgomery made no less than 18 titles at a single sitting, an unprecedented feat made more remarkable by their exceptional quality. *Something keeps a-worryin' me* (Bluebird 6658, 1936) had a typically high-pitched, whinnying vocal but a piano accompaniment that bore comparison with Earl Hines; *Farish Street Jive* (Bluebird 6894, 1936), on the other hand, had strong ragtime and boogie-woogie strains.

Though some maintained links with their southern home states, to which they returned in the harsh northern winters, hundreds of blues singers, pianists, guitarists and other instrumentalists went to Chicago and Detroit in the decade following World War I. The tide of immigrants forced up rent prices and pianists played for beer and tips at 'rent parties' organized in tenements for mutual aid. Many blues teams were formed by pianists and guitarists: Charlie Spand with Blind Blake, Big Bill Broonzy with Black Bob, Georgia Tom with Tampa Red.

Unique in having made a considerable reputation in both blues and gospel music, Thomas A. Dorsey, 'Georgia Tom' (*b* Villa Rica, Georgia, 1899), was the son of a revivalist preacher. In Atlanta about 1910 he came under the influence of local unrecorded blues pianists and when he migrated north during World War I he played the piano at clubs in Gary, Indiana. Later he studied at the Chicago College of Composition and Arranging and became an agent for Paramount records. Dorsey's compositions at this time included *Riverside Blues* recorded by King Oliver's Creole Jazz Band (Okeh 40034, 1923). He joined Les Hite's Whispering Serenaders as pianist, composer and arranger in 1923, and soon after formed his own Wildcat's Jazz Band, with which he worked with Ma Rainey. With the slide guitarist Tampa Red (Hudson Whittaker) he recorded with her. Their simple ditty *Tight like that* (Vocalion 1216, 1928), issued under Tampa Red's name, proved to be one of the best selling of all blues records; it combined sly urban sophistication and rural humour and was the inspiration for many of their 'hokum' records. Several of these were ribald songs, including *Selling that stuff* by the Hokum Boys (Paramount 11714, 1928) and *Terrible Operation Blues* (Decca 7259, 1930) with Jane Lucas.

It was a new formula for blues: entertainment with no serious intent. A healthy lust was expressed through hokum, which mildly ridiculed country manners while helping southern immigrants to cope with urban life. With Big Bill Broonzy, another member of the Hokum Boys, Georgia Tom and Tampa Red managed to go on making records when the financial crash of October 1929 stopped most blues recording.

IX Southern blues in the 1930s

Early in 1933, after a year of virtually no blues recordings, they appeared again in the monthly sheets announcing releases. The most popular blues singer was Leroy Carr (*b* Nashville, Tenn., 1905; *d* Indianapolis, 28 April 1935), a pianist who was accompanied with uncanny rapport by the guitarist Scrapper Blackwell. They met in their early 20s and though both recorded solo it was as a team that they were most impressive. Carr generally sang, accompanying himself in a smoothly rolling, boogie-woogie-influenced piano style. His melancholy voice was comparatively sweet for blues, and the lyrics (jointly composed) were reflective and poetic, coloured by a sense of disappointment rather than bitterness, reflecting the mood of many of their listeners. Blackwell's clearcut guitar picking acted as a strong foil. Their *How Long, How Long Blues* (Vocalion 1191, 1928), *Midnight Hour Blues* (Vocalion 1703, 1932), *Hurry Down Sunshine* (Vocalion 02741, 1934) and *Prison Bound* (Vocalion 1241, 1928) were among the compositions that passed rapidly into the repertories of many blues singers and that have still not lost their appeal. When Carr died from alcoholism, many blues were dedicated to his memory. Blackwell never recovered from the shock of Carr's death; he was murdered 30 years later. The fatalism of Carr's blues is found in the work of his principal imitator, Bumble Bee Slim (Amos Easton), in that of Walter Davis, a pianist based in St Louis, and in the recordings of Peetie Wheatstraw. They all had somewhat flat voices and a far less expressive delivery than that of the previous generation of blues singers.

Peetie Wheatstraw (William Bunch) (*b* Ripley, Tenn., 21 Dec 1902; *d* East St Louis, 21 Dec 1941) spent most of his life in East St Louis and was a popular singer in the notorious 'Valley' district. When he recorded *Tennessee Peaches Blues* (Vocalion 1552, 1930) at the age of 28, he gained wide fame and from then until a month before his death (in an accident on a railway crossing) he recorded over 160 titles. Billed as 'The Devil's Son-in-Law' on his records and once as 'The High Sheriff from Hell', Wheatstraw cultivated a nonchalant attitude that contrasted with the more passionate vocals of many Mississippi singers. Copied by others, some claiming a personal association with him on their records, he was reputedly a good guitarist though he was usually recorded playing the piano. He sang of gamblers, prostitutes, bootleggers and hoboes – *Kidnapper's Blues* (Vocalion 03249, 1936) being typical – and more than any other blues singer he was a spokesman for black working-class people. Employment, or unemployment, was a recurrent theme, for example in *Working on the project* (Decca 7311, 1937). Unfortunately Decca used more sophisticated accompaniments on his later records, which are interesting lyrically but less successful musically.

Wheatstraw often worked with James 'Kokomo' Arnold (*b* Lovejoy, Georgia, 15 Feb 1901; *d* Chicago, 8 Nov 1968), who was an accomplished musician. Arnold left the Georgia farm where he was raised to settle in Buffalo, New York, and in his 20s he travelled as far south as Mississippi. He played a steel-bodied guitar, laid horizontally across his lap, stroking the strings with a glass flask to produce a wailing sound. His vocals were pitched high on many of his records, but his natural voice was lower, with a buzzing tone that he often used as a drone in guitar solos. In Memphis, as 'Gitfiddle Jim', he recorded *Paddlin' Blues* (Victor 23268, 1930), an instrumental tour de force. Later he was recorded by Decca and *Old Original Kokomo Blues* (Decca 7026, 1934) was an immediate success; he made over 70 titles in the next four years, and several more with Wheatstraw, *Set down gal* (Decca 7361, 1937) being a fine example of their barrelhouse duets. The solo *Policy Wheel Blues* (Decca 7147, 1935) was typical of his lyrically original blues. *The Twelves* (Decca 7083, 1935), a version of *The Dirty Dozens*, used a traditional theme as a vehicle for his exciting playing. In 1936 Arnold began working in a steel mill, eventually giving up music.

Though the cooler, urbane singing of Leroy Carr and his followers was immensely popular, not only in the north but among young southerners who responded to their more sophisticated approach to blues, there were numerous singers besides Arnold who recorded in traditional manner with parochial lyrics and rural-style accompaniment. Among the more notable was John Adam 'Sleepy John' Estes (*b* Ripley, Tenn., 25 Jan 1899; *d* Brownsville, Tenn., 5 June 1977). With limited sight, he farmed when he could, but he learnt to play the guitar and performed for country picnics and parties in the Brownsville area. Accompanied by Yank Rachell, a local mandolin player, *Milk Cow Blues* (Victor 38614, 1930) had the punctuated phrasing, broken voice and compelling swing that characterized his best recordings. He made a number of them with the young harmonica player Hammie Nixon, *Drop down Mama* (Decca 7289, 1935) having beautifully integrated instrumental lines. Estes drew from his personal experience: *Floating Bridge* (Decca 7442, 1937) told of nearly drowning and *Brownsville Blues* (Decca 7473, 1938) and *Lawyer Clark Blues* (Bluebird 8871, 1941), with Brownsville Son Bonds playing second guitar, described local characters. Losing his sight completely during the following decade, he returned to Brownsville from Chicago.

Further east, in the Carolinas, younger singers included Buddy Moss and Josh White. 'Blind Boy' Fuller (Fulton Allen) (*b* Wadesboro, North Carolina, *c*1909; *d* Durham, North Carolina, 13 Feb 1941) was the most influential. Though not an innovator of the eastern, or Piedmont, style of blues, Fuller was its best-known exponent. Influenced by Blind Blake, Buddy Moss and the evangelist Blind Gary Davis, he formulated an eclectic style with fast guitar runs, swinging rag rhythms and gritty vocals, often against wash board cross-rhythms. Davis accompanied him on the traditional *Rag Mama Rag* (Vocalion 03084, 1935), one of his earliest successes. Fuller was probably at his best in fast, ragtime music such as *Step it up and go* (Vocalion 05476, 1940) but he was also a master of slow blues like *Weeping Willow* (Decca 7881, 1937). Generally he played with finger picks but on *Homesick and Lonesome Blues* (Vocalion 03234, 1935) he used the slide to brilliant effect. From late 1937 Fuller was regularly accompanied by Sonny Terry, a young blind virtuoso harmonica player, for example in *Pistol Slapper Blues* (Vocalion 04106, 1938).

Sonny Terry (Sanders Terrell) (*b* Greensboro, Georgia, 24 Oct 1911; *d* New York, 12 March 1986) was born and raised on a farm. Having lost his sight as a child he played the harmonica for money in the streets. Moving to North Carolina he joined Blind Boy Fuller playing in the tobacco towns, complementing Fuller's singing with wailing, strongly vocalized harmonica playing. In *Harmonica and Washboard Breakdown* (Okeh 05453, 1940) his virtuosity was fully apparent. Terry had evolved a technique of 'cross-note' playing (see p.170) which surpassed that of all his contemporaries, modulating and bending notes with breath control and fluttering fingers or cupped hands over the 'harp'. He interspersed shrill cries and could alternate harmonica and voice without a break, creating a continuous melodic flow. When Fuller died Terry formed a partnership with the guitarist Brownie McGhee (*b* 1915) that was to last 35 years, longer than any other in blues. Terry's crying harmonica and guttural, sometimes slightly off-key vocals were offset by McGhee's light, smooth guitar playing and mellow singing.

In Mississippi there were still scores of blues singers. Charley Patton made recordings in the year of his death, 1934, but 16 of the titles remained unissued; Tommy Johnson and Son House were active but unrecorded. Bo Carter however was recording steadily and Tommy Johnson's accompanist, Joe McCoy, had updated his image and was working with the Harlem Hamfats. While 'Big Joe' Williams was barking out rough country blues, Johnny Temple was singing to a succession of different accompaniments, not all of them satisfactory. Towards the end of the decade a new wave of 'downhome' singers, with their roots in the Patton–Brown–House tradition, appeared. Coarser and fiercer than their predecessors, they were a powerful stimulant to southern blues. Tommy McClennan's *New shake 'em on down* (Bluebird 8347, 1939), Robert Petway's *Catfish Blues* (Bluebird 8838, 1941) and Bukka (Booker) White's *Fixin' to Die Blues* (Vocalion 05588, 1940) had hard-driving guitar accompaniments to guttural vocals. White was especially noteworthy; his lyrics were often (as here) of great interest and his use of the slide, especially in train imitations like *Special Stream Line* (Vocalion 05526, 1940), was particularly effective.

Of these later singers, it was Robert Johnson (*b* Hazlehurst, Mississippi, *c*1912; *d* Greenwood, Mississippi, 16 Aug 1938), with his highly introverted, sometimes obsessional blues sung to whining guitar and throbbing beat, who left the deepest impression.

85

Ten years younger than Son House, he was the singer-guitarist who established the link between the rural Mississippi tradition and modern Chicago blues. But he was indebted too to the records of other singers. Influenced directly by Son House and by records of Lonnie Johnson, Leroy Carr and even Kokomo Arnold, he was also aware of the work of Skip James and Hambone Willie Newburn, whose themes he adapted in *32–20 Blues* (Vocalion 03445, 1936) and *If I had possession over judgement day* (Columbia CL1654, 1936). The latter, unissued in his lifetime, revealed an aspect of the tormented, even prophetic, theme of the haunted *Hell hound on my trail* (Vocalion 03623, 1937). Johnson's voice was taut and often strained, but he used falsetto to good effect, as on *Kind Hearted Woman* (Vocalion 03510, 1936). The persistent, walking-bass rhythm of *I believe I'll dust my broom* (Vocalion 03475, 1936) or *Ramblin' on my mind* (Vocalion 03519, 1936) profoundly influenced the postwar generation of blues singers, including Elmore James, his one-time companion Johnny Shines and his stepson Robert 'Junior' Lockwood. Johnson met a violent death, but his reputation rests on his remarkable recordings and not on the legends that have grown about him.

X Urban blues in the 1930s

During the Depression tough conditions in New York, Detroit and Chicago stimulated more aggressive and extrovert blues sounds and collective performance.. The centre of this development was Chicago, where the undisputed leader in the 1930s was

'Big Bill' (William Lee Conley) Broonzy (*b* Scott, Mississippi, 26 June 1893; *d* Chicago, 14 Aug 1958). Living on a farm in Arkansas until his late 20s, Broonzy was a link between the country and urban traditions. He was a fiddle player who settled in Chicago in 1920 and learnt to play the guitar, on which he was an outstanding performer when he began to record ten years later. One of the most recorded blues singers, he played in a light, lilting style. Some of his blues were wistful, poetic statements, complemented by moaning notes on the strings, like *Big Bill Blues* (Champion 16400, 1932) and *Friendless Blues* (Bluebird 5535, 1934), but Broonzy also recorded many songs of a gently ribald or hokum character, including *Keep your hands off her* (Bluebird 6188, 1935) or *Good Jelly* (Bluebird 5998, 1935), with Black Bob giving sympathetic piano support in a manner recalling the Leroy Carr–Scrapper Blackwell team.

By the mid-1930s the customary Chicago group of guitar, piano and often string bass had expanded to a five-piece band. Tampa Red seems to have pioneered these larger groups and it was *Let's get drunk and truck* (Bluebird 6335, 1936), made with his Chicago Five, that ushered in a new phase of urban blues. It was a swinging dance number, but it was followed by others with a tougher sound. Only a couple of weeks later, in April 1936, the Harlem Hamfats recorded *Oh Red* (Decca 7182, 1936), the first of over 70 titles. In spite of its name, it was a Chicago-based band with Herb Morand from New Orleans playing the trumpet and Odell Rand's reedy clarinet. Though it

87

often played swinging jazz, like *Tempo De Bucket* (Decca 7382, 1937), this seven-piece group included the guitar-playing brothers Joe and Charlie McCoy, who had played with Tommy Johnson and Ishman Bracey in Mississippi, and Joe took most of the vocals.

The jazz flavour of late 1930s Chicago blues was evident in many records by Tampa Red's Chicago Five with Arnett Nelson (clarinet) or Bill Owsley (tenor saxophone) and in Broonzy's recordings with the trumpeters Punch Miller or Alfred Bell. Broonzy's half-brother, Robert Brown (known as Washboard Sam), had a rough but musical voice that matched his washboard playing. Many of his records, among them *Washboard's Barrel House Song* (Bluebird 7291, 1937) and *Down at the Village Store* (Bluebird 7526, 1938), included Arnett Nelson (clarinet) or Buster Bennett (alto saxophone) and in some Herb Morand also played against a solid blues foundation laid by Broonzy and the pianists Blind John Davis, Horace Malcolm or Simeon Henry.

It was the emergence of the harmonica as a lead instrument in Chicago groups and the presence of some particularly strong blues and boogie pianists that turned blues away from the influence of jazz wind instruments. The harmonica's role was reflected in the nickname of William Gillum who, as 'Jazz' Gillum, began recording at this time. His *Sarah Jane* (Bluebird 6445, 1936) was an ironic country-dance tune but with Broonzy he was soon recording tougher, essentially urban blues. He was not a particularly inventive player, favouring short, piping high notes, but he was adequate in such recordings as *It sure had a kick*

88

(Bluebird 8505, 1940) and *War Time Blues* (Bluebird 8943, 1941).

Far superior was John Lee 'Sonny Boy' Williamson (ii) (*b* c1916; *d* Chicago, 1 June 1948), a highly influential harmonica player with a 'tongue-tied' voice. With the possible exception of Little Walter, on whom he was a strong influence, no harmonica player made as great an impact as Williamson, whose technique of squeezing notes and playing 'cross-harp' (e.g. the key of E on a harmonica in A) was widely imitated. *Good Morning School Girl* (Bluebird 7059, 1937), his first recording, introduced his unique instrumental style; his slight speech impediment gave his voice a distinctive quality in *Big Apple Blues* (Bluebird 8766, 1941). His lyrics were often extremely original; they included biographical themes like *Bad Luck Blues* (Bluebird 8265, 1939) on the murder of his cousin, such narratives as *Joe Louis and John Henry Blues* (Bluebird 8403, 1939) and the patriotic *War Time Blues* (Bluebird 8580, 1940). Many were taken at a brisk 'jump' tempo, such as *Sloppy Drunk Blues* (Bluebird 8822, 1941) and *Mellow Chick Swing* (Victor 202369, 1947), which gained from the presence of Broonzy or Willie Lacey (guitar) and Blind John Davis or Big Maceo (piano).

'Big Maceo' Major Merriweather (*b* Atlanta, 31 March 1905; *d* Chicago, 26 Feb 1953) was a forceful pianist who worked in Detroit before joining Tampa Red in Chicago. The contrast of Tampa's distinctive bottleneck guitar with Maceo's rumbling bass figures and wistful voice in *Worried Life Blues* (Bluebird 8827, 1941) set the pattern for a number of successful recordings by the duo, but they are probably best remembered for the headlong instrumental *Texas Stomp* (Victor 20-2028, 1945) and *Chicago Breakdown* (Bluebird 34-0743, 1945). Maceo suffered an incapacitating stroke and his last recordings were made with the young Eddie Boyd playing the piano. Memphis Slim was another of the young blues singers who made their début just before World War II. His loud voice and strong piano playing, modelled largely on Roosevelt Sykes, may be heard, for example, in *Beer Drinking Woman* (Bluebird 8584, 1940).

While some boogie-woogie pianists were playing at rent parties and others in expanding blues bands, a few gained more than local popularity. John Hammond traced Meade 'Lux' Lewis and Albert Ammons, who in 1935 were taxi drivers in Chicago. Their rediscovery led to that of others, including Jimmy Yancey, whose faintly Hispanic basses and elegantly simple right-hand figures provided a sober accompaniment to the hard-edged singing of his wife, Estelle 'Mama' Yancey. His contemplative approach was not suited to stage presentation. Lewis and Ammons were joined by a duo from Kansas City, the boogie pianist Pete Johnson and his vocalist Joe Turner. Ammons, Lewis and Johnson became popular at Café Society, New York, as the Boogie Woogie Trio. Linked to the swing craze, boogie enjoyed a brief vogue and many commercial and swing recordings were made, including *Boogie Woogie* by Tommy Dorsey and his Orchestra (Victor 26054, 1938) and Count Basie's *Basie Boogie* (Okeh 6330, 1941). Some, like Will Bradley's

Boogie Woogie Conga (Columbia 35994, 1941) and Charlie Barnet's *Scrub me Mama, with a boogie beat* (Bluebird 10975, 1940), bore little relation to the original piano idiom. A number of outstanding recordings were made by authentic boogie pianists, however, including Pete Johnson's *Goin' Away Blues* (Vocalion 4607, 1938), with vocal by Joe Turner, and Albert Ammons's *Chicago in Mind* (Blue Note 4, 1939).

The widespread popularity of boogie pianists did not outlast the swing craze, but the powerful singing of Joseph Vernon ('Big Joe') Turner (*b* Kansas City, 18 May 1911; *d* Inglewood, Calif., 24 Nov 1985) was an important influence on postwar blues. Starting his career at the age of 14 in Kansas City clubs, he became known as 'the singing bartender' and soon attracted the attention of the bandleaders Bennie Moten, Andy Kirk and Count Basie with whom he toured. From the mid-1930s he was frequently accompanied by Pete Johnson, with whom he appeared at the 'From Spirituals to Swing' concerts at Carnegie Hall in 1938. A few days later he made his first recordings: *Roll 'em Pete* (Vocalion 4607, 1938) features spectacular piano playing by Johnson and a forceful vocal by Turner in the style he made famous – half-shouted and with repetitive phrases building up tension at the close. Though he was best known as a blues 'shouter', Turner had a musical voice and was a sensitive singer in slow blues like *Lucille* (Decca 8577, 1941). Throughout the 1940s and 1950s he toured extensively with bands and solo pianists, his singing becoming recognized as a model of the jazz–blues approach in its strength, relaxed delivery, hot tone and subtle inflections. *Old Piney Brown is gone* (Swing-time 154, 1949) reflected his Kansas City background, while *You're driving me crazy* (Atlantic 1234, 1956) revealed his capacity to invest a popular song with blues quality. It was his *Shake rattle and roll* (Atlantic 1026, 1954) that anticipated rock-and-roll.

XI Postwar blues on the West Coast

Until the end of World War II the recording of blues had been controlled by a few large companies, but in the late 1940s small companies, many owned by Blacks, started commercial production. Some were in southern cities, like Memphis or Houston, others on the West Coast, where a smooth style of blues created by westward-moving migrants from Texas found a new market. New concerns operated in Chicago and Detroit, so the output of blues recording was considerable. Until then blues had been classified commercially as 'race music' (black music). This segregation, which was even used in record catalogues, was a factor in the popularity of postwar 'rhythm-and-blues', a term free of racial connotations.

The war, the 'Petrillo ban' imposed by the Musicians' Union on recording, and the advent of independent record companies, were factors that made it easy to distinguish postwar from pre-war blues on record, but there had in fact been a steady evolution that recordings do not reflect. There were also shortlived fashions that wartime entertainment may have encouraged, such as 'jive'. The word has many meanings in black American usage; it may be derived from the Wolof

(West Africa) *jev*, meaning 'to talk disparagingly', a usage it retains in the USA. It is also applied to witty or deceitful speech, to a form of stylized jitter-bugging or athletic dancing, and to marihuana. In black music it was especially applied to the lightweight, rhythmic 'hokum' blues popular in the 1940s during the 'swing era'. Though the words of jive songs were often insinuating, witty, sophisticated or sly, the music was associated with 'good times'.

The principal exponent of jive was the much-recorded singer and alto saxophonist Louis Jordan, whose *You run your mouth and I'll run my business* (Decca 7705, 1940), *The chick's too young to fry* (Decca 23610, 1945), *Let the good times roll* (Decca 23741, 1945) and *Saturday Night Fish Fry* (Brunswick 04402, 1949) are typically extrovert. Other jive artists included Phil Moore, whose *I'm gonna see my baby* (Victor 20-1613, 1944) is a patriotic wartime piece, and the white pianist Harry 'the Hipster' Gibson who recorded a number of outrageous songs like *Who put the Benzedrine in Mrs Murphy's Ovaltine?* (Musicraft 346, 1944).

Though jive as such declined, it survived as a vein in the rhythm-and-blues idiom, particularly through the recordings of Wynonie Harris, for example *Grandma plays the numbers* (King 4276, 1948) and *Bloodshot Eyes* (King 4461, 1951). *Bloodshot Eyes* was a 'cover' (a competitive version of another artist's song) of the original by the white singer Hank Penny; it is an indication of the convergence of white and black styles that had begun during the war and that culminated in rock-and-roll. The term 'rhythm-and-

93

blues' covered as wide a range of forms as did 'race music'. Not all were blues or blues related; many gospel records appeared in 'rhythm-and-blues' lists, as did those of innumerable vocal harmonizing quartets. These extremely popular groups were related to an earlier group, the Ink Spots, and the gospel quartets of the 1930s and 1940s, but their music had become more sophisticated, secularized and sentimental. Among them were such performers as the Moonglows, the Flamingoes, the Drifters, the Dominoes, the Four Buddies, the Five Satins, the Pelicans and the Platters.

Blues bands ranged from the large-scale aggregations of Lucky Millinder, Tiny Bradshaw and Todd Rhodes to those adopting a much cruder approach, with harshly played, 'honking' saxophones and riffing accompaniments, like the bands of Bill Doggett or Bull Moose Jackson. Closer to the blues tradition, yet showing an awareness of popular black entertainers, were the singers who recorded for Bob Geddins and other new record producers on the West Coast. It was the coupling of a ballad *I Wonder* with a strong piano piece *Cecil's Boogie* (both Gilt Edge 501, 1944), by the 'GI Sing-Sation' Private Cecil Gant, that pointed the way. Gant's formula combined a popular idiom with more solid blues, symbolizing the meeting of styles found in the playing and singing of several migrants from Texas who had settled in Los Angeles or Oakland, California. They were centred on Charles Brown, a pianist from Texas City whose piano style bore traces of the tradition as exemplified by Whistling Alex Moore but who owed much to Nat 'King' Cole for his vocal technique. Working with the Three Blazers (the guitarists Johnny and Oscar Moore and the bass player Eddie Williams), he made many hit records, including his influential *Drifting Blues* (Aladdin 112, 1946) and *Merry Christmas baby* (Exclusive 63, 1947). Another West Coast singer–pianist was Floyd Dixon, whose *Houston Jump* (Supreme 1528, 1947) made its Texas origins clear; his *Bad Neighbourhood* (Aladdin 3121, 1950) was one of several recordings made with the Three Blazers. Hadda Brooks's *Hollywood House Party Boogie* (Modern 157, 1946) lived up to its title, but she was not averse to 'boogie-ing' classical music, for example in *Grieg's Concerto Boogie* (Modern 145, 1946). Influenced by Charles Brown, Amos Milburn also came from Houston; his *Train Time Blues* (Aladdin 206, 1947) was one of several hit records but, like those of others of this group (who favoured colourful ties, white suits and a sophisticated club presentation) his later recordings tended to be more commercial.

Closely associated with these pianists was the guitarist Lowell Fulson, a part-Indian musician from Oklahoma who had worked with Texas Alexander before going to the West Coast. He had a skilful, fluent guitar style and a stronger vocal technique than other West Coast singers; notable among his extensive recordings are *Every day I have the blues*, in which the pianist Lloyd Glenn was one of the accompanying group (Swing-time 196, 1950), and his hit *Reconsider baby* (Checker 804, 1954).

But it was another singer and guitarist from Texas,

Aaron (Thibeaux) 'T-Bone' Walker (*b* Linden, 28
May 1910; *d* Los Angeles, 16 March 1975), who was
probably the most influential performer to record on
the West Coast. At the age of 19, under the name
'Oak Cliff T-Bone', he made his first record: *Witchita
Falls Blues* (Columbia 14506, 1929), which showed
his indebtedness to Blind Lemon Jefferson whom he
had followed in Dallas. He travelled widely with
medicine shows in the early 1930s; after hearing Les
Paul playing an amplified guitar he began to play the
instrument himself. Though he developed electric
guitar techniques in blues at the same time as Charlie
Christian in jazz, Walker did not record again until
the war and not steadily until 1945. *Call it Stormy
Monday* (Black and White 122, 1947) was a seminal
modern blues with a small-group accompaniment.
Walker generally used a band, which compensated
for the thinness of his vocals and allowed him to ex-
temporize guitar arpeggios. *Too Much Trouble Blues*
(Capitol 944, 1947) and *Alimony Blues* (Imperial 5153,
1951) are, characteristically, topical with slightly
hoarse vocals, witty lyrics and vibrant, rapid guitar
phrases answering each stanza. Capable of clearly
defined, elaborate improvisations even on fast
themes, Walker is heard at his best on *Strollin' with
Bones* (Imperial 5071, 1950). Often the strength of his
orchestras threatens to predominate, but remakes of
his best-known blues, *Stormy Monday* and *Mean Old
World* (Atlantic 8020, 1956), show his work to advantage. Walker is significant as the artist who bridged the
gap between the Texas folk tradition and modern blues,
as exemplified by the urban sophistication of Riley
'B.B.' King, who was much influenced by him.

Postwar blues on the West Coast

Numerous singers who recorded in the 1940s and 1950s on the West Coast and in Louisiana (especially New Orleans) had occasional hits, among them the pianist Roy 'Professor Longhair' Byrd, the band-shouter Roy Brown, Charles 'Crown Prince' Waterford, Eddie 'Mister Cleanhead' Vinson and the guitarist–violinist Clarence 'Gatemouth' Brown. Many women singers also recorded and were popular among black audiences, including the glamorous Ruth Brown, the generously built and broad-voiced 'Big Maybelle' Smith and the tough, harmonica-playing Willie Mae 'Big Mama' Thornton.

Most of these singers worked substantially in the blues idiom but there were others whose discs were listed as rhythm-and-blues but whose approach was more compromising. Aimed at teenage buyers and with increasing commercial exploitation to attract attention, such groups and singers were often on the fringes of blues in the blurred categories of pop and rock-and-roll. Though meriting attention as a social phenomenon or for its influence on pop music and culture, rock-and-roll falls outside the scope of blues proper. The distinction is sometimes arbitrary or difficult, as in the case of the New Orleans pianist 'Fats' Domino (*b* New Orleans, 26 Feb 1928) who sang a blues song like *Please don't leave me* (Imperial 5240, 1953) or a popular song like *Blueberry Hill* (Imperial 5407, 1956) with the same sweet nostalgia. His records had considerable middle-class appeal and such records as *Ain't that a shame* (Imperial 5348, 1955), *Bo Weevil* (Imperial 5375, 1956) and the blues 'standard' *Blue Monday* (Imperial 5417, 1956) were million-sellers. Little Richard's frenetic pounding of the piano and screaming vocals owed their form, at least, to the blues, while Chuck Berry and Bo Diddley (Ellas McDaniel) introduced witty lyrics with topical references modelled on blues as well as on popular ballads. Yet they were not primarily blues singers but rock-and-roll performers with strong appeal to young black and white audiences.

It may have been the ambiguity of blues within the context of rhythm-and-blues and its links with rock-and-roll that made rhythm-and-blues hard to define. There was a parallel desire for earthier, traditionally based 'downhome' blues, which singers who remained in Texas and Louisiana could provide. Lil Son Jackson's *Cairo Blues* (Gold Star 663, 1948), *I'm long gone* (Specialty 478, 1953) by Frankie Lee Sims and *Country Gal* (Modern 20-532, 1948), one of scores made by Andrew 'Smokey' Hogg, were representative of the many titles recorded in Texas that maintained the characteristics of the local tradition. Of the Texas guitarists, none was more famous than Sam 'Lightnin'' Hopkins (*b* Centerville, Texas, 15 March 1912; *d* Houston, 30 Jan 1982). Not only was he one of the most recorded blues singers of the postwar era, but he was also one of the most consistent. The arpeggio playing in *Short Haired Woman* and the basic boogie-rhythms of *Big Mama Jump* (both Gold Star 3131, 1947) introduced styles to which he repeatedly returned. One of the few direct protest blues issued on a postwar commercial 78 r.p.m. record was *Tim Moore's Farm* (Gold Star 640, 1947), but its appeal was local. Later, in New York, Hopkins made *Coffee Blues* (Jax. 635, 1950) which was among his first nationally selling records. Many items reflected his milieu, including the gambling theme of *Policy Game* (Decca 48842, 1953) and the slow blues *Lonesome in your Home* (Herald 471, 1954). *Penitentiary Blues* (Folkways FS3822, 1959) is among his finest recordings, with marked vibrato in the rough-textured voice and clear guitar arpeggios. Many of Hopkins's blues are extempore, and he was given to startling and poetic images, as in *Have you ever seen a one-eyed woman cry* (77 LA 12/1, 1959). He recorded with his blues guitarist brothers John Henry and Joel Hopkins and exchanged verses wittily with Brownie McGhee, Big Joe Williams and Sonny Terry on *Wimmin from Coast to Coast* (World Pacific 1296, 1960). Hopkins's mannerisms led to a certain repetitiveness but his original turn of phrase and profound feeling for the blues made some of his recordings masterpieces.

Because of the entrepreneurial activities of recording companies and trawls for new singers by talent scouts, recordings again do not necessarily give an accurate picture of the quantity or distribution of blues singers. However, when Crowley, Louisiana, became a centre of recording in the mid-1950s there was plenty of local talent on which to draw: Lightnin' Slim (Otis Hicks) from Baton Rouge, whose *Bad Luck and Trouble* (Excello 2096, 1957) was typically dark and rough in timbre; and others like Lonesome Sundown (Cornelius Green) and Slim Harpo (James Moore) who maintained the blues tradition but with a more modern image. Much the same could be said of Jackson, Mississippi, or Memphis, where the pianist Willie Love or the one-man band Joe Hill Louis were among the many singers from the Mississippi valley regions still performing in country jukes

99

and city clubs. There were occasional recording sessions in Atlanta (where the veteran blues singer Blind Willie McTell made many postwar titles), Nashville and elsewhere. But many of the southern rural-style blues were being recorded in northern cities. So the downhome blues of Gabriel Brown from Florida, for example *Down in the Bottom* (Joe Davis 5006, 1946), and *Church Bells* (Signature 32016, 1946) by Ralph Willis from Alabama, were recorded as early as the 1940s in New York, where Brown and Willis had settled, like many other blues singers.

It was this northward migration that led to rural-sounding blues by Doctor Isaiah Ross from Mississippi or J. P. 'Bobo' Jenkins from Arkansas being recorded in Detroit, where one of the most striking and prolific of downhome singers, John Lee Hooker (*b* Clarksdale, Mississippi, 22 Aug 1917), had lived since he was 30. Before moving to the motor industry in Detroit, Hooker worked in factories in Memphis and Cincinnati. His first recording, *Boogie Chillen* (Modern 20-627, 1948), was an outstanding success, preparing the way for his faster rhythmic items like *Wobbling Baby* (Chart 609, 1953). With a deep, rich voice he made effective use of vibrato in the slow blues *Cold chills all over me* (Modern 862, 1952). Though he recorded extensively on 78s, his work did not suffer when he started making albums. *Black Snake* (Riverside 12-838, 1959) is a typical blues in which he used suspended rhythm, hummed choruses, whispered lines and free-verse structure. When re-making themes in different versions, such as *Wednesday Evening Blues* (Riverside 12-321, 1960), Hooker was also an original composer of lyrics. Often irregular and non-rhyming, his blues stanzas are held together by insistent beat and hypnotic rhythm. *Birmingham Blues* (Vee Jay 538, 1963) is among his most impressive recordings, in which fierce indignation is unimpaired by the support of a full band. More widely heard than most blues singers, and with a mediocre hit *Boom Boom* (Vee Jay 438, 1961), he has been popular at blues concerts and festivals since 1960, but his later recordings are lack-lustre.

XII **Postwar Chicago**

By 1945 many blues singers who had been active before the war were still working in black clubs – Big Bill Broonzy, Sonny Boy Williamson (ii), Lonnie Johnson, Roosevelt Sykes, Big Maceo, Tampa Red and Memphis Minnie among them. They had a large following and the revived race record companies recorded many of them. Young blues singers were also gaining popularity, such as Eddie Boyd, Memphis Slim and 'Baby Face Leroy' Foster; and there were older men like Sunnyland Slim (Albert Luandrew) and Robert Nighthawk (Robert McCollum), playing the piano and the guitar respectively, who enjoyed a local reputation but made few records.

It was a session arranged by Sunnyland Slim that introduced a young blues singer (fostered in clubs by Broonzy) who soon played a large part in changing Chicago blues: 'Muddy Waters', whose real name was McKinley Morganfield (*b* Rolling Fork, Mississippi, 4 April 1915; *d* Chicago, 30 April 1983). Strongly influenced by Son House and by Robert Johnson's

records, Muddy Waters turned from the harmonica
to the guitar when he was 17. When he was recorded
in Clarksdale, Mississippi, for the Library of Congress his *I be's Troubled* and *Country Blues* (L. of
C. AAFS 18, 1941) revealed these influences. Two
years later he moved to Chicago where he began to
record in 1947. *Walkin' Blues* (Chess 1426, 1950) was
based on *Country Blues* but was now played on an
electric guitar with a vibrant slide technique and his
voice was louder and harder. This was the last recording he made with only bass support: the harmonica player Little Walter accompanied him on a
splendidly integrated *Louisiana Blues* (Chess 1441,
1950) and soon his half-brother Otis Spann and the
second guitarist Jimmy Rogers joined them to form
the nucleus of his powerful Chicago band. By 1953
Muddy Waters was performing dramatically phrased
songs which built to a forceful climax, like *I'm your
hoochie coochie man* (Chess 1560, 1953) and *Manish
Boy* (Chess 1602, 1955). They set the model for many
driving recordings like *Got my mojo working* (Chess
1620, 1956) or *Tiger in your tank* (Chess 1765, 1960)
which, in their declamatory style and volume, expressed the militant spirit of the ghetto at that time.
Later, Muddy Waters toured extensively but he
tended to lose contact with black audiences. Following a car accident in 1970 he was obliged to sing from
a chair.

Jazz Gillum and John Lee Sonny Boy Williamson
(ii) had shown the harmonica's potential for small-
group work, and there were several southern players,
like Snooky Pryor or Walter 'Shakey' Horton, who

102

followed suit. Their undisputed leader was 'Little Walter' Jacobs (*b* Alexandria, Louisiana, 1 May 1930; *d* Chicago, 15 Feb 1968). He began earning a living playing the harmonica at the age of eight. A decade later he was playing in Maxwell Street, Chicago, where he recorded *Ora Nelle Blues* (Ora Nelle 711, 1947). This showed his debt to Sonny Boy Williamson, but he soon developed his own technique of amplified harmonica playing, using the pronounced vibrato or 'warble' heard on *Mean Old World* (Checker 764, 1952). As a singer he had a somewhat characterless voice and was more expressive as an instrumentalist, especially in slow numbers like *Blue Lights* (Checker 799, 1954) with Robert Lockwood playing the guitar, which made use of heavy amplification and over-blowing. An outstanding band performer, Little Walter was at his best supporting other artists, as in his country-flavoured accompaniment to Leroy Foster on *Rollin' and Tumblin'* (Parkway 501, 1950) and the sessions with Muddy Waters that produced the superbly phrased support to *Long Distance Call* (Chess 1452, 1951) and *All Night Long* (Chess 1509, 1952). Many younger musicians were influenced by Little Walter, who was surprised to discover how well European audiences knew his recordings when he toured in the 1960s.

George Smith, who even called himself 'Little Walter Jnr', and 'Big Walter' Horton were two of the harmonica players who assumed Little Walter's mantle. Horton, whose curious movements earned him the name of 'Shakey', developed an individual and moving style of playing. The guitarist and

103

harmonica player Howling Wolf (blues singers were still expected to have colourful sobriquets), with his harsher, fiercer attack and commanding physical presence, became the principal challenge to Muddy Waters. Born Chester Burnett (*b* West Point, Mississippi, 10 June 1910; *d* Hines, Ill., 10 Jan 1976), he worked on a plantation in the Mississippi delta and heard the blues singers Charley Patton and Willie Brown. Possessing a coarse-textured voice, he imitated Patton's 'heavy' vocal style and his energetic movements. While travelling in Arkansas he met Sonny Boy Williamson (i) (Alex Miller), who taught him to play the harmonica. When he was nearly 40 he made his first recordings with a Memphis group that included the pianist and guitarist Ike Turner: *Moanin' at Midnight* (Chess 1479, *c*1950) was a dramatic performance and an instant success, the singer's baying cries earning him his nickname. He followed it with other versions of the same theme, including a forceful and rhythmic *Riding in the Moonlight* (RPM 333, 1951). He frequently pitched his vocals high to produce a strained, hoarse effect, as in *Smoke Stack Lightning* (Chess 1618, 1956), based on a Patton record, in which his son Hubert Sumlin played the guitar. With Muddy Waters and Elmore James, Howling Wolf shaped the sound of postwar Chicago blues, his direct harmonica playing, as in *Poor Boy* (Chess 1679, 1957), giving impetus to his supporting band. Though he played the guitar he seldom recorded with it; *The Red Rooster* (Chess 1804, 1960) was an exception but was more notable for its threatening vocal. Later records, like *Three*

Hundred Pounds of Joy (Chess 1870, 1963), often strained after novelty, while his stage performances could be physical to the point of being grotesque even if they were remarkable for a man of his years. But a slow blues like *My Country Sugar Mama* (Chess 1911, 1964) could still be impressive, with a firm harmonica lead and a rich vocal. During the last ten years before he died he toured widely, but he was at his best in Chicago clubs.

While Howling Wolf derived his style from Charley Patton and Muddy Waters looked to Son House, it was Robert Johnson who inspired Elmore James (*b* Richland, Mississippi, 27 Jan 1918; *d* Chicago, 24 May 1963), in many ways the archetypal postwar Chicago blues singer. Technically quite limited, he depended on a bottleneck slide and rhythms derived from Johnson. He sang in a taut, constricted voice and like many singers of his generation he paid greater attention to projection and volume than to content and subtle expression. The relationship of the blues singer to his audience had changed. The progression from front porch to local juke joint, from saloon to rent party, from casual employment to long stays at Chicago clubs, had led to an increasing emphasis on performance for an audience and a decrease in the expression of personal feeling. 'Blues' still represented both music and mood, but the blues singer came to articulate the mood of his hearers.

Some singers had a strong reputation in Memphis, or further south, but had to wait a long time for wider recognition, like Sonny Boy Williamson (i) (Alex 'Rice' Miller) (*b* Glendora, Mississippi, 5 Dec 1897; *d*

Helena, Arkansas, 25 May 1965). He borrowed the name of the younger, more famous recording blues singer in 1941 when he began to broadcast for the Interstate Grocer Company, which promoted his appearances on radio and travelling road shows in the 1940s. He was in his early 50s when he first recorded, but *Eyesight to the Blind* (Trumpet 129, 1951), made in Jackson, Mississippi, with a thrusting local band and featuring his trembling vocal and amplified harmonica, revealed a forceful and mature blues artist. *Mighty Long Time* (Trumpet 166, 1952), with only a vocal bass accompaniment, showed that he could be a subtle and sensitive performer. Moving to Milwaukee in 1955, he made a hit record with *Don't start me to talkin'* (Checker 824, 1955), backed by Muddy Waters and his band. Generally, Williamson's preferred guitarist was Robert Lockwood jr (his former companion and Robert Johnson's stepson), with whom he remade an earlier success, *Nine Below Zero* (Checker 1003, 1961). In 1963–4 he reached a new audience when he toured Europe. His popularity there brought him the satisfaction denied him in his youth, as he indicated on *On my way back home* (Storyville 671 170, 1963), one of many late recordings that showed his command of his instrument and a gentler side to his musical personality.

Another singer a little apart from the Chicago mainstream was Jimmy Reed (*b* Dunleith, Mississippi, 6 Sept 1925; *d* Oakland, Calif., 29 Aug 1976), who settled in Chicago in the late 1940s, eventually performing with an excellent guitarist and fellow

Mississippian, Eddie Taylor. Reed played the guitar and the harmonica, the latter in a high, piping style after the manner of Jazz Gillum. Though he was not an exceptional musician, he had an extremely relaxed manner and his 'mushmouth' style of singing contrasted with the ferocity of many Chicago singers of the period. With Taylor's guitar laying a solid foundation, he had the first of many hits with *I don't go for that* (Vee Jay 153, 1955); others include the rocking *Ain't that lovin' you baby* (Vee Jay 168, 1955) and a few instrumentals, the ethereal *Odds and Ends* (Vee Jay 298, 1957) with an added violin among them. At this time he recorded a popular ballad, *Honest I do* (Vee Jay 253, 1957), which indicated the direction many of his records were to take. Reed toured widely in the 1950s even though epilepsy hindered his career. He was among the first Chicago-based singers to realize that the future lay in touring the regions where records sold but where famous northern musicians were seldom heard.

Although over 200 clubs opened on the south side of Chicago during the 1950s, many lasted only for a season or two. Others ran for several years, giving employment to house bands and well-known singers and casual engagements to many others. 'Show lounge' and 'music bar' nightspots provided opportunities for many singers who worked in other jobs by day. Record companies, particularly Chess and Vee Jay, promoted their 'star' blues singers. Other performers, like the excellent guitarist J. B. Lenore (reserved and serious offstage but dynamic in performance), the coarser but irrepressible 'Hound Dog'

Taylor (who modelled his style on that of Elmore James) and the forceful J. B. Hutto, represented the vast reserves of black talent. Those who could not get engagements often played at the Maxwell Street open-air market, traditionally a place where blues singers tested their appeal and sought the attention of promoters.

XIII **Soul blues**

In the late 1950s a number of trends in black music gained momentum, contributing to a shift in popular taste and changes in the evolution of blues. They appear to have arisen partly from the merging of blues, gospel, vocal-harmonizing groups and other forms of black music into the general category of rhythm-and-blues. The rapid growth in popularity of these types of music was paralleled by the expansion of record markets. The increase in interest in gospel music was especially marked: many solo singers developed highly passionate and expressive styles while a number of groups employed instrumental accompaniments (see Chapter Four). As part of the process of secularization of religious music, some gospel singers combined the techniques of gospel and blues, often with little change in the lyrics. Soul music was largely the outcome of this synthesis of styles.

Discussion of soul music is beyond the scope of this chapter. It is a significant type of black music, however, and a number of singers and musicians still working largely within the blues idiom learnt much from it. Robert Calvin 'Bobbie Blue' (or Bobby) Bland (*b* Rosemark, Tenn., 27 Jan 1930) was among the most influential. Moving to Memphis as a teen-ager he sang with the Miniatures, a local gospel group. In 1949 he joined John Alexander (Johnny Ace) and Roscoe Gordon to form the Beale Streeters, performing on WDIA, a black radio station. In the early 1950s Bland toured with Ace, modelling his guitar style largely on that of T-Bone Walker and his vocals on B. B. King. He developed a style more in the manner of Nat 'King' Cole and Charles Brown, as in *It's my life baby* (Duke 141, issued 1955). He experimented with smooth, sentimental singing and harsher, crying vocals in the gospel manner, even-tually making a hit with *Cry Cry Cry* (Duke 327, 1960) which was further from the blues. Bland toured with the harmonica player Herman 'Little Junior' Parker, who organized a 'package show', Blues Con-solidated. Bland's stage manner, with its apparent warmth and close rapport with the audience, was carefully nurtured; like B. B. King he had become a professional entertainer.

Riley B. B. 'Blues Boy' King (*b* Indianola, Mis-sissippi, 16 Sept 1925), singer and guitarist, remained close to blues while exploiting his awareness of jazz, gospel and other idioms. Probably the best known and publicly exposed blues singer of any period, he was raised in Mississippi, and at the age of eight he was singing in church. He worked in Indianola as a sharecropper and tractor driver, learning to play the guitar and singing in gospel groups. He moved in 1946 to Memphis, where he was companion to his cousin Bukka White and made contact with other blues singers, including Sonny Boy Williamson (i).

Engaged by the newly formed WDIA radio station
he became a disc jockey known as 'Beale Street Blues
Boy', eventually shortened to 'B. B.' King. Influences
on his music were the innovatory electric guitarists,
among them T-Bone Walker, Lowell Fulson and the
jazz musician Charlie Christian. From them he developed a solo technique based on arpeggios, which
he used with large bands that included saxophones
and trumpet. B. B. King began recording late in 1949
and by early 1952 his *Three O'clock Blues* (RPM 339,
1952) was top of the rhythm-and-blues charts for 15
weeks; for the next 20 years he was seldom without a
record in the charts. He toured extensively in the
1950s and 1960s with Tiny Bradshaw's band and
others and appeared at the Fillmore Auditorium, San
Francisco, in 1968; from 1970 he gave innumerable
concerts overseas. He was awarded two honorary
doctorates and made over 400 records.

A considerable showman, King personalized his
guitar as 'Lucille' and developed a stage manner that
emphasized the apparent strain of playing. Single
'bent' and extended notes were contrasted with
cascades of descending arpeggios, and he made up
for a somewhat taut voice by singing in a high and
anguished style, for example in *Every day I have the
blues* (RPM 421, 1953), sung against a swinging band.
The difference between King's technique and that of
those with whom he worked is seen in *Lucille's
Granny* (Probe SPB1051, 1971) in which his solo
comes between others by the guitarists Jesse Davis
and Joe Welsh. His most popular and frequently
repeated themes include the slow blues *Sweet Little*

Angel (RPM 468, 1956), *My own fault baby* (Crown 5188, 1960) and *Confessin' the Blues* (ABC 528, 1966), which illustrate the inventiveness of his elegantly phrased guitar improvisations. King has been a significant influence on blues guitarists and many have also tried to emulate his appeal to white audiences.

Many singers, too, were influenced by King and instrumentalists like T-Bone Walker. Among them were two namesakes, neither related. Albert Nelson, a couple of years older and also from Mississippi, changed his name to Albert King. Heavily built, with a more traditional approach to blues singing, he used an elaborated single-string style clearly modelled on B. B. King's (he even named his guitar 'Lucy') with a speech-based phrasing, as in the *Blues at Sunrise* (Stax XATS 1002, 1969), recorded at the Fillmore Auditorium, San Francisco. A dozen years his junior, Freddie King similarly demonstrated his indebtedness to B. B. King in *Have you ever loved a woman* (Federal 12384, 1960), with crying introductory syllables to anguished vocals, followed by flourishes on the electric guitar. He preferred to play with a large band that set off the stinging quality of his instrumental work, as in *Wide Open* (Atlantic 588 186, 1969) made with a King Curtis orchestra; his ability to turn an older blues into a modern if still B. B. King-influenced interpretation was incisively demonstrated in his version of Eddie Boyd's *Five Long Years* (A & M Records AMLS65004, 1971). Freddie King died in his native Texas in 1976 at the age of 42.

Big-band settings using riffs, studied orchestrations and poised contrasts to display the singer and his elaborate guitar work were common. Albert Collins (*b* 1932), also from Texas where the inheritance of T-Bone Walker by way of B. B. King is still strongly evident, exploited the technique with *In love wit'cha* (Tumbleweed 3501, 1972). Recognition was slow for Collins, but his club and concert appearances in the 1970s won him progressive acclaim and many younger guitarists were indebted to his influence. He frequently used an organist in his accompanying orchestra and, like soul music performers, sometimes a vocal group.

Festivals and foreign tours have been important in promoting blues singers since the early 1970s and this has consequently encouraged stage presentation and virtuoso performances. Jimmy Dawkins (*b* 1939) (a contemporary of Albert Collins), known as 'Fast Fingers', typified this approach in *Lick for Licks* (Vogue (F) LDM30.149, 1971) made in Paris; in it Georges Arvanitas plays the organ and it includes, in an undeservedly minor role, the expatriate and underrated guitarist Mickey Baker. Dawkins is at best an average singer, but Luther Allison (*b* 1939), with whom he sometimes worked, is better, his voice having a sense of strain and roughness of texture in such songs as *The skies are crying* (Delmark DS625, 1969), which communicated effectively with his international audiences. While demonstrating the pervasive influence of B. B. King, Allison was also indebted to Otis Rush, one of the two or three outstanding talents of this generation.

Otis Rush (*b* Philadelphia, Mississippi, 29 April 1934) moved to Chicago at the age of 14 and soon obtained occasional engagements playing the guitar at neighbourhood clubs. His first record, *I can't quit you baby* (Cobra 5000, 1956), was a national hit, with its moody setting and trembling, agonized vocal. Though he was especially effective in slow blues, to which his tense singing was ideally suited, he also made forceful rocking numbers like *Jump Sister Bessie* (Cobra 5015, 1957), with a group that included Walter 'Shakey' Horton (1917–81) playing the harmonica. *So many roads, so many trains* (Chess 1751, 1960), with its high, nervous singing, was also a success, but Rush was often less impressive on record than in person. *All your Love* (Trio PA3086, 1975) displayed his excellent guitar playing. Basing his work on B. B. King and others, Rush has experimented in playing blues in minor keys and has placed much importance on his lyrics.

Many younger Chicago blues singers were divided between following the style of Bobby Bland towards soul music or by taking the lead of Otis Rush to a soul-influenced blues. The shortlived 'Magic Sam' Maghett was one who followed Rush; his original version of *All your Love* (Cobra 5013, 1957), made when he was 20, showed a singer of unfulfilled promise. Another disciple of Rush is George 'Buddy' Guy (*b* Lettsworth, Louisiana, 30 July 1936). Until he was 20 he lived in Louisiana, where he played the guitar and sang with the younger musicians who accompanied Lightnin' Slim (Otis Hicks, 1913–74). Moving to Chicago, he was influenced by Rush, whom he subsequently claimed to have defeated in a blues contest. His guitar playing was lyrical, finely executed

113

with clear notes that were allowed to 'hang' until they faded – a technique made possible by the use of well-amplified instruments. Sufficiently accomplished to be employed as resident guitarist for the Chess company, he recorded *First time I met the blues* (Chess 1735, 1960), notable for its high, intense vocal and expressive guitar playing. Guy provided fluent support for Sonny Boy Williamson (i) in *Trying to get back on my feet* (Checker 1080, 1963) and was particularly sensitive as an accompanist to Amos 'Junior' Wells (*b* 1934) in the slow blues *Ships on the Ocean* (Delmark DL612, 1965). A successful partnership with Junior Wells was aided by the ability of both musicians not only to play with great skill but also to perform before large audiences as popular entertainers. They were in great demand for concerts and overseas tours, during which Guy made some of his best recordings: *Ten Years Ago* (Red Lightnin' (F) RL0034, 1974), recorded in Montreux, remade a theme they had first recorded in 1961, while the rock standard *High Heel Sneakers* was played with great aplomb in Japan (Bourbon (J) BMC2001, 1975). However, some of their recent performances have been crowd-pleasing rather than of quality.

The blues of the generation of singers born in the late 1930s and the 1940s has been substantially coloured by soul music. Typically, James Copeland (*b* 1937) from Texas, after a career working in Houston bands, began touring in the 1960s with Percy Mayfield, Freddie King and his own band, drawing on a range of contemporary styles, with rock, soul and blues freely exploited. At his best, as in *Third*

Party (Rounder 2025, 1981), he can sing forcefully and play with skill and feeling. A similar eclecticism was to be found in the work of Z. Z. Hill (1941–84), also from Texas, who adopted the soul style of Bobby Bland; *Down Home Blues* (Malaco 7406, 1981) signalled a step towards soul blues, welcomed by an expanding, if largely white, audience. Hill's early death robbed blues of one of its more promising younger talents.

Frank 'Son' Seals (*b* 1942) from Osceola, Arkansas, had a more solid blues background, working with Earl Hooker and 'Hound Dog' Taylor before touring with Albert King in the late 1960s. He developed a thrusting guitar technique that reflected these associations and an emotional singing style. *Your love is like a cancer* (Alligator 4703, 1972) showed him at his best, but some later recordings were not up to the standard of his live appearances.

Field trips in the south continue to uncover local and previously unrecorded veteran singers (mostly guitarists but a few harmonica players), but younger blues men are fewer. There are indications of a renewal of interest in blues among young Blacks in the 1980s, whether in the playing of *Saddle up my pony* (High Water 1001, 1983) by a southern band like the Fieldstones, from Memphis, or the soul-based blues of Robert Cray (*b* 1952) whose *Phone Booth* (Hightone 301, 1984) has been regarded as an encouraging sign of a blues revival. Yet it is undeniable that blues has a minority appeal among Blacks and that this has been the case since the 1960s. Its future as a music of black Americans must be in doubt.

XIV Field recording

Field recordings have been an important influence on the perception of the blues. Blues benefited greatly by its coincidence with developments in popular music but, as noted above, record companies promoted some singers and styles to the detriment of others. This process in turn created markets and may substantially have influenced taste. Location units in the 1920s enabled many rural blues singers to make recordings, confirming that blues was already current in rural communities. However, record companies sponsored and encouraged the new music, inviting songsters to record blues and embracing non-blues types of black secular song as 'blues' in their promotional literature and advertisements. Not only was it a 'new' music, and hence attractive to young people, but it also permitted record companies to copyright blues as new songs and music publishers to secure royalties from them; commercial concerns had a vested interest in promoting 'originals', or blues that did not share title or lead verses with other compositions.

There is evidence of the influence of recorded blues on folk traditions and the passing of stanzas or lines from the 'classic' urban idiom to folk usage. The extensive distribution of records and the high proportion of homes with phonographs (up to 30% of families owned one even in poor rural areas) probably did much to disseminate blues and to harden its form. It was also instrumental in promoting the 'name' artist and therefore advancing the career of the professional blues singer. The roles of talent scouts and music salesmen such as Polk Brockman in Atlanta, H. C. Speir in Jackson, Mississippi, Arthur Laibley in Chicago and Frank Walker in New York both in promoting and, by the limitations of their taste and spheres of contact, in limiting the range of singers who recorded the material they put on wax, has only slowly been recognized.

Recordings in the field may give a more accurate picture of blues in its context than commercial recordings do. Unfortunately nothing apart from written notes survives of the earliest field recordings, made before World War I by John A. Lomax and Howard Odum. The disclosure of a large number of field recordings made between 1924 and 1933 by Lawrence Gellert might suggest that some blues forms have been in circulation at an earlier date and that blues were used for protest and social comment of a more incisive kind than on commercial record. As the dating of many of Gellert's records is unspecific and details of the singers' identity and even their location is often missing, the value of Gellert's recordings as evidence is reduced. The earliest were made in Greenville, South Carolina, and included vocals with guitar accompaniment in a light ragtime style not unrelated to that of Blind Blake, who first recorded commercially two years later. An example is *Down in the Chain Gang* by an unknown singer (Heritage 304, *c*1924). Apparently Gellert was unique in winning the confidence of his singer informants, many of whom were working on convict gangs. A large number of titles were work songs or, as he called them, 'negro songs of protest' like *Cap'n got a Lueger* (Rounder

117

4004, 1933). Others revealed an awareness of commercially issued blues, such as *Standin' on the streets of Birmingham* (Rounder 4013, 1930s), which derived from Blind Lemon Jefferson's *One Dime Blues* (Paramount 12578, 1927).

When the Archive of Folksong was initiated at the Library of Congress, Richard Gordon, its first curator, made a number of field recordings, including some in Darien, Georgia. Most were sacred, though *Glory to God my son's come home*, based on the story of the Prodigal Son, by J. D. Purdy (L. of C. AFS L68, 1926) is mainly secular. In 1933 John A. Lomax and Alan Lomax started recording systematically for the archive in the southern states, frequently setting up their recording machines in penitentiaries with large black convict populations. Among the several thousand discs cut by the Lomaxes, Zora Neale Hurston, Elizabeth Barnicle, John Work and others for the Library of Congress were many blues, though they represented a relatively small proportion.

As a corpus, the most remarkable collection from a single source were the songs recorded by the songster known as 'Leadbelly' (Huddie Ledbetter) (*b* Mooringsport, Louisiana, 21 Jan 1885; *d* New York, 6 Dec 1949). By the age of 15 Ledbetter was well known as a musician in the Caddo Lake region of Louisiana. He learnt to play the 12-string guitar and sang in the streets and bars of Dallas. In 1918 he was sentenced to the Texas State Penitentiary for murder, and though he was reprieved in 1925 he was again sentenced in 1930 for intent to murder, to the Loui-

siana State Penitentiary, Angola. There he was
recorded by John A. Lomax, who assisted in gaining
his parole. The recordings Leadbelly made for the
Library of Congress were remarkable in their variety
and included a beautiful version of Jefferson's *Match
Box Blues*, played with a knife across the strings, and
a haunting *If it wasn't for Dicky* (both Elektra
301, 1935). He made several commercial recordings,
among them a powerful mule-skinner's holler *Honey,
I'm all out and down* (Melotone 3327, 1935) and
a ballad *Becky Deem, she was a gamblin' gal* (ARC
6-04-55, 1935); but though they were dramatically
performed they were anachronistic and unsuccessful.
In New York the self-styled 'King of the Twelve-
string Guitar Players of the World' was in demand
for his *Good Morning Blues* (Bluebird 8791, 1940)
and he found a welcome audience among jazz historians, who viewed him as the last of the blues
singers. Extensive recording coverage for the Library
of Congress and small folk labels ensured adequate
documentation of the most prolific of all songsters.
On a Monday (Asch 343-3, 1943), with Sonny Terry,
and an early version of his best-known song, *Good-
night Irene* (Asch 343-2, 1943), were typical with their
full-throated vocals and excellent rhythmic accompaniment. Recalling early traditional songs and work
songs for his 'Last Session' he sang a moving *I ain't
goin' down to the well no more* (Folkways 241, 1948).
Among many other songs, *Rock Island Line* (Playboy
119, 1949), recorded in this version shortly before his
death, became an anthem of 'skiffle' followers. After
he died there was a temporary devaluation of his

119

importance, but in 1975 the film *Leadbelly* (directed by Gordon Parks) was released with vocals by the blues singer 'Hi Tide' Harris.

In 1934 the Lomaxes recorded the Texas songster Pete Harris, whose *Blind Lemon's Song* was recorded with slide guitar (Flyright (E) SDM265). The following year in Belle Glade, Florida, they recorded *Alabama Blues*, by a fierce country band led by Booker T. Sapps, a harmonica player (Flyright (E) SDM258, 1935). Unfortunately the condition of the recording betrays the serious deterioration of many of the Library of Congress discs. Jimmie Strothers, a veteran singer and inmate of the State Farm at Lynn Virginia, recorded a long blues, *Goin' to Richmond* (Flyright (E) LP259, 1934). Considered by the Lomaxes to be as fine a guitarist as Leadbelly, Gabriel Brown (discovered by Zora Neale Hurston), recorded *Education Blues* (Flyright (E) SDM257, 1936) at the all-black township of Eatonville, Florida; five years later he was in New York where he made a number of commercial recordings. In Detroit the Lomaxes met Calvin Frazier, a singer who later made commercial records, though his companion Sampson Pittman, whose *Cotton Farmer Blues* was a version of the *Boll Weevil Ballad* (Flyright (E) LP542, 1938), was no less interesting. They came from Mississippi where the Lomaxes later recorded. Earlier, the guitarist Smith Casey at the Clemens State Farm, Brazoria, Texas, made a beautiful version of a local ballad *Shorty George* with a soaring vocal line (L. of C. AAFS 17, 1938). Some singers recorded by field units had previously recorded commercially: Bukka White, who made a recording in Parchman Farm State

Penitentiary, Mississippi, Oscar 'Buddy' Woods in Shreveport and Blind Willie McTell in Atlanta, whose score of discs included several interviews, blues ballads and ragtime pieces, such as *Kill it Kid Rag* (Melodeon 7323, 1940).

Notable sessions were held at the State College, Fort Valley, Georgia, which was unique among black colleges in recognizing blues and other rural idioms and which promoted annual festivals in the 1940s. Among many significant items is *Fort Valley Blues* (Flyright (E) SDM250, 1943) by Blind Billy Smith's String and Washboard Band from Macon, Georgia, which confirms that rural string bands were still active at this time for square dances.

In Mississippi the field units encountered Son House and Willie Brown; *Government Fleet Blues* (Flyright (E) LP541, 1941) was made by both men, accompanied by Fiddlin' Joe Martin, but they also recorded powerful solo items: *Depot Blues* by House and Brown's *Mississippi Blues* (both L. of C. AFS L59, 1942) among them. Historically, the most notable discovery was McKinley Morganfield, whose *Rambling Kid Blues* (Testament 2210, 1942) was accompanied by a primitive country band, the Son Simms Four. Morganfield, under the name Muddy Waters, changed the course of blues when he moved to Chicago soon afterwards.

By the early 1940s the field recording trips made for the Archive of Folksong were virtually at an end. Thousands of recordings of work songs, hollers, plantation songs, ballads, folksongs, children's game chants, monologues, tall-tales, toasts, sermons, spirituals

121

and gospel songs as well as blues were recorded in penitentiaries, churches, work camps, private homes and elsewhere. They constituted an incomparable documentation of black rural traditions. Yet all but a small proportion remains unissued – and largely unissuable. Of the blues recordings most of those issued have been by independent record labels, particularly in England, catering for minority interests.

XV Research and rediscovery

Interest in blues outside black culture had been minimal, and generally misinformed, before World War II. But a few enthusiasts wanted to locate singers and bring them before recording microphones and white audiences. As early as 1933 John Hammond was responsible for Bessie Smith's last recording session, organized on behalf of the English company, Parlophone. He later hoped to trace Robert Johnson for the celebrated 'From Spirituals to Swing' concerts at Carnegie Hall in 1938; Johnson had been killed, but Big Bill Broonzy and Sonny Terry were among those who performed.

In the 1940s the best-known blues musician was Josh White, who broadcast regularly. As a child Joshua Daniel 'Josh' White (*b* Greenville, South Carolina, 11 Feb 1915; *d* Manhasset, NY, 5 Sept 1969) led street evangelists and blind gospel singers in South Carolina towns. From them he learnt a wide range of songs and he eventually acquired a prodigious guitar technique. He was only 13 when he recorded with Blind Joe Taggart, singing falsetto and playing the guitar in *There's a hand writing on the wall* (Para-

mount 12717, 1928). In 1932 he began a long recording career, often using the pseudonym Pinewood Tom
for blues, for example in *Mean Mistreater Mama*
(Banner 32918, 1933). He had a light voice with a
glottal catch which he used to great – if sometimes
excessive – effect. By 1940 he was well established in
New York where he performed with his Carolinians,
with whom he recorded some unauthentic work songs,
like *Told my cap'n* (Columbia 35562, 1940). *Southern
Exposure* (Keynote 514, 1941) was from an album of
socially committed songs. His work became more
sophisticated, appealing to a wide audience. He popularized folksongs and blues, for instance in his version
of *The House of the Rising Sun* (ABC-Paramount 124,
1957), but his commercialized approach alienated
blues audiences.

Josh White worked frequently with Brownie
McGhee and Sonny Terry, the white protest singer
Woody Guthrie and with Leadbelly. In 1949 Leadbelly performed in France and in 1951 Big Bill
Broonzy was invited there. In Europe Broonzy recalled
his old country songs and in his last years he was as
much a folksinger as a blues singer, making well over
200 recordings: *John Henry* (Vogue (F) 118, 1951)
and the protest song *Black, Brown and White* (Vogue
(F) 125, 1951) were typical. Brownie McGhee and
Sonny Terry went to England in 1958 for the first of
many visits and the same year Muddy Waters and
Otis Spann played in Europe. At first Waters's electric
guitar was unacceptable to many listeners unaware of
the changes that had taken place in Chicago blues.

Knowledge and recognition of blues outside the

123

black (mainly working-class) community was limited by the lack of research. Jazz magazines in the USA and Europe paid some attention to blues and some writers on folk music acknowledged it as a late, perhaps declining, tradition.

Although the Library of Congress ceased field recording, Alan Lomax continued to record along similar lines. In 1947 at the Parchman State Penitentiary he taped important examples of work songs and hollers (see §II above). Three years later Harold Courlander recorded a range of sacred and secular songs in Livingston, Alabama (see Chapter One, §IV above), among them a long, slow unaccompanied blues *Black Woman* by Rich Amerson (Folkways FE 4417, 1950), distantly based on a Texas Alexander recording. Blues that may have been beyond the influence of commercial records were also sought by Frederic Ramsey jr in an extended field project of 1951–7 supported by the Wenner-Gren Foundation. His survey of the repertory of an Alabama field-hand, Horace Sprott, included several unaccompanied blues which nevertheless betrayed the influence of Blind Lemon Jefferson and Blind Boy Fuller, for example *My little Annie, so sweet* (Folkways FA 1659, 1954). When Lomax returned to the south and re-created Sea Islands singing of the slave era he also discovered, in Mississippi, the blues singer Fred McDowell, whose *Shake 'em on down* was a forceful blues with slide guitar (Atlantic 1348, 1959). Between 1959 and 1961 Harry Oster of Louisiana State University continued the tradition of recording in state penitentiaries but concentrated less on work songs and more on blues compositions. Among the singers he heard at Angola and elsewhere in Louisiana was Robert Pete Williams (*b* Zachary, 14 March 1941; *d* Zachary, 31 Dec 1980), a singer of great creative ability, evident in his *Death Blues* (Prestige Bluesville 1026, 1960). Convicted of murder in 1956, he was sentenced to Angola State Prison. Williams's improvisations were marked by an unusual contemplative guitar style and freely associated, structurally loose stanzas, like *Farm Blues* (Ahura Mazda (E) AMS2002, *c*1976).

Research that considered blues as music in its own right, not part of folksong or jazz, began in the late 1950s. Much of it was based on knowledge of commercially recorded blues singers, so that 're-discovery' became important. The taping by Samuel Charters of Gus Cannon and Will Shade (1956) and of Furry Lewis and Lightnin' Hopkins (1959) were significant, as were the recordings of 'Poor Joe' Williams by Bob Koester in St Louis (1958). The following year Georges Adins and Yannick Bruynoghe from Belgium conducted research in Chicago, and the French writers Jacques Demêtre and Marcel Chauvard undertook research there and in Detroit; they did not record the singers they interviewed but their reports conveyed the extent of urban blues activity at the time. In 1960 Paul Oliver made an extensive research trip to Detroit and Chicago and was later joined in Memphis and Mississippi by Chris Strachwitz and in Texas by Mack McCormick; this trip resulted in the recording of Sam Chatmon, Whistling Alex Moore, Black Ace, Lil Son Jackson, Henry Brown and many other previously commercially recorded singers.

A number of formerly unknown singers were taped, the most important being Mance Lipscomb (*b* Navasota, Texas, 9 April 1895; *d* Navasota, 30 Jan 1976). He was 66 when he was first recorded and he represents the songster tradition in its purest form. His reputation was extensive in Texas as much for his effortless playing for dances, for example *Buck Dance* (Reprise 2012, 1961) and *Sugar babe it's all over now* (Arhoolie 1001, 1960), as for his singing of old ballads like *Ella Speed* and the only collected version of *Freddie* (Arhoolie 1001, 1960). For over 40 years he was a share-cropper and his *Captain Captain* (Reprise 2012, 1961) recalls working on a Brazos plantation before he had his own smallholding. As a guitarist Lipscomb must be numbered among the most gifted on record in the black folk idiom, perhaps re-flecting the proximity in Texas of Mexican guitarists, as his *Spanish Flang Dang* (Arhoolie 1023, May 1964) suggests. He drew on his earliest recollections for *Take me back*, but like all songsters his range was catholic and he could follow with *Shine on, Harvest Moon* (composed 1908) or the spiritual *Motherless Children* (all on Arhoolie 1026, Nov 1964). The subject of the film *A Well Spent Life* (1971; produced by Les Blank), Lipscomb was popular at concerts and festivals until 1973, when ill-health forced him to retire.

Apart from the autobiographies of W. C. Handy (1957), Ethel Waters (1951) and Big Bill Broonzy (1955), the first books devoted to blues were pub-lished in 1959 and 1960. A rapidly expanding audience for the music led to the establishment of the first specialist magazines: *Blues Unlimited* (founded

1963) was published monthly for 20 years and less regularly thereafter, *Blues World* appeared from 1965 to 1973, and *Rhythm and Blues Monthly* from 1964 to 1966 – all British publications. *R & B Panorama* appeared in Belgium and *Jefferson* in Sweden; blues magazines were later published on a regular basis in France, Germany, Italy and even Finland and Japan. The USA had to wait until 1972 for its first regular blues magazine, *Living Blues*. The large number of publications not only indicated an ever-expanding international interest but a growth in the number of contributors whose personal (and generally un-subsidized) research led to the features, interviews and discographies that most contain. Research projects include those of Bengt Olsson from Sweden into medicine shows and drum and fife bands, Bruce Bastin and Pete Lowry into the musical traditions of the Carolinas, Karl Gert zur Heide and John Broven into Louisiana blues, Mike Leadbitter into Houston blues, and William Ferris into blues as social activity in Mississippi, David Evans into the complex around the Crystal Springs and Jackson region of Mississippi and Gayle Dean Wardlow into the Alabama and Mississippi traditions.

A significant outcome of research based on the study of records led to the 'rediscovery' of many prominent figures in early blues. Thus Sleepy John Estes was traced to Brownsville, Tennessee, in 1962. With his old companions Hammie Nixon (harmonica) and Yank Rachell (mandolin) he made many recordings. *Rats in my Kitchen* (Delmark DL-603, 1962) and *Easin' back to Tennessee* (Storyville (D)

172, 1964), the latter made on a European tour, are among moving performances from this late stage of his career. Mississippi John Hurt was discovered in 1963 still playing in a manner uncannily similar to that of his 1928 discs; his later recordings include the ballad *Louis Collins* (Piedmont 13157, 1963) and the mildly erotic *Candy Man Blues* (Vanguard CRS9220, 1964). Among other notable items was a version of the often remembered Mississippi theme *Slidin' Delta* (Piedmont 13161, 1964), which demanded nimble fingering. Hurt's amiable disposition and gentle playing endeared him to eastern audiences. In 1963 he recorded over 90 items for the Library of Congress but, tired of the limelight, he returned to Mississippi.

Perhaps the most remarkable rediscovery was that of Son House in 1964. For a decade he played to festival, club and college audiences, making European visits in 1967 and 1970. The majestic quality of his steel guitar playing and the moving intensity of his singing was captured on *Empire State Express* (Columbia 2417, 1965). Failing health forced him to retire in the mid-1970s but he is remembered as the epitome of delta blues. Among other notable rediscoveries that led to recording sessions were those of Victoria Spivey and Whistling Alex Moore (1960), Sippie Wallace (1962), Bukka White (1963) and Skip James (1964).

Between 1960 and the mid-1980s over 100 books were published on blues, many initiated outside the USA. Only a few of those doing research were based in the south and, until the 1980s, none were black.

Blues research has therefore been dominated by students from outside the cultural regions that have inspired the music and outside the ethnic Afro-American milieu in which it originated and flourished. Many are untrained in musicology or anthropology.

Complementary with research was the organization of international tours and concert appearances for the singers who had been located. During the 1970s many blues singers found it profitable to play exclusively for white audiences, performing on the 'college circuit' and not in black clubs. This tendency became more marked as soul music gained ground and older blues singers became of no interest to young Blacks and of diminishing appeal to the middle-aged. Inevitably, writing on blues and the presentation of singers in concerts threatened to place the music at some distance from its cultural context. All these factors have affected, and even distorted, the perception of blues. When, in the later 1960s, record companies issued blues largely for white collectors and enthusiasts, singers were recorded whose records might have been unsaleable in a black store. In consequence the extensive recorded output of even such singers as Lightnin' Hopkins and Big Joe Williams, while revealing their many-sided talents, did not necessarily reflect their popularity among black audiences.

XVI White blues

Blacks and Whites were in close contact in the south; in the country townships Blacks worked for, and often alongside, Whites. That there was an exchange of musical forms is hardly surprising. More remarkable, superficially, is how little the so-called 'cross-over' occurred in blues. The music of the songster generation, including ragtime songs, coon songs, ballads, dance tunes and novelty items, was common to both black and white singers, who took them from similar sources. Thus versions of ballads like *John Henry* or *Railroad Bill*, coon songs like *Chicken you can roost behind the moon*, ragtime songs like *Furniture Man* and numerous ragtime instrumental pieces were recorded by Whites and Blacks. But the specifically black identity of blues may have inhibited some white musicians, who showed little direct influence of blues singing and instrumentation until the commercial recordings of blues and white country 'old time music' of the mid-1920s.

By the late 1920s a number of white singers were using blues form frequently; among them were the brothers Austin and Lee Allen, whose *Reckless Night Blues* (Victor 40303, 1930) had a steady two-beat guitar and banjo rhythm but a more fiercely blue-toned harmonica. Their *Chattanooga Blues* was issued in the Columbia race series (Columbia 14266, 1927), an 'insult' for which they unsuccessfully sued the company for $250,000. This was not the sole example: Buster and Jack was the pseudonym under which Jack Cawley's Oklahoma Ridge Runners appeared in the Victor race series. Their *Cross Tie Blues* (Victor 23540, 1930) used the traditional form but was relatively conventional white string-band music. Closer to black blues feeling was the playing of Frank Hutchinson from Virginia; his *Cannonball Blues* (Okeh 45378, 1929) owed form and technique to Furry Lewis. Blind

Lemon Jefferson was the most frequently mentioned influence on white blues, and some recordings, like Larry Hensley's *Match Box Blues* (Vocalion 02678, 1934), were direct imitations. Blues were recorded by several white string bands such as the Leake County Revelers and the Carolina Tar Heels and country duets like Darby and Tarlton or Narmour and Smith.

Early white blues has not received much attention, but there is evidence of a separate white genre characterized by steady and inflexible rhythms, markedly grainy accents that could not be confused with those of Blacks, and a dispassionate, narrative style of singing. Blues was seldom used as an expressive medium but as a loose form that allowed for descriptive lyrics. Even so, traditional verses occur with great frequency, suggesting that some may be white in origin. Blues also concealed suggestive lyrics, sometimes sung with arch selfconsciousness, as in the Carolina Tar Heels' *Farm Girl Blues* (Victor 23516, 1930) and many recordings by Cliff Carlisle, like *Ash Can Blues* (Vocalion 02910, 1932) and *Mouse's Ear Blues* (Vocalion 02656, 1933).

Though Carlisle acknowledged the influence of black musicians, the chief source of his playing and singing style was Jimmy Rodgers (*b* Meridian, Mississippi, 8 Sept 1897; *d* New York, 26 May 1933). No other white singer was as admired by Blacks as Rodgers, who worked with Frank Stokes and other songsters in medicine shows during his brief career. At his second session Rodgers sang a *Blue Yodel* (Victor 21142, 1927) that combined blues verses with

131

yodelled refrains. The formula was repeated many times – 13 *Blue Yodels* were issued – but Rodgers recorded many other blues. The ease with which he worked with black musicians is evident from the accompaniments by Louis Armstrong on *Blue Yodel no.9* (Victor 23580, 1931) and the eminently relaxed *My Good Gal's Gone Blues* made with Clifford Hayes's black Louisville Jug Band (Bluebird 5942, 1935). Black musicians tried to mimic Rodgers's blue yodelling, for example Mae Glover in *Pig Meat Mama* (Gennett 6948, 1929) and the Mississippi Sheiks with *Yodeling Fiddling Blues* (Okeh 8834, 1930).

Perhaps the most unlikely examples of a white singer working with black musicians were recorded by Jimmie Davis, later twice governor of Louisiana. *Down at the Country Church* (Victor 23628, 1931) was a hokum version of a rural service with the moaning of the congregation imitated on a slide guitar by the black musician Eddie Shaffer. He and Oscar 'Buddy' Woods provided a beautifully integrated accompaniment to Davis's *Red Nightgown Blues* which concluded with a quick instrumental section (Victor 23659, 1932).

Further from black traditions is 'talking blues', another form of white blues that gained some currency. It was first recorded by Chris Bouchillon, a guitarist and motor mechanic from South Carolina. His *Talking Blues* (Columbia 15120-D, 1926) was spoken rather than sung, in a laconic, dry manner to a guitar accompaniment. Other white performers used the idiom, including Lonnie Glosson whose *Arkansas*

Hard Luck Blues (Conqueror 8732, 1936), spoken over rapid fingering, was witty and ironic. But the style was made popular by the 'Okie' folk poet Woody Guthrie, whose *Talkin' Dust Bowl Blues* (Victor 26619, 1940) made its points with wry humour. Guthrie performed in New York in the 1940s with Leadbelly, Sonny Terry and Brownie McGhee and other white banjo players or guitarists of the period including Pete Seeger; he played at concerts and festivals with these singers or with Big Bill Broonzy and his records were an important influence on Bob Dylan in the 1960s.

Few white performers appeared contractually on race records or accompanied blues singers. Best known of those who did was Eddie Lang (Salvatore Massaro), who recorded instrumental duets with Lonnie Johnson, including *Have to Change Keys to Play these Blues* (Okeh 8637, 1928) and *A Handful of Riffs* (Okeh 8695, 1929). The two worked well together, Lang being an inventive guitarist if rhythmically somewhat stiff by comparison with Johnson. He accompanied a number of blues singers including Texas Alexander in *Work Ox Blues* (Okeh 8658, 1928), Bessie Smith in *Kitchen Man* (Columbia 14435, 1929) and items by Gladys Bentley, Coot Grant and Sox Wilson. Closer to the blues idiom, Frank Melrose recorded a couple of piano solos under the name 'Broadway Rastus', issued in the race series, including *Whoopee Stomp* (Paramount 12764, 1929), and other items as by 'Kansas City Frank' with a Herb Morand band. A greater contribution was made by George Barnes, who played with the mandolin player Charlie McCoy on Big Bill Broonzy's *You know I got a reason* (Conqueror 8767, 1936). He was a pioneer of the electric guitar in blues and made several recordings as accompanist to Blind John Davis, Jazz Gillum, Washboard Sam and Merline Johnson, in whose *About my time to check* he took a well-phrased but restrained solo (Vocalion 04150, 1938).

During the boogie-woogie era many white jazz pianists played in the idiom and some attempted blues solos, one of the better ones being Joe Sullivan, whose *Gin Mill Blues* (Columbia 2876-D, 1933) gained him early fame. Some years later he recorded with a band consisting mostly of black musicians, his Café Society Orchestra; on *Low Down Dirty Shame* (Vocalion 5531, 1940) with this group Joe Turner contributed the vocal line. Other white pianists, such as Stan Wrightsman and Art Hodes, though they worked for the most part as jazz musicians, could perform a good blues solo. Hodes, in particular had considerable respect for blues performers and modelled his simple style on Jimmy Yancey's. However, little was added to blues by these modest forays.

Of marginal interst was the blues element in the music of 'Western swing' bands of the 1940s. The 'hot string bands' were eclectic, drawing on jazz, blues, cowboy songs and country music to create a lively if superficial synthesis. Bob Wills and his Texas Playboys had considerable success with *Steel Guitar Rag/Swing Blues no.1* (Okeh 03394, *c*1939), which drew on music by the blues guitarist Sylvester Weaver and verses from Blind Lemon Jefferson. Milton Brown and his Musical Brownies was another Western swing band that derived a substantial amount of its material from blues. However, these groups did not contribute to blues; they popularized and thereby diluted it.

Early in the 1950s there were signs of a more direct response to blues among white country musicians. Though the identity of Monroe 'Moe' Jackson is uncertain and the elements of parody are near the surface of his *Go 'way from my door* (Mercury 8127, 1951), the variety of blues techniques in his vocal and guitar accompaniment are impressive. His approach suggests that he may have had experience of medicine shows; this was certainly the case with 'Harmonica Frank' Floyd (*b* Tucapola, Mississippi, 11 Oct 1908; *d* Memphis, Tenn., 7 Aug 1984) who performed in shows, roadhouses, barbershops and in the streets. In constant contact with black blues singers, he was influenced by Blind Boy Fuller in his *Step it up and go* (Chess 1475, 1951), while *Howlin' Tom Cat* (Chess 1494, 1951) was loosely based on a Bo Carter blues but with vocal effects and fine harmonica playing. Floyd's guitar playing was still in the white tradition and the combination of rhythm-and-blues and country guitar have led some to consider his *Rockin' Chair Daddy* (Sun 205, 1954) the first rock-and-roll record by a white singer. It did not have the impact of a contemporary recording from the same studios, Elvis Presley's *That's all right* (Sun 209, 1954), based on a blues by Arthur 'Big Boy' Crudup. Presley's other records for Sun were also derived from blues: *Good Rockin' Tonight* (Sun 210, 1954) from Roy Brown and Wynonie Harris and a fast version of *Milkcow Blues Boogie* (Sun 215, 1954)

135

from Kokomo Arnold's hit. Elvis Presley continued to sing versions of standard blues for the next few years, and the rock-and-roll performers Carl Perkins, Jerry Lee Lewis, Eddie Cochran, the Everly Brothers and Gene Vincent all included blues among their recordings.

'Skiffle' enjoyed extraordinary popularity in England during the late 1950s following the success of Lonnie Donegan's *Rock Island Line* (Decca (E) F10647, 1955) based on a song by Leadbelly. The term appears to have come from *Home Town Skiffle* by the Paramount All Stars (Paramount 12886, 1929) and *Skiffle Blues* (Arkay 1001, 1947) by the pianist Dan Burley with his Skiffle Boys. Donegan's record was also a hit in the USA and by the following year there were several hundred skiffle bands, using home-made instruments such as washboards, jug, kazoo and tub bass to augment guitars and harmonica. Its makeshift nature resulted in many poor recordings but skiffle was a practice-ground for young musicians who soon turned to rhythm-and-blues.

The Beatles drew inspiration from the 'Tamla-Motown' version of rhythm-and-blues popularized in Detroit but the Rolling Stones turned to Louisiana blues. Several members of the group had worked briefly with Alexis Korner in the late 1950s who with the harmonica and 12-string guitarist Cyril Davies had run blues clubs to which visiting singers went. Korner moved from a blues style based on that of the guitarist Scrapper Blackwell to form his Blues Incorporated band in 1962. Its approach was experimental; *Blue Mink* (Ace of Hearts (E) ACL1187, 1963) was a synthesis of elements derived from rural blues, Charlie Mingus and Thelonious Monk. Though the Rolling Stones made their reputation with a sensuous and high-volumed form of 'rock' blues, they could play powerfully in the blues idiom, for example Lightnin' Slim's *Little Red Rooster* (Decca TXS101, 1964). The Yardbirds and The Who were among other blues-styled 'beat' groups. Probably the most admired guitarist in Britain apart from the expatriate black American Jimi Hendrix, was Eric Clapton (formerly with the Yardbirds), who joined John Mayall's Blues Breakers. *All your Love* (Decca (E) LK4804, 1966), first recorded by Magic Sam, demonstrated Clapton's excellent guitar playing to Mayall's piano. *Crossroads*, a Robert Johnson blues (Polydor (E) 583.060, 1967) made with his group Cream, conveys the group's strength but reveals the thinness of Clapton's vocals.

In the USA a similar development took place. Young white guitarists had imitated rural blues singers, as they had in Britain, but the Paul Butterfield Blues Band, with the leader playing the harmonica and Mike Bloomfield the guitar, broke new ground. *I got a mind to give up living* (Elektra 7315, c1967) was a slow blues in which the playing of the black Chicago musicians Jerome Arnold (bass) and Billy Davenport (drums) enabled the band to get away from a dragging beat. Again the vocal contributions were the weakest aspect, but the band's ability to play blues was demonstrated in its support of Muddy Waters with Otis Spann (piano) in the slow blues *Mean Disposition* (Chess SRLS4556, 1969), which also confirmed the superiority of the black singer's timbre and expression and his relaxed mastery of the slide guitar.

Of the other white American groups who experimented with blues, including the Grateful Dead, Captain Beefheart and the Jefferson Airplane, possibly the most able was Canned Heat, with the guitarists Al Wilson and Henry Vestine; their *Refried Boogie* (Liberty 84001, *c*1968) lasted some 40 minutes though much of it was drum solos. The martyr of white blues was Janis Joplin, at one time vocalist of Big Brother and the Holding Company. Her passionate, extravagant performances seemed expressive not only of her tortured personality but also of the dilemma of white blues: if it kept within the limitations of black tradition it was uncomfortably restricted (for many white blues performers were musically educated beyond the demands of the idiom), but if it was extended it lost its identity as blues. The meeting of instrumental and lyric expression which in the finest blues singers was the peak of their achievement seemed denied white players when they kept close to the blues idiom. Most moved outside it to the expanding fields of rock music.

For blues singers there were initially a number of advantages in the wider interest in their music; those that travelled to Europe gained prestige and more engagements in the USA. Some, among them the pianists Champion Jack Dupree, Memphis Slim, Curtis Jones and Eddie Boyd and the guitarist Mickey Baker, settled in Europe where they found enthusiastic audiences and wider acceptability. But they were separated from the sources and social contexts of their

138

music, which were undergoing considerable change. White interest in black music always presages or coincides with a departure from the idiom by the black population; when blues gained white enthusiasts it lost black audiences.

XVII Zydeco

Only one form of black blues can be said to have been substantially influenced by white music: 'zydeco' (also 'zodico'). The word is believed to be a corruption of the phrase 'Les haricots sont pas salés', meaning 'times are not good', the title of a popular dance tune in French Louisiana. Zydeco derives from the dance music of the descendants of the Acadians who were expelled from Nova Scotia by the British in the 18th century. Settling in Louisiana, the Acadians (corrupted as 'Cajuns') intermarried with Indians and later with Blacks. They were mainly hunters, trappers and fishermen whose descendants still live in the bayou country of southwest Louisiana. Cajun music takes several forms; the *fais dodo*, or country dance, is traditionally performed to button accordion, guitar and sometimes fiddle and rhythm accompaniment.

Early field recordings of black Cajun music made in Louisiana by John Lomax include Ellis Evans (harmonica) with Jimmie Lewis (washboard) playing a *Cajun Negro Fais Dos-dos Tune* (L. of C. unissued, 1934) at New Iberia and French negro ring dances with (probably) Austin Coleman and Joe Washington Brown singing unaccompanied the earliest collected version of *Les haricots sont pas salés* (L. of C. LBC 13, 1934) at Jennings, Louisiana. The button accordion

139

was played occasionally by Leadbelly, whose *Corn Bread Rough* (Asch 101, 1942) was a rural dance theme.

In the 1920s the black accordion player Amadé Ardoin from Eunice, Louisiana, played with a fellow share-cropper and white fiddle player Dennis McGee. His repertory and playing style were strongly in the Cajun tradition, featuring waltzes and two-steps, rhythmic accordion accompaniment and called vocals with descending lines that merged with the accordion's notes. Though he played regularly for white dances at Abe's Place, Eunice, he also performed at black house parties. Ardoin was famed both for his playing and for his crying hollered vocals. Apart from many dance tunes he recorded a number of themes that were blues in feeling if not in structure, for example *Les blues de la prison* (Decca 17014, 1934) made with McGee and *Les blues de voyages* (Bluebird 2189, 1934). Ardoin's first cousin, Alphonse 'Bois Sec' Ardoin, with an all-black group, was still playing essentially Cajun music in the mid-1960s – mainly waltzes and two-steps but including some blues-influenced items, among them *Les blues du voyageur* and *La robe barrée* (both Melodeon 7330, 1966), recorded in Mamou, Louisiana, with Ardoin (accordion) and Conray Fontenot (fiddle).

Blues increasingly infiltrated black Cajun music in the 1940s and early 1950s, but postwar rhythm-and-blues with its rocking rhythms facilitated a blend that led to zydeco. Among the earliest recordings were Clarence Garlow's *Bon ton roula* ('Let the good times roll'), with Latin rhythm and English vocal (Macy's 5001, 1950), and *Paper in my Shoe* by the accordionist

140

Boozoo Chavis (Folk Star 1197, 1954), a local hit. It was the recordings of a young share-cropper Clifton Chenier (*b* Opelousas, Louisiana, 25 June 1925) that established zydeco in its blues-Cajun form. *Cliston Blues* (Elko 920, 1954), recorded with his cousin Morris 'Big' Chenier (guitar), was a strong, slow blues. Whereas Cajun and black Cajun musicians played the simple four-stop diatonic German C button accordion, Chenier used the versatile piano accordion which allowed him to play in 'blues' keys. He performed numerous dance pieces such as *Rockin' Accordion* (Zynn 1011, 1961) with a fuller band. In 1956 he had moved to Houston, Texas, which already had a sizable Louisiana French (black) population and numerous zydeco dance halls. He was joined by his younger brother Cleveland Chenier who played a corrugated metal 'chest washboard' worn like a breastplate. Its staccato rhythms, augmented by drums, were heard on many of Clifton's best records, including his hit *Louisiana Blues* (Bayou 509, 1965), sung with a rich timbre and in heavy patois. *Black Gal* (Bayou 704, 1966) was an even greater success (with Morriş Chenier playing fiddle), based on a Joe Pullem blues from the 1930s. Chenier's eminently danceable music, such as the fast number *Tu le ton son ton* (Arhoolie 1082) and the slow drag *Monifique* (Arhoolie 1038, 1967) with its heavy beat, was characteristic of 'bal de maison' music. During the 1970s Chenier toured extensively in the USA and elsewhere. *Jambalaya* (Arhoolie 1086, 1975), recorded in Montreux, Switzerland, demonstrated the effect of wider exposure; it is jazz-influenced but with a lively

141

rock beat and flourishing guitar solo by Paul Senegal. Chenier was the undisputed 'King of Zydeco', whose appeal and improvisational ability are captured in the film *Hot Pepper* (1973; directed by Les Blank).

Chenier's dominance has drawn attention away from other performers, many of whom have recorded. The old country tradition of fiddle playing represented by Conray Fontenot has been faithfully documented, as in his *Bee de la manche* (Arhoolie (F) 5031, 1981), while the dance-hall music of Houston was first captured in its raw intensity in the playing of Sidney Babineaux and Albert Chevalier, including the latter's *Les haricots sont pas salé* [*sic*] (Arhoolie (F) 1009, 1961). Marcel Dugas from Church Point was one of the best-known accordion players; he recorded with a tough rural band led by the fiddle player Wild Bill Pitre whose vocal showed the influence of Jimmy Reed in *Purty lil red dress* (Flyright (E) LP543, 1969). Another, Alton Rubin, known as 'Rockin' Dopsie', played in the Lafayette region from the 1940s; his *Ma negresse* (Sonet (E) SNTF718, *c*1975) is typical of the strong two-beat music and shouted vocals of the country juke.

Many other zydeco bands have undiminished popularity in Louisiana. Lawrence 'Black' Ardoin (*b* 1946), son of Bois-Sec Ardoin, who plays the traditional button accordion with a band that included the fiddle and electric guitar, demonstrates the strong links of contemporary zydeco with its roots. *Bayou Two Step* (Arhoolie (F) 1091, 1984) is typical of this hybrid music which in the 1980s was the most flourishing of all blues forms.

XVIII **Composition**

Most blues singers take pride in their ability to 'rhyme up a song' and to invent new stanzas on any theme. Nevertheless, there is considerable repetition in blues composition and many singers depend substantially on songs learnt from others, either directly or through records. Only a small number, Blind Lemon Jefferson, Lonnie Johnson, Sleepy John Estes, Peetie Wheatstraw, Lightnin' Hopkins and Robert Pete Williams significant among them, seem to have had the ability to devise new blues at will. Even they had blues by which they were well known and which they were often called on to repeat. While blues audiences clearly liked new compositions they also drew great satisfaction from hearing singers repeat in person the songs they made popular on record or on the stage. So Sippie Wallace would be required to sing *Up the Country*, Tommy Johnson *Big Road Blues* or Muddy Waters *Hoochie Coochie Man*. A number of blues seem to have had special appeal, and these are often related to the success of an initial record release. Some are dance pieces, like *Pine Top's Boogie Woogie* (Vocalion 1245, 1928) by Pinetop Smith, Tommy McClennan's *Bottle up and go* (Bluebird 8373, 1939) and John Lee Hooker's *Boogie Chillen* (Modern 20-627, 1948). Others have an arresting structure that has made them a test piece for a blues player's skills, for example the guitar part to Tommy Johnson's *Big Road Blues* (Victor 21279, 1928) or the train imitation of Cow Cow Davenport's *Cow Cow Blues* (Vocalion 1198, 1928).

Certain songs gained currency for their risqué

143

implications or thinly veiled suggestiveness, such as Speckled Red's *The Dirty Dozen* (Brunswick 7116, 1929), James 'Stump' Johnson's *The Duck-Yas-Yas-Yas* (QRS R7049, 1929) and Robert Johnson's *Terraplane Blues* (Vocalion 03416, 1936). Other blues are notable for a turn of phrase or the use of unexpected imagery. Blind Lemon Jefferson's *One Dime Blues* (Paramount 12578, 1927) and *Match Box Blues* (Okeh 8455, 1927) are among the best known of his recordings. Charlie McFadden's *Piggly Wiggly Blues* (Bluebird 5160, 1933), with its boast 'My name is Piggly Wiggly, I've got groceries on my shelf', recorded after the development of the first supermarket chain, appealed for its witty topicality. Joe Pullem's *Black Gal* (Bluebird 5459, 1934) was as popular for his vocal resemblance to Charlie McFadden as for the high, pure-toned delivery of its key line 'Black gal, black gal, what makes your nappy head so hard?'

Some blues appear to have been popular for their departure from standard form, like Richard M. Jones's composition *Trouble in Mind* (Okeh 8312, 1926) recorded by Bertha Chippie Hill, Big Bill Broonzy's *Key to the Highway* (Okeh 06242, 1941) and Leroy Carr's *How Long, How Long Blues*, all of which are in eight-bar form. The verse and chorus structure of *Kokomo Blues* may have been part of its appeal but it is also linked with the versions of *Red Cross Blues* (Melotone 12753, 1933) by Walter Roland and his contemporaries Walter Scott and Lucille Bogan. Subsequently recorded in various versions, it spoke of the Blacks' resentment of charitable handouts in the 1930s and it also provided a

1. Fisk Jubilee
Singers, 1872

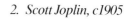
2. *Scott Joplin, c1905*

3. *Joseph F. Lamb, c1910*

4. Ida Cox

5. Son House,
1967

6. Thomas A. Dorsey

7. Minnie McCoy,
c1941

8. *Jimmy Reed*

9. *B. B. King, c1980*

10. Robert Pete Williams,
Montreal, 1971

11. Clifton Chenier, c1981

NORFOLK JAZZ QUARTETTE

These rollicking, jazzing boys from the Sunny South must have been born singing, you will say. When it comes to harmony—they invented it. They sing exclusively, of course, for Paramount and they are known as the finest male quartette of the Race.

NORFOLK JAZZ QUARTETTE

12032—AIN'T IT A SHAME Vocal Quartette   **Norfolk Jazz Quartette**
       RAISE R-U-K-U-S TONIGHT Vocal Quartette **Norfolk Jazz Quartette**
12054—STOP DAT BAND Vocal Quartette   **Norfolk Jazz Quartette**
       SAD BLUES Vocal Quartette   **Norfolk Jazz Quartette**
12055—DIXIE BLUES Vocal Quartette   **Norfolk Jazz Quartette**
       QUARTETTE BLUES Vocal Quartette   **Norfolk Jazz Quartette**

EXCELSIOR NORFOLK QUARTETTE

12131—JELLY ROLL BLUES Male Quartette   **Excelsior Norfolk Quartette**
       CONEY ISLAND BABE Male Quartette   **Excelsior Norfolk Quartette**

FOUR HARMONY KINGS

12009—DON'T CRY MY HONEY Quartette   **Four Harmony Kings**
       SWEET ADELINE Quartette   **Four Harmony Kings**
12104—AIN'T IT A SHAME Male Quartette   **Four Harmony Kings**
       GOODNIGHT ANGELINE Male Quartette   **Four Harmony Kings**

12. A Paramount advertisement for quartette recordings, 1923

13. The Staples Singers: (left to right) Mavis, Roebuck (guitar), Purvis and Yvonne, c1951

14. Mahalia Jackson

structure on which other topical songs could be built, for instance Speckled Red's *Welfare Blues* (Bluebird 8069, 1938) and Sonny Boy Williamson's *Welfare Store Blues* (Bluebird B8610, 1940).

Williamson's *Good Morning School Girl* (Bluebird 7059, 1937) gained from its structure with repeat half lines and chord sequence. Jazz Gillum's *Look on Yonder Wall* (Victor 20-1974, 1946) and Big Bill Broonzy's *I'm gonna move to the outskirts of town* (Okeh 6651, 1942) were other examples of recurrent blues that retained their popularity after World War II. Nevertheless the postwar period had its own canonical blues like T-Bone Walker's *Call it Stormy Monday* (Black and White 122, 1947), Lightnin' Slim's *Rooster Blues* (Excello 2169, 1960), Lowell Fulson's *Reconsider Baby* (Checker 804, 1954) and Magic Sam's *All your Love* (Cobra 5013, 1957), which were popular among a great many singers. None was more so than Elmore James's *Dust my Blues* (Flair 1074, 1956), perhaps the most frequently played and overworked of postwar themes, which nevertheless derived from Robert Johnson's *I believe I'll dust my broom* (Vocalion 03475, 1936).

In some cases it was not the original record but a particularly effective derivation that became the basis of a blues 'standard'. Standards were the mainstays of many singers' repertories. However, the demands of the record industry to produce a dozen or more titles for one long-playing record and the pressure to produce more albums when the first has been a commercial success, has meant that the requirement for a handful of songs at one session has been superseded by a thirst for new titles that by no means all singers can satisfy. But it also reflects a greater emphasis on solo improvisation on an instrument, usually the guitar, as blues has become musical rather than verbal expression.

The work of blues composers should receive greater attention. Not all composers were good executants and not all made the best versions of their songs: some wrote blues for other singers. In the 1920s Perry Bradford, Tom Delaney, Porter Grainger, Richard M. Jones, Clarence Williams and Wesley Wilson were among the many blues writers. During the 1930s Walter Roland, Jimmie Gordon, Big Bill Broonzy, Robert Brown (Washboard Sam) and St Louis Jimmy (James Oden) were active. Dave Bartholomew, Arthur 'Big Boy' Crudup, Jimmy Rogers (James A. Lane) and Jimmy Reed in the postwar era all composed popular blues but the most prolific is probably Willie Dixon (*b* Vicksburg, Mississippi, 1 July 1915), a bass player who has written songs for Muddy Waters, Howling Wolf and other blues singers, as well as for rock-and-roll performers like Bo Diddley and Chuck Berry.

The customary omission of blues composers' names from discographies has contributed to the disregard of their role. It should be noted, however, that composer credits often indicate the session organizer or talent scout and not necessarily the original composer. Most blues singers have been at best only partly literate and unfamiliar with commercial methods, so few understood royalties or copyright, which were claimed by many of those who brought them to the microphone.

Composition

The status of blues as folk or popular music has often been ambiguous: many of the early classic blues singers were stage entertainers and later singers of the rhythm-and-blues and soul blues eras were inextricably involved with contemporary popular music. Blues as entertainment offered a route for some singers to enter the world of professional music, but for countless Blacks blues enabled the less privileged to develop the skills and artistry that provided them with a vehicle for personal expression. In this sense for at least half a century it remained a folk music that afforded opportunities for creative endeavour within a form with its own continuity and tradition.

Though the number of blues stanzas on record may exceed a quarter of a million, there have been few attempts to trace their origins. Until the 1950s, and in many cases much later, most blues singers came from the south and had been engaged in manual labour for much of their lives. Clearly some blues originated in work song and probably from songs of the earlier slave and plantation economy that survived on the southern penitentiaries (see §II above). This appears to be the source of Tom Dickson's *Worry Blues* (Okeh 8570, 1928):

> 'Good Mornin' Captain', said 'Good Mornin' Shine' (*twice*)
> T'ain't nothin' the matter Captain but I just ain't gwine'.
>
> I don't mind workin' Captain, from sun to sun (*twice*)
> But I wants my money, Captain, when pay-day comes.

Although the earliest blues derived from field hollers, blues were recorded long before them. Recordings of camp hollers were made in Clarksdale, Mississippi, in 1941 by an unknown singer (possibly Son House), with spoken comments (italicized) by other members of the camp (L. of C. AFS59, 1941):

Well if I had-a follered, boys, my ol' second mind . . .
I said I'd a been up the country my old second time . . .
yeah, yeah –
Well I'm feelin' low down today
I know you is Son, go sing them ole levee camp blues;
I know you got em; sing em;
Oh Mister Charlie, Mister Dud Low Joe . . .
I done decided, oh boys, I won't work no mo' . . .
Boy look-a hyah
Oh I'm gonna get levee camp [Bodosha] Lord for to hold my
    head
Sleep yo' own, boy
I'm gonna get [Bodosha] women for to make up my bed.
eeh, get up there will ya!
Well look-a here boy
Well that ole mule ain't gonna get back
he ain't gonna drive no more.
Oh I see . . .
Yeah I done walked this ole levee boys till my feet got numb
If you see Mister Charlie, ask him did his money come?

In spite of their extended syllables and loose structure such hollers were frequently sung in couplets. References to singing and having the blues may indicate the relationship of hollers to blues or, bearing in mind the date, perhaps the influence of blues on them. Moreover, there are indications that the field recordings were not made while the men were actually at work.

Many holler-like extended blues in free form were

148

recorded in the field for Harry Oster by Robert Pete Williams, a prisoner at Angola penitentiary when Oster first heard him. His appeals for a pardon had been rejected three times, as he recounted in *Pardon Denied Again* (Arhoolie 2015, 1960):

> Well, I know my case is ain't too bad, Lord
> I just can't see, I just can't see,
> Why they treat me this away,
> Lord have mercy on my dyin' soul.
> I got, I got a big family on my hand(s)
> They's out there in that free worl'
> Waitin' on me to re-'pear
> Oh Lord they wan' me to return again, back to my home
> Oh Lord, have mercy on me,
> I got a man, tol' me that he would write
> Now, a letter to the governor for me,
> And I hope he would help me along.
> Grant to the Lord he hear my prayer
> I wish that governor would take sides with me,
> Lord have mercy on me.

Though his stanzas were irregular and there was no rhyme scheme, Williams's improvised song was held secure by the strong rhythmic unity of his guitar playing. Instrumental accompaniment may have contributed to the fixing of blues form, but early blues were often less thematically consistent than this one. Many examples from the 1920s were of stanza chains which were only loosely related though they included verses in wide currency, some of them dating back to the beginning of the century.

Henry Thomas, for example, had a typical songster's approach to blues when he sang his version of *Red River Blues* (Vocalion 1137, 1927):

> Look where the sun done gone, (*twice*)
> Look where the sun done gone, poor girl
> Look where the sun done gone.
>
> Yes it's gone, God knows where, (*twice*)
> Look where the sun done gone darlin'
> Look where the sun done gone.
>
> Lovin' babe I'm all out and down, (*twice*)
> I'm all out and down, I'm layin' on the ground
> Look where the sun done gone.

The rest of the song had fragments of traditional stanzas drawing on *Poor Boy Long Ways from Home* and the customary 'Which away do the Red River run?'. Yet verses similar to those quoted above were sung in somewhat different order in his *Lovin' Babe* (Vocalion 1468, 1928), which included a stanza also heard in his *Texas Worried Blues* (Vocalion 1249, 1928), 'got the worried blues, God, I'm feeling bad', which in turn incorporated a 'fare thee well' verse and other stanzas noted since early in the century. As a songster, Thomas characteristically used elements or whole stanzas that floated freely between blues songs and were readily available to all singers, parts of traditional or ragtime songs and images or fragments probably of his own devising.

Other blues appear to have late 19th-century ragtime and 'coon' song origins adapted to meet the singer's taste. The following words are from Joe Calicott's *Fare thee baby* (Brunswick 7166, 1930):

> Told me early spring, when the birds begin to sing,
> Fare thee baby, fare thee well.
> Told me early spring, when the birds begin to sing,
> Well it's the last chance to be, my gal, with me.

They may be compared with similar songs by the Memphis Jug Band (*I'll see you in the spring, when the birds begin to sing*, Victor 21066, 1927) and Johnnie Head (*Fare thee Blues* parts 1 and 2, Paramount 12628, 1928).

'Fare thee well' phrases appear in many white songs ranging from the 19th-century dance tune *Old Joe Clark* to the morbid ballad *Death is a Melancholy Call*. The recorded examples are all linked in some way with *Dink's Blues*, noted by John A. Lomax from a Mississippi migrant woman worker on the Brazos River, Texas, c1904–7. They are also linked with a number of published 'fare thee well' songs from the turn of the century, including *Fare thee honey, fare thee well* by the white coon-song composers Walter Wilson and John Queen.

The 12-bar, three-line stanza with an *aab* rhyme scheme was well established by World War I but recordings in the 1920s suggest that other structures were also used. A number of early blues appear to have been eight-bar couplets. Tommy Johnson's celebrated *Cool Drink of Water Blues* (Victor 21279, 1928) was sung and recorded by him with successive stanzas in the schemes *aaa*; *aa*; *ab*; *aa*; *ab*, *bb*, *b*. None was in the well-established *aab* formula.

XIX Form and content

Why the 12-bar, three-line form predominated is a matter of conjecture. Published blues may have played a part in crystallizing the form, which was presumably based on folk sources. The structure permitted singers to improvise new lines to rhyme with the repeat couplet, and this undoubtedly assisted blues composition. Though improvisation may not be as fundamental to blues as to jazz, some singers being content to repeat their songs and accompaniments with little variation, extempore playing and verse making is an essential element of the tradition.

Many blues singers used one or two stanzas as the core of their songs and added others that were often related in mood if not directly in content. Thus in his first issued record *Cloudy Sky Blues* (Columbia 14205-D, 1927), using the customary *aab* form, Barbecue Bob sang a number of stanzas that combined to create an image of separation and disquiet:

It seems cloudy, brown, I believe it's goin' to rain,
Seems cloudy now, I believe it's goin' to rain,
Goin' back to my reg'lar 'cause she got everything.

Hey, hey mama, mama, that ain't no way to do,
Hey, hey, pretty mama that ain't no way to do,
You tryin' to quit me, mama you know I've been good to you.

Hello Central, give me long, long distance phone, (*twice*)
I wanna hear from my sweet mama back home.

When your brown gets funny, everything you do – she gets sore
(*twice*)
You can hunt another home 'cause she don't want you no more.

The third verse was probably ultimately derived from Charles K. Harris's *Hello Central, give me heaven*, published in 1901, which inspired a number of 'Hello Central' songs; the verse, in slightly different form, occurs in several blues.

By the time this blues was recorded, such collections of stanzas linked primarily by mood were becoming somewhat anachronistic; thematic blues with a narrative or a succession of verses conveying a specific message were now common. Evans has noted that Blind Lemon Jefferson's recordings of 1926 included none that were purely thematic and five that were partly so; of those none were original, all but three were wholly traditional and 11 were non-thematic. Three years later the balance was reversed; of the 22 items recorded by Jefferson that year all but one was original and all were thematic.

Not all singers showed such a marked progression or change of approach. Charley Patton's *Stone Pony Blues* (Vocalion 02680, 1934) is non-thematic but *High Sheriff Blues*, on the other side of the record, is thematic and to some extent a remodelling of an earlier recording, *Tom Rushen Blues* (Paramount 12877, 1929).

Lay down last night hopin' I would have my peace, peace (*twice*)
When I woke up Tom Rushen was shakin' me.

When you get in trouble it's no use a-screamin and cryin, mm-mm   (*twice*)
Tom Rushen will take you back to prison house flyin'.

It was late òne night Holloway was gone to bed – mm-mm
Mr Day brought whiskey taken from under Holloway's head.

Aw it's boozy booze, now Lord to carry me through
It takes boozy booze, Lord to carry me through,
But each day seems like years in a jailhouse where there is no booze.

I got up this mornin', Tom Day was standin' roun' – mm-mm
(*twice*)
Say, if he lose his office now, he's running from town to town.

Let me tell you folkses just how he treated me – mm
I'm gonna tell you folkses just how he treated me – mm-mm
He caught me yellin', I was drunk as I could be.

Though there is some narrative the listener is let in on part of a story rather than the whole, as he might be when hearing a ballad.

In blues the narrative is frequently condensed, the meanings codified, so that the verses stand as a succession of cameos. Each may be related to a theme or themes, though apparently inconsequential verses simply contribute to the overall expression of mood and content. Frequently someone is addressed: sometimes the listener, sometimes another person, and often both, as in Charley Jordan's *Hungry Blues* (Vocalion 1657, 1931):

Let me get out on the street baby, Lord and see what I can do,
                                                              (*twice*)
Well I don't mind being hungry, but my baby she'll be hungry
    too.

Now today is Thursday, let's all give a helping hand (*twice*)
I'm talking to all you girls, oh' that's got a hungry man.

Now if it wasn't for you baby, Lord what would I do? (*twice*)
I wouldn't be walking round here, ragged and broken and hungry
    too.

Now if you ever been hungry, Lord you know just how I feel
                                                              (*twice*)
I got so hungry last winter 'til I went out and I tried to steal.

Stealin' was a good job 'til the police got on my trail (*twice*)
But the next thing I knew, I was all locked up in jail.

Now if you got a good woman, better treat her nice as you can
I say if you got a good woman, better treat her as nice as you can

154

Because I got so hungry last winter, 'til I had to eat from a
    garbage can.

While most of the verses are original to this blues,
variants of the first lines of verses 4 and 6 are found
in many others.

The use of clichés in terms of full or partial expression enables the singer to insert words or ideas appropriate to his theme. So a singer may start a verse
with the line 'don't the moon look lonesome shinin''
through the trees' and follow it with 'don't your house
look lonesome' or 'don't your home seem lonesome'
or merely 'ain't it lonesome, ain't it lonesome', to
which the conclusion of the line may be 'when your
woman gets up and leaves' or 'when your biscuit-
roller leaves'. Such formulae are aids to invention but
some singers depended on them with little originality.
The blues stanza itself was a formula, its lines
composed of iambic pentameters with a momentary
caesura in the middle that divided the line and
enabled the singer to add half-line invented phrases
to standard half lines.

Thematically, blues realized its greatest potential
during the 1930s when the movement of thousands of
migrants, the loss of jobs and the fruitless seeking for
new work provided subjects for scores of records.
Travelling, especially by box car or 'riding the rods'
on freight trains and moving between the 'jungles' or
hobo camps, figured prominently; so too did petty
crime, gambling and the 'policy' racket, bootlegging
and alcohol addiction. Prostitution and 'hustling'
were frequent themes and the subject of many blues by
women singers. In many cases the themes were gener-

alized but a number were more specific; there were several blues on the mid-1930s 'bonus marches' by war veterans, others on hurricanes, fires and named disasters.

An example of a topical theme is labouring for organizations under the New Deal, which employed a quarter of a million Blacks in the Public Works Administration, the Works Projects (Progress) Administration and the Civilian Conservation Corps. Peetie Wheatstraw recorded several blues on this theme, among them *Working man* (*doing the best I can*) (Decca 7200, 1936), *Working on the project* (Decca 7311, 1937) and *New working on the project* (Decca 7379, 1937), which summarized the effects of receiving a '304' slip with a final pay cheque, indicating the loss of employment:

Working on the project – what a scared man, you know (*twice*)
Because every time I look around, ooh well, well somebody's
   getting their 304.

Working on the project, the rent man is knocking on my door
                                                        (*twice*)
'I'm sorry, Mister Rent Man, ooh well, well, I just got my 304'.

Working on the project, a 304 can make you cry (*twice*)
There's one thing sure, you can tell the project 'Good-bye'.

It was the subject to which he returned in *304 Blues* (*Lost my job on the project*) (Decca 7453, 1938) and the fact that all were recorded while he was under contract to Decca indicates the popularity of this theme. But Wheatstraw was not the only singer on the subject: the earliest was Walter Roland's *CWA Blues* (Melotone 13103, 1931) and others followed, including Jimmie Gordon's *Don't take away my PWA* (Decca 7230, 1936), Casey Bill's recitative about the destruction of his house by a wrecking crew, *WPA Blues* (Vocalion 3186, 1936) and his *New WPA* (Vocalion 03950, 1937), Bill Gaither's *Lazy Woman Blues* (Decca 7668, 1939), Washboard Sam's *CCC Blues* (Bluebird 7993, 1938), Big Bill Broonzy's *WPA Rag* (Vocalion 04429, 1938) and *WPA Blues* (ARC 6-08-61, 1938). These songs on the problems of marginal employment and unemployment during the Depression might seem to have been unwelcome reminders to the black audience, even if they could afford the records. But it seems such blues were popular and, when radio still rarely employed Blacks, records were the only means whereby Blacks could hear the voices and share the experience of others in their predicament in different parts of the country.

The increasing popularity of radio programmes for black audiences may have contributed to the decline of blues with documentary or social significance in the mid-1950s. But blues of social content were seldom sung objectively; even when a disaster was described the singer himself was usually central to the theme, either from personal experience or from projection into the situation. Such blues as J. B. Lenoir's *Eisenhower Blues* (Parrott 802, 1954) and Bo-bo Jenkins's *Democrat Blues* (Chess 1565, 1954), which were politically motivated, or Floyd Jones's *Ain't times hard* (Vee Jay 111, 1955) and John Brim's *Tough Times* (Parrott 799, 1953), which reflected economic pressures on the poor and black in the mid-

157

1950s, were all sung from a personal standpoint; they were also among the last significant commercially issued 78 r.p.m. records of this type.

Through blues there runs a strong vein of complaint which sometimes finds expression in words of anger. Frequently it tends to be laconic or passive and occasionally has more than a note of self-pity. If blues was expressive of the human condition of individuals rather than the orchestration of protesting voices, it did have much to say about personal relationships. Often chauvinistic and blatantly sexual, but gaining from its honesty and forthrightness, blues was affirmative in its glorification of the life-force. Probably three-quarters of recorded blues are about the relationship between the sexes, but the high proportion of these that convey sublimated aggression, bitterness and disappointment suggests that they are symbolic of more profound psycho-social problems. Seldom does the blues have more than an oblique element of protest which is communicated more by canalizing frustration or anger into statements of broken relationships than through overt declarations of resistance or defiance. In this respect blues was overtaken by gospel music.

XX Music and techniques

No aspect of blues has been so neglected as the analysis of the idiom as music. This reflects the interests of writers and critics, who have largely focussed on biographical data. But it is also an outcome of the inherent nature of the music: placing a high premium on micro-tonal variations for expressive purposes, it has not lent itself to presentation in conventional musical notation.

Blues is dominated by the vocal: instruments are largely used to accompany singing and the 'blues singer' is more readily recognized than the 'blues musician'. Later this relationship changed to some extent; larger bands with four, five or even a dozen musicians sometimes performed instrumental items. But even in such cases a lead singer, often a singer–guitarist, would lead the band with the instrumentalists in a supporting role. The use of tones and inflections derived from or related to those of the blues voice is evident in the instrumental work.

Long before blues was recognized as a distinct genre, writers on black music expressed despair in their attempt to notate the singing of slaves. Lucy McKim commented on the 'odd turns made in the throat and the curious rhythmic effect produced by single voices chiming in at regular intervals . . . They seem almost impossible to place on the score' (1867). Later, when a collection of black songs was published, Jeanette Robinson Murphy observed (1899) that the compilers did not explain to the singer 'that he must make his voice exceeding nasal and undulating, that around every prominent note he must place a variety of small notes, called "trimmings", and he must sing notes not found in our scale'. These characteristics of earlier black song, which demonstrate links with vocal practice in some regions of West Africa, suggest a tradition that not only goes back to the import of slaves but also looks forward to blues, where in some respects the techniques were probably extended and exaggerated.

There have been many attempts to account for the origins of 'blue tonality' and to identify its character. In conventional terms blues singers are inclined to disregard pitches as fixed points and to treat them with a fluidity expressed in slurs and fluctuations about the note. This is especially evident in the blues singer's approach to the third degree of the scale and frequently to the seventh, which is flattened or 'wavers' between flat and natural. However, neutral thirds and sevenths are used by folksingers in many cultures without displaying blues tonality; they are present, for example, in much Anglo-American folksong. William Tallmadge observed that 'when the savannah slaves arrived in this country, they found a musical culture which, instead of suppressing their own inflected musical practice, actually sustained and reinforced it'; but, he concluded, blues tonality arises when the inflected pitches are used within European harmony: 'An unique polychordal effect is occasioned by discrete neutral pitches sounding against the regular pitches of the accompanying chords'. He concluded that 'all discrete neutral pitches, when regular chords are present or *implied* are blue notes'.

A number of musicologists have attempted to define 'blues scale', perhaps the best known being Winthrop Sargeant (1938), who argued the meeting of an African pentatonic scale with the European diatonic one. Hatch and Watson, using sol-fa notation (*do, ra, re, me, mi, fa, fi, sol, la, le, te, ti, do*), concluded that the 'tonal distribution frequency' of country blues was *do, sol, me/mi, fa, te, lah, re, ti*; from this they derived a 'country-blues scale' in which the bracketed notes occurred with comparative rarity: *do, (re), me, mi, sol, (la), te, (ti)*. Comparing this with other blues forms, they observed that *me* and *te* were much less frequently used in the female, urban classic blues while *la* and *re* appeared much more so. On the other hand, male, urban blues of the 1930s used a somewhat reduced scale of *do, re, me, mi, fa, sol, (la), (te), (ti)* derived from the relatively frequent sequence *do, sol, mi, fa, me, re, te/la, ti*. Theoretically, because the relationship between instrumental and vocal blues is so close, the issue of blues tonality applies as much to the characteristics of instrumental accompaniment and performance as it does to singing.

Before discussing instrumental work it is necessary to mention blues structure, outlined in §II above. As noted, the most prevalent structure is a three-line stanza, sung and played in the harmonic sequence of tonic, subdominant and dominant chords (I, IV and V), generally as I, I, I, I; IV, IV, I, I; V, V, I, I. But there are many variations, such as I, I, V, V; I, I, IV, IV; I, I, I, I; and many eight-bar blues have a I, I, IV, IV; I, V, I, I sequence or a variant of it.

A number of late 19th-century ballads assumed a three-line form often with a couplet and refrain line, presaging blues, and it seems that the conjunction of this ballad type and the meandering free-form vocal improvisations of the holler bred the blues form proper. It was noted early in the century and, as dis-

161

cussed in §IV above, appeared in published form before World War I. It is tempting to think that publication hastened the popularization of blues, but few rural singers are likely to have had access to published blues or have been interested in sheet music; verbal and instrumental transmission through travelling shows, including medicine shows, is more likely. Exchanges of song among black servicemen during World War I may have contributed to the spread of the idiom, and the popularization of classic blues on phonograph record in the early 1920s and of folk idioms from 1925 seems to have aided the crystallizing of the form. Departures from the standard 12-bar blues form were relatively rare in the 1930s and the structure still predominates.

As a sequence it has a certain inevitability, an inexorable yet anticipatory resolution that both prepares the listener – or the performer – for the subsequent stanzas and permits the termination of the blues at any verse. While it is sufficiently simple to allow novice guitarists to perform blues with three basic chords, it also permits considerable variation and inflection. In fact it is the capacity of the framework to allow individual interpretation in performance that has made it so suitable a vehicle for folk creativity. Almost invariably blues vocals follow a descending melodic contour, both in the individual lines and in the shape of the stanza. This contour, which arises from vocals that start at a high pitch and climb slightly or descend steadily to a lower one, combines with blues structure and timbre to give musical unity. This is reflected in the accompaniments

162

which, however, rarely departed from local traditions until the wide availability of records afforded easy access to other sounds and styles. Mississippi guitarists, for instance, appear to favour opening their first line of a blues on the chord of E moving to the dominant 7th, and they frequently begin with a one- or two-bar anticipation of the first stanza. Most Mississippians also favoured descending phrases on the bass strings. This predilection for descending runs corresponding to the vocal contour is to be heard in all other traditions, on the top strings among many East Coast blues guitarists.

The blues chord sequence can be easily learnt but most blues guitarists develop complex right-hand fingering techniques. The 'claw-hammer' style, in which the forefinger is crooked and draws up the string, is the most common, often enriched by picking with the second and third fingers to give intricate patterns within the chord. Some singers used fingerpicks, like Blind Boy Fuller; others developed horn-like fingernails and eschewed picks, like Sleepy John Estes. Some guitarists, including Big Bill Broonzy, used the plectrum or flat pick for specific tunes or rhythms. To obtain the desired blue tonality, which could make virtually every note a slurred blue note, most guitarists would slide the stopping finger on the string or 'choke' the string by pushing it laterally across the fret while depressing it, thus raising the note a quarter-tone or more or creating a wavering, whining sound. Many 'hammer' on the string, allowing a double note to occur naturally when the string is released. Some guitarists, for instance

163

Lonnie Johnson, used these techniques almost habitually; others made expressive devices out of them, as did Josh White, sometimes to excess.

Many guitarists achieved blue tonality by using a slide on the strings, an old technique first noted by W. C. Handy in 1903, when he heard a Mississippi guitarist using a quill. A length of copper tubing or a glass bottleneck, its rough edges annealed by heat, would be slid over the third or fourth finger and used to touch the strings in a slide action which imparted a characteristic wailing sound. The technique of holding a clasp-knife or blade or even a nail between the fingers, as used by the Arkansas bluesman CeDell Davis, prevents the forming of conventional chords; it is closer to the Hawaiian bar technique and may have been introduced by Hawaiian guitarists after the annexation of Hawaii in 1898 and the subsequent popularity of island musicians. Some blues guitarists, including Black Ace, Oscar Woods and Kokomo Arnold, used the Hawaiian bar technique, with the guitar laid flat across the lap; Black Ace (B. K. Turner) substituted an aspirin bottle for a bar.

When using the bar or slide laid across the full width of the strings, it is necessary to retune a guitar from a standard tuning (*E–A–d–g–b–e'*) to one of a number of 'cross-note' tunings. Among the most common are 'Sebastapol' (or 'Vastapol'), in which the guitar is tuned to an open E chord (*E–B–e–a♭–b–e'*) or open D (*D–A–d–f♯–a–d'*), or 'Spanish', tuned to open A (*E–A–e–a–c♯–e'*) or open G (*D–G–d–g–b–d'*). The widespread popularity among songsters of 'Spanish flang-dang' (Fandango) and *Talking in*

Sebastapol suggests that the tunings were named after instrumental pieces, as was the open D (*D, A, d, g, b, e'*), known as 'Poor boy' tuning, in which the early blues *Poor Boy Long Ways from Home* was often played. This use of the slide has been among the most persistent of blues guitar techniques, being widely adapted to the electric guitar by Elmore James and his imitators and successors and maintained by white blues and rock groups and such guitarists as Eric Clapton and Pete Townshend.

The choice of an instrument was often conditioned by economic constraints and the first guitar was usually a 'diddley bow' – a strand of baling wire nailed to a fence, a small rock for a bridge and a bottleneck slide drawn along the 'string'. The 'cigar-box' instrument with one or more strings was frequently the next stage, followed perhaps by a mail-order guitar kit from Sears or a second-hand 'Kalamazoo' Gibson. American Martin and Gibson guitars were favoured, including the large Gibson 'Dreadnought', but in the days before amplification street musicians and juke-joint guitarists sought the National or Dobro chrome steel-bodied guitars with metal resonators or diaphragms to amplify the sound. Blues guitarists almost invariably used steel wound strings, and a second guitarist, using the flat pick and providing a rhythmic support, would back up the lead in country juke playing. When the electric guitar first became popular in the late 1930s it was adopted by a few blues singers; in the postwar years it was used widely in Chicago where it ousted the acoustic instrument. Amplification permitted lighter, more deft fingering and this was reflected in a greater sophistication of performance by some guitarists and more extended solo work.

In general, early blues guitarists were sparing with instrumental solos while accompanying blues vocals though not when playing for dancing. The standard 12-bar structure sustained a vocal generally in the first two, fifth and sixth, and ninth and tenth bars, allowing a short instrumental phrase or 'break' in the intervening bars. The break was often used rhythmically by Mississippi guitarists and frequently used for an answering phrase by Texas players. Most guitarists followed this formula only loosely, singing across, or into, the instrumental bars or, as in Blind Lemon Jefferson's *Bad Luck Blues*, singing responses in them, so that the vocal line was virtually continuous throughout the verse (ex.5*a*). He interpolated an instrumental break of thirteen bars – which followed a conventional blues sequence C, C, C, C; F, F, C, C; G7, G7, C, C – into the succession of verses, its particular quality arising from clean fingerpicking and an expressive tone rather than complexity (ex.5*b*). While this was recognizably Jefferson's personal style of playing, the instrumental work was characteristically early Texan.

The way in which blues guitar playing developed as a result of the meeting of the intermediate style of the younger singer Aaron T-Bone Walker and that of the Mississippi–Memphis guitarists of the 1950s may be seen in B. B. King's complex improvisations in *Gonna keep on lovin' you* (Blues Way 60001) (fully discussed by Sawyer), which demonstrates the

Music and techniques

Ex.5 Blind Lemon Jefferson: *Bad Luck Blues,*
transcr. Happy Traum (1968)

(a) Vocal line

1. I wanna go home but I ain't got suf-fi-cient clothes doggone my

bad luck soul_ Wan-na go home but I ain't got suf-fi – cient

clothes   I mean suf-fi – cient   Sold my clothes and I

wan-na go home but I   ain't got suf-fi-cient   clothes.

(b) Instrumental break

gui

guitarist's sense of structure and dynamics. In the key
of G, it follows the standard 12-bar blues progression
over four stanzas: the first part is played with great

167

Ex.6 B. B. King: *Gonna keep on lovin' you*, transcr. C. Sawyer (1980)

168

economy, steady beat and with silent pauses that suspend the melodic line; the second and third are in Hypophrygian mode, creating dramatic contrast between syncopated rhythm and characteristic cascading phrases, with marked dissonances and a rapid resolution; the fourth part is a final restatement of earlier phrases (ex.6).

In a number of ways the guitar is ideal for the blues; it sustains notes longer than the banjo and it offers more range. It can provide rhythmic and melodic accompaniment, and the techniques summarized above permit expressive use of its tonal qualities. It is light, portable and loud enough for most functions at which bluesmen work. In some respects the harmonica was no less appropriate, combining portability, volume, expressive potential and a similar suitability for blues tonality. It can be used as a solo instrument with vocal only with difficulty, though many harmonica players from Jaybird Coleman to Sonny Boy Williamson (i) have so managed to alternate voice and harmonica phrasing as to give an impression of accompaniment and almost unbroken melodic line.

Some harmonica players use the instrument 'straight', playing in C on an instrument in C, or in E on an E harmonica. But most play 'crossed harp'; that is, on an instrument tuned a 4th above the key being used, for example on a harmonica tuned to the subdominant (A) of the key (E) in which the piece is to be played. Crossing is accomplished by drawing or sucking on the tonic and subdominant notes, allowing the blues tonality of bending and wailing to be achieved more readily. It is customary to block the apertures with the tongue so that slight tongue movements alter the sound as the breath is drawn, a technique that is much more difficult on blown notes. By cupping the hands over the instrument and opening and shutting the cup, by fluttering the fingers or rocking the harmonica between the lips, sounds may also be altered. In particular, the 'warbling' or tremolo effect much exploited by Little Walter and later Chicago players was achieved by hand vibrations while cupping the instrument and made more pronounced by holding a microphone in the cupped hands.

Though the sources of blues harmonica styles have not been positively traced it seems likely that the techniques were arrived at by mimicry, for example 'mocking the trains' in imitation of whistles and engine sounds, as in Palmer McAbee's *Railroad Piece* (Victor 21352, 1928), in which he apparently used cyclic breathing. All harmonica players learnt a version of *The Fox Chase*, formerly a showpiece for fiddle players. It seems likely that the harmonica, which became increasingly popular with the inflow of German immigrants at the close of the 19th century, ousted the fiddle when it was adopted by black players. Cheap and manufactured in millions, the popular 'Marine Band', a ten-hole, 20-reed Höhner, could be obtained in a range of keys, and it was customary for 'harp players' to carry several in an adapted cartridge belt or rack. A neck-harness, which allowed a guitarist to play the harmonica while maintaining an accompaniment, was popular among one-man band musicians, like Drifting Slim (Elmon Mickle), Doctor Ross and Juke Boy Bonner.

While the essence of blues guitar and harmonica playing lies in adapting notes by 'bending' them, blues pianists are denied such measures by the fixed notes of the piano. As discussed above, blues pianists achieve illusions of bent and passing notes by

171

'crushing' adjacent keys or sliding the third finger across them, for example between G and G♭ or E♭ to E. Dissonances were exploited to impart blues tonalities; compelling rhythms would be placed against right-hand tremolos and simple alternating chords in the left hand against elaborate treble configurations. Most blues pianists played in the keys of C, F and G (the easiest), which did not fit well with the guitarist's preference for E and A. Though some blues guitarists played in C when working with a pianist, it was customary to use a capo, or clasp, across the strings to change the key while the player could retain preferred fingering; thus a capo at the third fret allowed the guitarist to play in C while fingering as he would for the key of E.

Mention has already been made of the 4/4 and 'eight to the bar' bass figures used by boogie-woogie pianists. Though some of these pianists performed as soloists for dances and rent parties, most of them knew and used boogie basses, often interpolating them after the third or fourth chorus of a piece to give additional impetus towards the close. Although the walking octave bass was the most dramatic, and perhaps the most memorable, of the left-hand figures used by blues and boogie pianists, a variety of chordal and single-note bass figures were played which displayed dotted quaver rhythms and a generous use of major and minor 3rds and 7ths. An accomplished pianist like Roosevelt Sykes or Leroy Carr would use all these devices, from steady 4/4 time with a solid, stomping accompaniment, to light and economical left-hand support to filgree right-hand passages, to drone accompaniments on a single chord, or to fast and exhilarating boogie basses.

Not all blues pianists were as versatile: many were relatively limited but individual within their own style, for example Cripple Clarence Lofton, whose repertory consisted of a few pieces in C, G and F which he played effectively at different tempos, occasionally to different bass figures, sometimes with his own vocal. Many pianists exploited particular phrases or sequences as personal trade marks, using these recognizable signatures to introduce the majority of their records, for example Peetie Wheatstraw's introduction to *Road Tramp Blues* (ex.7). Others, perhaps through dependence on an effective passage they could play with ease, introduced the same breaks into most of their recordings, as did

Ex.7 Introduction to Peetie Wheatstraw: *Road Tramp Blues*, transcr. P. Garon (1971)

Speckled Red with the fast final four bars of *The Dirty Dozen*, which crept into many other titles. In nearly all his recordings Charlie Spand used a characteristic phrase, also in the last four bars of a stanza, from *Soon this Morning* (ex.8).

Ex.8 Phrase from C. Spand: *Soon this Morning*, transcr. B. Hall (Hall and Noblett, 1976)

That some blues pianists were technically limited does not detract from the quality of their work, which in many instances gained in depth of feeling from the lack of sophistication. But blues pianists were competitive while they worked on similar circuits. The Fort Bend County pianists of Texas, who in the 1930s worked in the sawmill towns of the eastern part of the state, included Son Becky, Pinetop Burks, Robert Shaw, Buster Pickens and Black Boy Shine (Harold Holiday); they had elements of style in common but they competed for attention and engagements. However their repertory was also a defence against interlopers whose skills were put to the test by their ability to play such standard pieces as *The Cows* or

174

Hattie Green. Among Mississippi pianists a similar group development of skills was demonstrated by their ability to perform certain pieces, notably the *Forty-Fours*. As *44 Blues* by Roosevelt Sykes and *Forty-four Train* by Lee Green, it was recorded as *Vicksburg Blues* by Little Brother Montgomery (ex.9). Played in F, the piano accompaniment is closely integrated with the vocal, the held notes of which are matched by repeated quavers in the right hand, resolving into triplets for the passage between the lines. In the left hand the climbing bass figure, uniquely associated with the piece, maintains the beat but builds up tension, its rumbling, even threatening, character impressively contrasted with Montgomery's taut, braying vocal with its marked vibrato. By such means blues pianists created an idiom as significant and individual as that of the guitarists, though it has taken longer for it to be recognized.

Blues techniques seem to have developed and spread through emulation and competition but some musicians devised their own styles and means of expression. Some adapted their instruments, adding strings, fitting crude amplifiers or removing the front panel of pianos. Others developed flamboyant techniques, playing the guitar behind their backs or necks, whirling the instrument without missing beats, and other tricks. In postwar Chicago and Detroit players like Howling Wolf lay on the floor while performing, posturing and even playing the electric guitar with the teeth. Much of this display was competitive, a demonstration of the performer's mastery

175

Ex.9 Little Brother Montgomery: *Vicksburg Blues,* transcr. D. Kincaid (Oliver, 1968)

176

I sing— 'em—— my babe says she did-n't

want me— no more——

of his instrument. The use of the 'wah-wah' pedal and 'fuzz box' to extend sounds has also been prevalent among younger musicians (contributing to the complexities of transcribing blues).

A number of instruction books and manuals aimed at the aspiring guitarist, pianist and harmonica player have been published, some analysing and transcribing techniques and recorded performances. Though no blues musician learnt from a manual, these analyses make a contribution. Musicological analyses are few and mainly restricted to a small number of country bluesmen mainly from Mississippi (Fahey 1970; Titon 1977; Evans 1982). A considerable but essential task awaits the ethnomusicologist prepared to make a stylistic, evolutionary and structural analysis of blues music.

XXI Bibliography

GENERAL HISTORIES

S. B. Charters: *The Country Blues* (New York, 1959/*R*1975)

——: *The Bluesmen* (New York, 1967)

P. Oliver: *The Story of the Blues* (London, 1969)

E. Southern: *The Music of Black Americans: a History* (New York, 1971, 2/1983)

G. Oakley: *The Devil's Music: a History of the Blues* (London, 1976)

L. Levine: *Black Culture and Black Consciousness* (New York, 1977)

BIOGRAPHICAL DICTIONARIES AND RECORD GUIDES

A. McCarthy, A. Morgan, P. Oliver and M. Harrison: *Jazz on Record: a Critical Review of the First 50 Years, 1917–1967* (London, 1968)

J. C. Arnaudon: *Dictionnaire du blues* (Paris, 1977)

K. Bogaert: *Blues Lexicon: Blues, Cajun, Boogie Woogie, Gospel* (Antwerp, *c*1979)

P. Guralnick: *The Listener's Guide to the Blues* (New York, 1979)

S. Harris: *Blues Who's Who* (New Rochelle, NY, 1979)

G. Herzhaft: *Encyclopédie du blues* (Lyons, 1979)

DISCOGRAPHIES

J. Godrich and R. M. W. Dixon: *Blues and Gospel Records, 1902–1942* (Hatch End, nr. London, 1963, rev. and enlarged 3/1982 as *Blues and Gospel Records, 1902–1943*)

M. Leadbitter and N. Slaven: *Blues Records, 1943–1966* (London, 1968)

ORIGINS

J. R. Murphy: 'The Survival of African Music in America', *Popular Science Monthly*, lv (1899), 660

F. Olmsted: *A Journey in the Seaboard Slave States in the Years 1853–1854*, xi (New York, 1904), 19f

A. Lomax: 'Murderer's Home', Tradition 1020 [disc notes]

H. Nathan: *Dan Emmett and the Rise of Early Negro Minstrelsy* (Norman, Oklahoma, 1962)

J. H. Dormon: 'The Strange Career of Jim Crow Rice', *Journal of Social History*, iii/2 (1969–70)

D. Evans: 'Afro-American One-stringed Instruments', *Western Folklore*, xxix (1970)

178

Bibliography

P. Oliver: *Savannah Syncopators: African Retentions in the Blues* (London, 1970)

B. Jackson: *Wake Up Dead Man: Afro-American Worksongs from Texas Prisons* (Cambridge, Mass., 1972)

W. K. McNeil: 'Syncopated Slander: the Coon Song 1890–1900', *Keystone Folk Quarterly* (1972), no.17, p.12

J. S. Roberts: *Black Music of Two Worlds* (New York, 1972)

D. Epstein: *Sinful Tunes and Spirituals* (Urbana, 1977), 181ff

D. Evans: 'African Elements in Twentieth-century United States Black Folk Music', *Jazzforschung*, x (Frankfurt, 1978), 85

S. B. Charters: *The Roots of the Blues: an African Search* (Boston, Mass., 1981)

S. Dennison: *Scandalize my Name: Black Imagery in American Popular Music* (New York, 1981)

M. T. Coolen: 'The Fodet: a Senegambian Origin for the Blues?', *Black Perspective in Music*, x/1 (1982), 69

FROM SONGSTERS TO BLUES SINGERS

D. Scarborough: *On the Trail of Negro Folk-songs* (Cambridge, Mass., 1925)

H. W. Odum and G. B. Johnson: *Negro Workaday Songs* (Chapel Hill, 1926)

N. I. White: *American Negro Folk Songs* (Cambridge, Mass., 1928)

L. Cohn: 'Mississippi John Hurt', *Sing Out!*, xiv/5 (1964), 16

M. McCormick: 'Henry Thomas, Ragtime Texas', Herwin 209 [disc notes]

P. Oliver: *Songsters and Saints: Vocal Traditions on Race Records* (London, 1984)

PUBLICATION AND RECORDING

Anon: 'Origin of "Blues" Numbers', *Sheet Music News*, v (1923), Oct, 8

W. C. Handy: *A Treasury of the Blues* (New York, 1925) [ed. with an essay by A. Niles]

——: *Father of the Blues* (London, 1957)

P. Oliver: 'Special Agents: an Introduction to the Recording of Folk Blues in the Twenties', *Jazz Review*, ii/2 (1959), 20

D. Mahony: *The Columbia 13/14000-D Series: a Numerical Listing* (Stanhope, NJ, 1961)

S. B. Charters and L. Kunstadt: *Jazz: a History of the New York Scene* (Garden City, NY, 1962)

179

P. Bradford: *Born with the Blues* (New York, 1965)

R. C. Foreman jr: *Jazz and Race Records, 1920–1932* (diss., U. of Illinois, Urbana, 1968)

R. M. W. Dixon and J. Godrich: *Recording the Blues* (London and New York, 1970)

M. E. Vreede: *Paramount 12000/13000 Series* (London, 1971)

CLASSIC BLUES

E. Waters and C. Samuels: *His Eye is on the Sparrow* (New York, 1951)

G. Avakian: 'The Art of Jazz: Bessie Smith', CL-855-8 [disc notes]

P. Oliver: *Bessie Smith* (London, 1959)

G. Schuller: *Early Jazz: its Roots and Musical Development* (New York, 1968)

R. Groom: 'Lonnie Johnson', *Blues World*, no.35 (1970), p.4

D. Stewart-Baxter: *Ma Rainey and the Classic Blues Singers* (London, 1970)

——: 'Ida Cox 1923 Recordings', FB-301 [disc notes]

C. Albertson: *Bessie* (London and New York, 1972)

P. Oliver: 'The Thomas Family 1925–1929', PY4404 [disc notes]

S. Lieb: *Mother of the Blues: a Study of Ma Rainey* (Amherst, 1981)

E. Brooks: *The Bessie Smith Companion* (Wheathampstead, St Albans, 1982)

SOUTHERN FOLK BLUES

P. Oliver: 'Barbecue Bob', *Music Mirror*, v/8(1958), 6

—: 'Blind Lemon Jefferson', *Jazz Review*, ii/4 (1959), 19

G. D. Wardlow: 'Biographical Notes', OJL 2, 5, 8 [disc notes]

R. Groom: 'The Legacy of Blind Lemon', *Blues World*, nos.18–40, (1968–71)

J. Fahey: *Charley Patton* (London, 1970)

D. Evans: *Tommy Johnson* (London, 1971)

P. Lowry: 'Some Cold Rainy Day', *Blues Unlimited*, no. 103(1973), 15

'Son House', *Living Blues*, no.31 (1977), 14 [interview]

D. Evans: 'Blind Willie McTell', JEMF 106 [disc notes]

G. van Rijn and H. Vergeer: 'Texas Troublesome Blues: Alger "Texas" Alexander', Agram (H) AB 2009 [disc notes]

G. D. Wardlow: 'Ishmon Bracey', *Blues Unlimited*, no.142 (1982), 4

180

Bibliography

STRING, JUG AND WASHBOARD BANDS

P. Oliver: 'Tub Jug Washboard Bands 1924–1932', RLP 8802 [disc notes]

B. Rust: 'Clarence Williams Jug and Washboard Band', Philips 13653 AJL [disc notes]

G. Mitchell: 'An Interview with Peg Leg Howell', Testament T-204 [disc notes]

B. Olsson: *Memphis Blues and Jug Bands* (London, 1970)

——: 'Cannon's Jug Stompers and Gus Cannon as Banjo Joe, 1927–30: Biography', Herwin 208 [disc notes]

——: 'South Memphis Jug Band', FLY (E) 113 [disc notes]

P. Oliver: 'Coley Jones and the Dallas String Band 1927–1929', Matchbox (E) MSE 208 [disc notes]

PIANO BLUES AND THE NORTHERN MIGRATION

E. Borneman: 'Boogie-Woogie', *Just Jazz*, ed. S. Traill and G. Lascelles (London, 1957)

P. Oliver: 'Mr Sykes Blues 1929–1932', Riverside 8819 [disc notes]

M. Harrison: 'Boogie Woogie', *Jazz: New Perspectives*, ed. A. McCarthy and N. Hentoff (New York, 1959/*R*1974)

K. Gert zur Heide: *Deep South Piano: the Story of Little Brother Montgomery* (London, 1970)

J. Bentley: 'The Honey-dripper: Roosevelt Sykes', *Living Blues*, no.9 (1972), 21

E. Kriss: *Six Blues-roots Pianists* (New York, 1973)

S. Calt, J. Epstein and N. Perls: 'Barrelhouse Blues 1927–1936', Yazoo L-1028 [disc notes]

E. Kriss: *Barrelhouse and Boogie Piano* (New York, 1974)

R. Hall and R. Noblett: 'A Handful of Keys', *Blues Unlimited*, no.113 (1975) 14

SOUTHERN BLUES IN THE 1930s

P. Oliver: 'Key to the Highway', *Jazz Monthly* (1958), Aug, p.2

——: 'Peetie Wheatstraw', *Jazz Monthly*, v/3 (1959), 2

D. P. Schiedt: 'Blues Before Sunrise: Leroy Carr', CL 1799 [disc notes]

P. Oliver: 'Kokomo Arnold', *Jazz Monthly* (1962), May, p.11

B. Groom: 'Robert Johnson', *Blues World Booklet*, no.1 (1967)

J. Shines: 'The Robert Johnson I Knew', *American Folk Music Occasional*, no.2 (New York, 1970), 30

B. Bastin: *Crying for the Carolines* (London, 1971)

P. Garon: *The Devil's Son-in-law* (London, 1971)

181

B. Hall and R. Noblett: 'Leroy Carr, 1930–1935', PY4407 [disc notes]

P. Guralnick: 'Searching for Robert Johnson', *Living Blues*, no.53 (1982), 27

URBAN BLUES IN THE 1930s

W. Russell: 'Boogie Woogie', *Jazzmen*, ed. F. Ramsey jr and C. E. Smith (New York, 1939)

Y. Bruynoghe and W. Broonzy: *Big Bill Blues: mes blues, ma guitare et moi* (Brussels, 1955, 2/1956; Eng. trans., 1955/R1964)

P. Oliver: 'Big Maceo', *The Art of Jazz*, ed. M. Williams (New York, 1959), 109

P. Clinco: 'Joe Turner', *Living Blues*, no.10 (1972), 3 [interview]

M. Rowe: 'Tuff Luck Blues', *Blues Unlimited*, no.106 (1974), 5

J. and A. O'Neal: 'Georgia Tom Dorsey', *Living Blues*, no.20 (1975), 17 [interview]

M. Harrison: 'The Blue Note recordings of Albert Ammons and Meade Lux Lewis: an idiom's apotheosis', Mosaic MR3-103 [disc notes]

P. Oliver: 'Sales Tax on it: Race records in the New Deal Years', *Nothing Else to Fear: new perspectives on America in the Thirties*, ed. S. Baskerville and R. Willett (Manchester, 1985)

POSTWAR BLUES ON THE WEST COAST

D. Burley: *Dan Burley's Original Handbook of Harlem Jive* (New York, 1944)

C. Calloway: *The New Cab Calloway's Hepster's Dictionary* (Derby, Conn., 1945)

M. McCormick: 'Lightnin' Hopkins: Blues', *Jazz Panorama*, ed. M. Williams (New York, 1962)

C. Gillett: *The Sound of the City: the Rise of Rock and Roll* (New York, 1970, rev. 3/1983)

M. Leadbitter: *Nothing but the Blues* (London, 1971)

'T-Bone Walker', *Living Blues*, no.11 (1972), 14 [interview]

J. Broven: *Walking to New Orleans: the Story of New Orleans Rhythm and Blues* (Bexhill-on-Sea, 1974)

C. Gillett: *Making Tracks: Atlantic Records and the Growth of a Multi-billion-dollar Industry* (New York, 1974)

'Charles Brown', *Living Blues*, no.27 (1976), 19 [interview]

A. Shaw: *Honkers and Shouters: the Golden Years of Rhythm and Blues* (New York, 1978)

Bibliography

A. O'Neal: 'John Lee Hooker', *Living Blues*, no.44 (1979), 14 [interview]

R. Palmer: *Deep Blues* (New York, 1981/*R*1983)

M. Leadbitter and G. D. Wardlow: 'Canton Mississippi Breakdown', *Blues Unlimited*, no.144 (1983), 4

I. Whitcomb: 'Legends of Rhythm and Blues', *Repercussions: a Celebration of Afro-American Music*, ed. G. Haydon and D. Marks (London, 1984), 54

J. Hannusch: *I hear you knockin': the Sound of New Orleans Rhythm and Blues* (Ville Platte, Louisiana, 1985)

POSTWAR CHICAGO

P. Oliver: 'Muddy Waters, Hoochie-coochie Man', *Jazz Monthly* (1959), Jan, p.2

——: *Muddy Waters*, Collectors Classics, i (Bexhill-on-Sea, 1964)

——: 'Remembering Sonny Boy', *American Folk Music Occasional*, ii, ed. C. Strachwitz and P. Welding (New York, 1970), 39

P. Guralnick: *Feel Like Going Home: Portraits in Blues and Rock 'n' Roll* (New York, 1971)

J. Rooney: *Bossmen: Bill Monroe and Muddy Waters* (New York, 1971)

M. Leadbitter: 'Bring it on Home', *Blues Unlimited*, no.98 (1973), 4

M. Rowe: *Chicago Breakdown* (London, 1973)

R. Neff and A. Connor: *Blues* (Boston, Mass., 1975)

B. Turner: 'Howling Wolf: an Appreciation', *Blues Unlimited*, no.118 (1976), 4

L. Fancourt: *Chess Blues Discography* (Faversham, England, 1983)

SOUL BLUES

C. Keil: *Urban Blues* (Chicago, 1966)

S. Dance: 'B. B. King: the King of the Blues', *Jazz* (1967), Feb, p.15

'Buddy Guy', *Living Blues*, no.2 (1970), 3 [interview]

A. Shaw: *The World of Soul: Black America's Contribution to the Pop Music Scene* (New York, 1970)

M. Leadbitter: 'Madison Night Owl: Freddie King', *Blues Unlimited*, no.110 (1974), 5

M. Haralambos: *Right On: from Blues to Soul in Black America* (London, 1974)

'Otis Rush', *Living Blues*, no.28 (1976), 10 [interview]

D. Lewis and C. Huggins: 'A Long Conversation with Collins', *Blues Unlimited*, nos.135–6 (1979), 4

C. Huggins and W. Greensmith: 'I'm Still Struggling for What I Started With: Luther Allison', *Blues Unlimited*, no.139 (1980), 4

C. Sawyer: *The Arrival of B. B. King* (New York, 1980)

V. Pearlin: 'Johnny Copeland', *Living Blues*, no.52 (1982), 12

'Z. Z. Hill', *Living Blues,* no.53 (1982), 17 [interview]

FIELD RECORDING

H. W. Odum and G. B. Johnson: *The Negro and his Songs* (Chapel Hill, 1925)

A. Lomax: 'Sinful Songs of the Southern Negro: Experiences Collecting Secular Folk-music', *Southwest Review*, xix (1933–4), 105

L. Gellert: *Negro Songs of Protest* (New York, 1936)

J. A. and A. Lomax: *Negro Folk Songs as Sung by Leadbelly* (New York, 1936, 3/1959)

J. A. Lomax: 'Field Experience with Recording Machines', *Southern Folklore Quarterly*, i (1937), 57

L. Gellert: *Me and my Captain* (New York, 1939)

J. A. Lomax: *Adventures of a Ballad Hunter* (New York, 1947)

L. Cohn: 'Leadbelly: the Library of Congress Recordings', EKL-301/2 [disc notes]

J. Cowley: 'The Library of Congress Recordings', *Blues and Gospel Records, 1902–1942*, ed. J. Godrich and R. M. W. Dixon (Hatch End, nr. London, 1963, rev. and enlarged 3/1982 as *Blues and Gospel Records, 1902–1943*)

R. Groom: 'The Library of Congress Blues and Gospel Recording', *Blues World*, no.38 (1971), 8

D. Evans: 'An Interview with H. Speir', *JEMF Quarterly*, viii (1972), 117

N. Cohen: ' "I'm a Record Man": Uncle Art Satherly Reminiscences', *JEMF Quarterly*, viii (1972), 18

M. Seeger: 'Who Chose those Records?: a Look into the Life, Taste, and Procedures of Frank Walker', *Anthology of American Folk Music*, ed. J. Dunson and E. Raim (New York, 1973)

C. Lornell: 'J. B. Long', *Living Blues*, no.29 (1976), 9 [interview]

D. Evans: 'Fieldwork with Blues Singers: the Unintentionally Induced Natural Context', *Southern Folklore Quarterly*, xlii (1978), 9

L. S. McMurray: *Living Blues*, no. 67 (1986), 15 [interview]

Bibliography

RESEARCH AND REDISCOVERY

F. Ramsey jr: *Been Here and Gone* (Brunswick, NJ, 1960)

M. McCormick: 'Mance Lipscomb, Texas Sharecropper and Songster', F1001 [disc notes]

H. Courlander: *Negro Folk Music, USA* (New York, 1963)

——: *Negro Songs from Alabama* (New York, 2/1963)

P. Oliver: 'Eagles on the Half', *American Folk Music Occasional*, i (1964), 91

R. Koester: 'Brownsville Blues', DL613 [disc notes]

P. Oliver: *Conversation with the Blues* (London and New York, 1965)

S. House: 'I Can Make my own Songs', *Sing Out!*, xv/3 (1965), 38

P. Welding: 'Mance Lipscomb, Vol.4', F1033 [disc notes]

M. Jones: 'Josh White Looks Back, Parts 1–2', *Blues Unlimited* (1968), no.55, p.16; no.56, p.15

S. Calt: 'Bill Williams', Blue Goose 2004 [disc notes]

W. Ferris: *Blues from the Delta* (London, 1971)

G. Mitchell: *Blow my Blues Away* (Baton Rouge, 1971)

B. Bastin: 'Black Music in North Carolina', *North Carolina Folklore Journal*, xxvii/1 (1979), 3

P. Oliver: 'Blues Research: Problems and Possibilities', *Journal of Musicology*, xi (1983), 377

B. Bastin: 'Mississippi John Hurt, Library of Congress Recordings, Vol.1', FLY 553 [disc notes]

P. Oliver: *Blues off the Record: Thirty Years of Blues Commentary* (Tunbridge Wells, 1984)

WHITE BLUES

P. Welding: 'The Rise of the White Blues Performer', *Down Beat Music '65* (Chicago, 1965), 55, 85

J. Litweiler: 'The Soul of the New White Blues', *Sounds and Fury*, ii/2 (1966), 28

H. Traum: 'The Art of the Talking Blues', *Sing Out!*, xv/6 (1966), 53

R. Groom: *The Blues Revival* (London, 1970)

T. Russell: *Blacks, Whites and Blues* (London, 1970)

J. S. Otto and A. M. Burns: 'Black and White Cultural Interaction in the Early Twentieth Century South: Race and Hillbilly Music', *Phylon*, xxxv (1974), 407

P. Oliver: 'Blue-eyed Blues: the Impact of Blues on European Popular Culture', *Approaches to Popular Culture*, ed. C.W.E. Bigsby (London, 1976), 227

C. R. Townsend: *San Antonio Rose: the Life and Music of Bob*

Wills (Urbana, Ill., 1976)

N. Porterfield: *Jimmie Rodgers: the Life and Times of America's Blue Yodeler* (Urbana, Ill., 1979)

C. Escott and M. Hawkins: *Sun Records: the Brief History of the Legendary Record Label* (New York, 1980)

E. Ward: *Michael Bloomfield: the Rise and Fall of an American Guitar Hero* (Port Chester, NY, 1983)

ZYDECO

R. Reed: 'Les blues de Bayou', MLP 7330 [disc notes]

C. Strachwitz: 'Zydeco', F1009 [disc notes]

——: 'Zydeco Music, i.e. French Blues', *American Folk Music Occasional*, ii, ed. C. Strachwitz and P. Welding (New York, 1970), 22

C. Strachwitz and M. Goodwin: 'Classic Clifton', F1082 [disc notes]

M. Doucet: 'Amadé Ardoin', Old-Timey 124 [disc notes]

J. Broven: *South to Louisiana: the Music of the Cajun Bayous*, ii (Gretna, Louisiana, 1983)

B. Ancelet and E. Morgan: *The Makers of Cajun Music* (Austin, Texas, 1984)

BLUES COMPOSITION

I. Lang: *Jazz in Perspective: the Background of the Blues* (London, 1947)

F. Driggs and K. Shirley: *The Book of the Blues* (New York, 1963)

P. Oliver: *Screening the Blues: Aspects of the Blues Tradition* (London, 1968)

H. Oster: *Living Country Blues* (Detroit, 1969)

J. Titon: *Early Downhome Blues: a Musical and Cultural Analysis* (Urbana, Ill., 1977)

D. Evans: *Big Road Blues: Traditions and Creativity in the Folk Blues* (Berkeley, Calif., 1982)

P. Oliver: *Early Blues Songbook* (London, 1982)

FORM AND CONTENT

S. Brown: 'The Blues as Folk Poetry', *Folksong: a Regional Miscellany*, ed. B. A. Botkin (Norman, Oklahoma, 1930)

M. Jones: 'On Blues', *PL Yearbook of Jazz 1946*, ed. A. McCarthy (London, 1946), 72–107

P. Oliver: *Blues Fell this Morning: the Meaning of the Blues* (London, 1960)

186

Bibliography

S. B. Charters: *The Poetry of the Blues* (New York, 1963)

E. Sackheim: *The Blues Line: a Collection of Blues Lyrics* (New York, 1969)

W. Ferris: 'Racial Repertoires among Blues Performers', *EM*, xiv (1970), 439

R. Gruver: 'The Blues as Dramatic Monologues', *JEMF Quarterly*, vi/2 (1970), 129

J. Titon: 'Autobiography and Blues Texts; a Reply to "The Blues as Dramatic Monologues" ', *JEMF Quarterly*, vi/3 (1970), 79

S. Calt: 'The Country Blues as Meaning', *Country Blues Songbook*, ed. S. Grossman, H. Grossman and S. Calt (New York, 1973), 8

P. Garon: *Blues and the Poetic Spirit* (London, 1975/R1979)

J. Titon: *Downhome Blues Lyrics: an Anthology from the Post-World War II Era* (Boston, Mass., 1981)

P. Oliver: 'Blues, and the Binary Principle', *Popular Music Perspectives*, ed. P. Tagg and D. Horn (Gothenburg and Exeter, 1982)

——: 'Twixt Midnight and Day: Binarism, Blues and Black Culture', *Popular Music 2*, ed. R. Middleton and D. Horn (Cambridge, 1982)

——: 'Can't even Write: the Blues and Ethnic Literature', *MELUS*, x/1 (1983), 7

M. Taft: *Blues Lyric Poetry: an Anthology* (New York, 1983)

——: *Blues Lyric Poetry: a Concordance* (New York, 1984)

BLUES MUSIC AND TECHNIQUES

W. F. Allen, C. P. Ware and L. McKim Garrison: *Slave Songs of the United States* (New York, 1867/R1971)

W. Sargeant: *Jazz: Hot and Hybrid* (New York, 1938, rev. and enlarged 3/1964/R1975)

T. Glover: *Blues Harp: an Instruction Method* (New York, 1965)

D. Hatch and J. Williams: 'The Country Blues: a Musical Analysis', *Blues Unlimited*, no.21 (1965), 8

J. Lester and P. Seeger: *The 12-string Guitar as Played by Leadbelly* (New York, 1965)

P. Welding: 'Stringing the Blues: the Art of the Folk Blues Guitar', *Down Beat*, xxxii/19 (1965), 22, 56

D. Garwood: *Masters of the Instrumental Blues Guitar*, i (Lagura Beach, Calif., 1967)

S. Grossman: *The Country Blues Guitar* (New York, 1968)

H. Traum: *The Blues Bag* (New York, 1968)

E. Helfer: 'Basic Blues Piano Techniques', *Living Blues*, no.3 (1970), 22, 28

J. Silverman: *Folk Blues: 110 American Folk Blues* (New York, 3/1971)

E. Kriss: 'Early Barrelhouse Piano', *Living Blues*, no.16 (1974), 14

D. J. Hatch and D. R. Watson: 'Hearing the Blues: an Essay in the Sociology of Music', *Ars sociologica*, xvii (1974), 162

E. Kriss: 'Blues Tremolo', *Living Blues*, no.20 (1975), 38

R. Hall and R. Noblett: 'A Handful of Keys: Charlie Spand', *Blues Unlimited*, no.117 (1976), 22

A. Funaro and A. Traum: *Chicago Blues Guitar* (New York, 1980)

A. M. Dauer: *Blues aus 100 Jahren: 43 Beispiele zur Typologie der vokalen Bluesform* (Frankfurt am Main, 1983)

W. Tallmadge: 'Blue Notes and Blue Tonality', *Black Perspective in Music* (New York, 1984)

CHAPTER FOUR

Gospel

I Origins

Gospel song is a type of religious folk or popular music, the origins of which are inextricably bound up with the development of fundamentalist religion within rural southern communities in America after the Civil War. Though sung by both Afro-American and white soloists, groups and congregations, it has found its richest expression in black churches and communities. Gospel song largely replaced spirituals but has drawn considerably from them.

During the 1870s the religious revival led by Dwight Lyman Moody (1837–99) was impelled by the conviction that social reform would be the outcome of moral and spiritual regeneration. But Moody and later Billy Sunday (both white) discouraged emotional outbursts and replaced the 'fire and damnation' preaching of earlier generations with compassion and sentimentality. Though their songs and those of Homer Rodeheaver and their white contemporaries were intended, in the words of Ira David Sankey (1840–1908), Moody's partner, 'to implant the gospel in the hearts of the people', their music drew on marching tunes, popular and 'heart' songs for form and melody; some were rousing, others maudlin.

Published collections of the new hymns considerably advanced their popularity. Among them were *Gospel Songs*, compiled by P. P. Bliss and D. W. Whittle in 1874, and *Gospel Hymns and Sacred Songs*, assembled by Bliss with Ira Sankey the following year. *Gospel Hymns,* in six volumes, was first published by Sankey, McGranahan and Stebbins between 1878 and 1891. In 1894 they were issued as a combined work, like Henry Date's *Pentecostal Hymns*, in canvas-covered editions directed at the new churches. These collections were all by white composers, but in 1893 W. Henry Sherwood compiled a new hymnal with lively arrangements; it was adopted by the loose federation of black Baptist churches, the National Baptist Convention and the Baptist Young People's Union, and published as *The National Harp of Zion and BYPU Hymnal*, indicating the tentative recognition by the Baptist Church of the new wave of what were now being termed 'gospel songs'.

At the turn of the century the first compositions of a black gospel songwriter appeared. Charles Albert Tindley (7 July 1851 or 1859–1933) was a Methodist preacher from Maryland who gained experience at rural camp-meetings. In the 1870s he established his East Calvary Methodist Episcopal Church in Philadelphia, where he had a choir that gave occasional concerts that may have included his early compositions. Some of his gospel songs became 'standards', including *I'll overcome some day* (1901), *What are they doing in heaven today* (?1905), *Stand by me* (1905); probably the most popular was *Leave it there*, which, as *Take your burdens to the Lord*, was to be recorded many times. These and 30 others were published in his *New Songs of Paradise* (1916), intended for Sunday schools and social gatherings.

While Sankey and Moody's gospel song suppressed emotional outbursts and passionate singing, influencing the development of white gospel song for a century, black gospel assumed a character of its own. The rise of black gospel song coincides with the beginnings of ragtime, blues and jazz and it sprang from similar roots of segregationalism. Establishing their individual identity, black musical cultures flourished. Though trained choirs such as the Fisk Jubilee Singers and the Utica Jubilee Singers continued to perform spirituals and absorbed new gospel songs by white composers, their techniques were not those of folk music. They used conventional harmonies, diatonic scales and pure vocal tones though with tonal inflections and modified responses.

At the same time black harmonizing quartets grew rapidly in popularity. James Weldon Johnson recalled hearing 'the crack quartets made up of waiters in the Jacksonville hotels' in the 1870s and by 1886 he and his 13-year-old brother were in a quartet competing against others. The origins of white barbershop harmonizing have not been thoroughly investigated. Johnson noted that 'when a white barber was unknown in the South, every barber shop had its quartet, and the men spent their leisure time playing on the guitar . . . and "harmonizing" '. Part-singing had not been considered a characteristic of black singing, but Natalie Curtis Burlin noted (*c*1915) that as many as 900 black students at Hampton University, Virginia, sang the 'old plantations' without training, with no choral divisions but spontaneously harmonized. She recorded and transcribed the singing of a quartet consisting of an agricultural student, a tinsmith, teacher and blacksmith, one of 'several self-organized and self-trained quartets at Hampton'. Their effects were 'not thought out or consciously achieved by the singer – it is entirely emotional. For the Negroes always explain: "We sing the way we *feel*" ', a recurrent observation in the following 60 years.

Competition between groups seems to have promoted harmonizing skills and hearing travelling quartets extended their techniques. They not only performed religious songs; quartets like Scott Joplin's Texas Medley Quartette (with which he toured between 1895 and 1897 from Texarkana to Syracuse, New York, and back to Louisiana and Texas before disbanding in Missouri), appear to have used both plantation and popular songs. They also toured with minstrel and vaudeville shows. In the 1880s W. C. Handy left school in Florence, Alabama, to join a quartet in a local touring minstrel show. Though he had 'learned all the songs in *Gospel Songs*, one to six', the minstrel songs were secular; in 1892 he joined the Lauzetta Quartet in a saloon in Birmingham, Alabama, which performed the religious parody *Gwine chop 'em in the head with a golden ax.*

It seems that early quartets may have had a secular origin but sang sacred and secular songs. This is reflected in the repertories of early recording vocal groups. Of the first two dozen recordings by the Norfolk Jazz Quartet only four were sacred, including

Who built the ark? (Okeh 4400, 1921) and *My Lord's gonna move this wicked race* (Paramount 12035, 1923), and they were issued as by the Norfolk Jubilee Quartet. Other groups such as the Excelsior Quartet also had a mixed but predominantly secular repertory. The links with earlier forms of jubilee singing arising from the Fisk University and other college singers was reflected in the groups' names: at least 40 of those who recorded between 1920 and 1940 called themselves 'Jubilee Singers' or 'Jubilee Quartet' or a variant of those names. Most drew on spirituals, jubilee songs, white gospel hymns and the newer songs of Albert Tindley, Lucie Campbell or William Herbert Brewster for their repertories as well as composing their own songs. They sang at social gatherings, church meetings and charity functions until some were sufficient attraction to sing in Baptist churches.

II Black churches and preachers
Black churches had begun to break away from white Protestant churches as early as the late 18th century when, in 1796, the African Methodist Zion Church was formed in New York. Early in the 19th century the rival African Methodist Episcopal Church was founded and by 1880 it had 400,000 members, double its rival's. The Wesleyan Methodist revival, including the spontaneous testifying initiated by the white George Whitefield in the 18th century, inspired black theology and practice. A century later the Methodists were challenged by the growth of the Baptist churches, which did not follow a single doctrine or

policy. They united, split and combined again as the National Baptist Convention which was incorporated with 3 million members in 1915. Subsequently it was split into two, and later three, national conventions which claimed a membership of over seven and a half million by the 1960s. The freedom of Baptist churches to worship as they wished made the faith attractive to Blacks. At revival meetings and in southern black churches many preachers developed dramatic styles of delivery, encouraging spontaneous responses and affirmations from their congregations. Many Baptist preachers were popular on record in the 1920s, among them the celebrated Reverend A. W. Nix, from Birmingham, Alabama, whose forceful, growling and intimidating sermon *The Black Diamond Express to Hell* (Vocalion 1098, 1927) was issued in six parts. It was complemented by an equally passionate *White Flyer to Heaven* (Vocalion 1170, 1927). Other remarkable sermons by Nix with congregational support and singing included *Your bed is too short and your cover is too narrow* (Vocalion 1159, 1928) and *Sleeping in a dangerous time* (Vocalion 1247, 1928).

Equally popular was Reverend J. C. Burnett, whose *Drive and go forward* (Columbia 14173, 1926) and *The Downfall of Nebuchadnezzar* (Columbia 14166, 1926) were powerful examples of the genre, with responses by Sisters Odette Jackson and Ethel Grainger. Burnett's *You are sleeping in a dangerous time* (Columbia 14474, 1929) was his version of the theme Nix had used; preachers often competed in their interpretations of biblical subjects. By far the

194

most widely recorded was Reverend J. M. Gates, who was responsible for a quarter of the 700 sermons issued on race records between 1925 and 1941. *Death's black train is coming* (Victor 20211, 1926), *You midnight ramblers* (Okeh 8684, 1929) and *Did you spend Christmas day in jail?* (Okeh 8753, 1929) were among his best, strongly and clearly expressed with support from Sisters Jordan and Norman and Deacon Leon Davis from his own congregation at the Mount Calvary Church, Atlanta, where he was pastor for nearly 30 years. Some of his recordings, like *Scat to the cat and Suie the hog* (Okeh 8844, 1930), were bizarre and even self-parodying. Like several other Baptist preachers, Gates drew heavily on contemporary events and secular material as well as biblical stories. Few if any of the recorded preachers were Methodists, for they tended to follow white middle-class patterns of worship and song.

At the end of the 19th century the Baptists faced powerful competition with the rise of the Holiness movement and the Pentacostalist churches. Their services were characterized by the gift of 'speaking with tongues'; members of the congregation uttered pronouncements in 'unknown' languages while in a hysterical, hypnotic or trance-like state. Musically, these ecstatic services probably relate most closely to the plantation 'shouts' or ring-dances of African origin, characterized by stamping and singing while moving in a circle anti-clockwise in a loose-limbed, shuffling dance. Though the circular dance has not been performed since the 1930s, the term 'shouting' still applies to the ecstatic singing and dancing, accompanied by hand-clapping, that are a feature of Holiness services and that frequently end in the dancers being overcome by 'spirit possession'. Common in the Holiness and Sanctified churches (in which the dancing and exultation takes place in the church aisles), such extravagant possession leads to jerking, rhythmic movements, babbling, involuntary cries and perspiring before succumbing to the trance. Sheets are often laid out for those whom the Holy Spirit has thus entered and such churches have been nicknamed 'Holy Roller'.

Many of the earliest black churches of this kind were founded by dissatisfied Baptist preachers, among them Reverend C. P. Jones, who in 1894 formed the Church of Christ Holiness, in Selma, Alabama, and Reverend William Christian who founded the Church of the Living God at Wrightsville, Arkansas, in 1899. Most influential of these new denominations was the Church of God in Christ, founded in 1895 by a black Memphis Baptist minister, C. H. Mason, near Lexington, Mississippi. Other churches of this sect developed rapidly, particularly in southern rural communities. With the migrations to northern cities during and after World War I, the denomination became well established in Chicago, Detroit and elsewhere. Its services are typified by the dramatic and forceful exhortations of the preachers, whose message is fundamentalist and often puritanical. Member churches thrived principally in lower-class neighbourhoods as 'store-fronts' in converted shops, stores, garages and private dwellings; they comprised four-fifths of the 500 black churches in Chicago in 1945, according to Drake and Cayton. Many were related to the Church of God Holiness, Church of Christ Sanctified and Pentecostal churches which had the most dramatic services and the strongest emotional appeal to black people in the lower-income groups. They have continued to increase and have traditionally provided a base for gospel music. Census figures never credited the Sanctified, Pentecostal and Holiness churches with a total of more than half a million members, but the proliferation of store-front churches made them very conspicuous in black communities.

In Sanctified and Holiness churches music plays an important part, as do the exhortations of the preachers who, in the hoarse and 'straining' voices by which their quality is measured by their congregations, bark the message of the Gospels. Their services differed from those of the Baptists in a significant respect that contributed to their popularity: their gospel songs were accompanied by musical instruments, the preachers following Psalm cl: 'Praise him with the sound of the trumpet; praise him with the psaltery and harp. Praise him with the timbrel and dance; praise him with stringed instruments and organs. Praise him with the loud cymbals; praise him with the high sounding cymbals. Let everything that hath breath praise the Lord'. The timbrels (tambourines ringed with cymbals) were probably the first instruments used in black Pentecostal churches and they are still the accompaniment for many gospel quartets and choirs, shaken in the air and rattled against the hip, struck with the ball of the hand and the fingertips. Pianos preceded electric organs, but small domestic harmoniums were soon in use. Banjo- and guitar-playing evangelical singers were brought in from the streets and many churches employed trumpet and trombone players.

Reverend D. C. Rice, who recorded extensively, was accompanied by the trumpet (possibly Punch Miller), trombone, piano, bass and percussion in *I'm on the battlefield for my Lord* (Vocalion 1262, 1929). He was from Alabama but moved to Chicago in World War I to join Bishop Hill's Church of the Living God, Pentecostal. Though not inventive he was a strong preacher and was prompted to record by the success of Reverend, later Bishop, Ford Washington McGee (*b* Winchester, Tenn., 5 Oct 1890; *d* Chicago, 8 April 1971). McGee was raised in Texas and became a faith healer and evangelist, establishing himself in Oklahoma City with the support of the blind woman pianist Arizona Dranes. Moving to Chicago in 1925 he opened a church in a tent, where his preaching and rousing services attracted large congregations. He was recorded for the first time two years later and *Lion of the tribe of Judah* (Victor 20858, 1927) was a remarkable success. A bishop of his denomination, McGee built his Chicago Temple in 1928 and it remained his headquarters for over 40 years. His combination of hoarse exhortation and melodious singing is especially evident in the sermon *Holes in your pockets* (Victor 38583, 1930). Excitement builds up from sermon to congregational singing on *Death may be your pay check* (Victor 21656, 1928), and the responses to the chanted message of Jesus, *The Light of the World* (Victor 38513, 1929), are followed by a gospel song in which McGee's piano playing is prominent. Few records can convey the excitement of his live services but it is superbly captured in *Fifty miles of elbow room* (Victor 23401, 1930), which has trumpet, guitar and piano accompaniment to strong, rhythmic congregational singing.

III The rise of gospel song

If the message of spirituals is endurance of the trials of this life with the reward of life after death, that of gospel songs is more immediate. Though the themes are often similar, and many gospel songs are little more than spirituals with a modern beat, their spirit is infinitely more optimistic. Gospel songs bring a message of 'good news' and are so called, according to some preachers, because they state the 'gospel truth'. The promise of a better life hereafter still pervades them but their joyousness and extrovert character suggest happiness achieved in this life in preparation for the next.

Much of the growing popularity of gospel song was due to the publication by the Sunday School Publishing Board of the National Baptist Convention of the collection *Gospel Pearls* (1921), which included over 160 songs popular in black churches. The principal composer in the new idiom was the former blues and hokum singer and pianist 'Georgia Tom' Thomas A. Dorsey (*b* Villa Rica, Georgia, 1899), son of a revivalist preacher. As early as 1921 Dorsey had heard Reverend A. W. Nix preaching in Chicago and was inspired to write songs for the Morning Star Baptist Church. In 1932 he was appointed choral director of the Pilgrim Baptist Church in Indiana Avenue, a post he held for over 40 years. His earliest compositions, strongly influenced by C. A. Tindley, include *If I don't get there* and *We will meet him in the sweet by and by*. They were based on hymns and spirituals and did not have the swing and open structure that permitted responses, as his later songs did. In the early 1930s he made a few gospel recordings, including *How about you* and *If you see my Saviour* (Vocalion 1710, 1932), and a song recorded by many other artists, *If I could hear my mother pray* (Vocalion 02729, 1934). His light voice, suited for hokum, lacked the necessary conviction or excitement for gospel singing and wisely he concentrated instead on writing songs. Of these his most successful was *Precious Lord, take my hand*, written when his first wife died. As his compositions became known, Dorsey toured with Mahalia Jackson and Roberta Martin, selling sheet music of the songs he wrote and they sang. Among the best known were *Peace in the valley*, *I will put my trust in the Lord* and *The Lord has laid his hands on me*. As president of the National Convention of Gospel Choirs and Choruses and as a composer Dorsey has been the most influential figure in the gospel song movement. Blues and jazz coloured his compositions, adding to their appeal.

Dorsey tried to popularize the term 'gospel', crediting his own recordings as by 'Thomas A. Dorsey and the Gospel Singers' and a couple with his blues companion Tampa Red (guitar) as by the Gospel Camp Meeting Singers. But fewer than a dozen of 150 recorded groups before World War II called themselves 'gospel' and some 40 clung to the word 'jubilee'. The music was changing, however. Jubilee singing was giving way to more complex harmonizing by 'quartets'; about 80 groups recorded before 1940 used this name. Barbershop harmonizing, white 'glee clubs', concert appearances and contests all contributed to the evolution of quartet singing for as the groups became more competitive they became more experimental. It was customary for a deep, rich bass to be established by one singer while a tenor sang extended and elaborated verses of the song. Early recordings by the Biddleville Quintette (four male singers and one female) show a wide range of influences with evidence of shape-note singing style in *Coming to Christ* (Paramount 12480, 1929), lining-out in *I heard the voice of Jesus say* (Paramount 12396, 1928), preaching and increasing vocal range in *Wasn't that a mighty day* (QRS R7070, 1929) and repeat lines and responses in *I'm going up to live with the Lord* (Paramount 12969, 1929).

Groups adopted a variety of approaches, for example Bryant's Jubilee Quartet, which used piano accompaniment in the bouncily rhythmic *Oh rocks don't fall on me* (Banner 32266, 1931), the Pilgrim Jubilee Singers, with their chime-like vocalizing in *I'm in his care* (Vocalion 1118, 1927) and the jazz-influenced version of *See how they did my Lord* by the Dunham Jubilee Singers (Columbia 14605, 1931), from Birmingham, Alabama, led by Charles 'Son' Dunham. The Birmingham Jubilee Singers, whose repertory, like that of the Dunham group, was largely secular, showed jazz quartet characteristics. But they also produced carefully styled and close-harmony pieces like *He took my sins away* (Columbia 14140, 1926), the first of over 50 recordings. The Ravizee Singers, Bessemer Sunset Four and the influential Famous Blue Jay Singers, who later settled in Texas, were among Alabama groups.

Another concentration of gospel quartets was in Virginia, focussed on the long-established and much-travelled Norfolk Jubilee Quartet. Others included the Peerless Four Quartette and the Silver Leaf Quartet, which included the remarkable falsetto singer William Thatch. The Silver Leaf's recording of *Sleep on mother* (Okeh 8644, 1928) was the first to use the rhythmic vocal phrase 'clank-a-lanka'; it was much copied by other groups such as the Famous Blue Jay Singers, whose version was strongly reminiscent of *The Old Folks at Home* and simply entitled *Clanka-a-lanka* (Paramount 13119, 1932). The phrase remained popular for over 20 years though its meaning is unclear (it was probably based on train rhythms).

Most of the vocal quartets of the 1920s and early 1930s sang unaccompanied but occasionally a piano was used and, more rarely, other instruments. Jazz tone and inflections had become increasingly common for expressive purposes, as had rhythmic vocalizing, for example Willie Johnson's 'vocal percussion' in the early recordings of the first Golden Gate Jubilee Quartet. Their sophisticated version of Thomas Dorsey's *Bedside of a Neighbour* (Bluebird 7278, 1937) shows the changes taking place in some groups after the mid-1930s. It is likely that the contrasts of falsetto and bass on the recordings of the Ink Spots and the vocal imitations of instruments and strong rhythmic emphasis of the Mills Brothers were influences on gospel groups. The Alphabetical Four used a guitar for additional rhythmic support and jazz technique was clearly evident in the comb-and-paper vocalized muted 'trumpet' accompaniment of their first recording, Dorsey's *Precious Lord hold my hand* (Decca 7546, 1938), and many others. Most recording quartets of the 1930s appear to have been Baptist, but the Golden Eagle Gospel Singers led by Thelma Byrd was probably Sanctified. Their *Tone the bell* (Decca 7314, 1937) is a driving performance, with congregational singing behind the lead, and piano, guitar, harmonica and tambourine accompaniment. In *He's my rock* (Decca 7787, 1940) the blues harmonica player Hammie Nixon not only played the accompaniment but took a blues-style solo over a humming chorus. Novelty techniques were also being extensively exploited, for example in the skilful but highly secularized later recordings of the popular Golden Gate Jubilee Quartet and the first recordings of the Dixie Hummingbirds, which ranged from the extraordinary, sustained falsettos of *Soon will be done with the troubles of this world* (Decca 7746, 1939) to the nostalgic sentimentality of *Little Wooden Church* (Decca 7667, 1939).

Musicological analysis of gospel song and its relation to jubilee singing has begun; Richard M. Raichelson, George Robinson Ricks, William H. Tallmadge and Horace C. Boyer have made initial, specialized studies. Tallmadge distinguished between 'folk-styled jubilee quartets', 'jazz-styled jubilee quartets', 'jubilee gospel quartets' and 'gospel-jubilee quartets', further dividing 'jubilee-gospel' groups (with jazz terminology) into 'hot' and 'cool'. But he had to resort to cumbersome further definitions using almost mutually exclusive terms: the Birmingham Jubilee Singers were identified as 'trained-folk-jazz-styled'.

Though gospel quartets tried to establish their identity through aspects of 'style' – featured bass or falsetto for example – and through dress (porters' uniforms, white tuxedos etc.) their approaches were experimental. By the end of the 1930s harder tones and rhythmic complexity were common, anticipating characteristics of postwar gospel singing.

IV Evangelists and soloists

Itinerant evangelists who had no church but gained converts by preaching and singing in the streets were known as 'jack-legs'. They included Washington Phillips from Texas, whose reproachful and pre-judiced *Denomination Blues* (Columbia 14333, 1928) was delicately accompanied on his home-adapted dulcimer, the 'dulceola'. Another was the 'Guitar Evangelist', Reverend Edward Claiborn, who played the slide guitar in a sombre *Death is only a dream* (Vocalion 1096, 1927). Many were blind and made a living from charity. Prominent was Blind Joe Taggart, in whose *There's a hand writing on the wall* (Paramount 12717, 1928) a youthful Joshua White played the second guitar and sang responses. White acted as 'lead boy' for a number of such blind singers. Wistfully appealing is Blind Mamie Forehand's *Honey in the rock* (Victor 20574, 1927), accompanied by her own hand-cymbals and the guitar playing of her blind husband A. C. Forehand.

Among earlier evangelists 'Blind' Willie Johnson (*b* Marlin, Texas, *c*1902; *d* Beaumont, Texas, *c*1950) was outstanding. He accompanied himself on the guitar when singing at Baptist Association meetings and in country churches around Hearne, Texas. He was led by his wife Angeline who accompanied him on several of the recordings he made on location between 1927 and 1930. Johnson had a remarkably deep yet lyrical voice with a pronounced rasp, as heard in his extraordinary narrative of the story of Samson and Delilah, *If I had my way I'd tear that building down* (Columbia 14343, 1927). His guitar technique was unique, often with pronounced rhythmic emphasis, but he also played the slide guitar sensitively, as in his haunting evocation of spiritual 'moaning' *Dark was the night, cold was the ground* (Columbia 14303, 1927) and *Bye and bye I'm going to see the King* (Columbia 14504, 1929). His wife, Angeline Johnson, sang antiphonally with him in several recordings, including *The rain don't fall on me* (Columbia 14537, 1930) and *Church I'm fully saved today* (Columbia 14582, 1930). Johnson's records were influential on other gospel singers and all were of exceptional quality. After the Depression he continued to beg as a street singer but did not record again.

During the 1930s there was a marked reduction in the number of evangelists recorded though there is no evidence that they had declined in numbers. In Hattiesburg, Mississippi, Blind Roosevelt Graves and his half-blind brother Uaroy Graves had an exhilarating small band, the Mississippi Jook Band; they played ragtime and blues themes but as a duo they principally recorded gospel songs such as the syncopated *I'll be rested (when the roll is called)* (Melotone 6-11-44, 1936). Many blues singers became preachers, including Walter Davis, Blind Roosevelt Darby and Robert Wilkins. The links between blues and gospel song are evident in Wilkins's beautiful recording of *The Prodigal Son* (Piedmont PLP 13162, 1964).

The blues singer Blind Boy Fuller and later Bull City Red and Brownie McGhee recorded sacred items as by 'Brother George and his Sanctified Singers'. They had been influenced by their fellow Eastern singer, Reverend Gary Davis (*b* Lawrence County, S. Carolina, 30 April 1896; *d* Neutonville, NJ, 5 May 1972), an outstanding guitarist. Blind from childhood, he was adept at playing the harmonica, banjo and guitar by the age of seven. A distorted left wrist enabled him to use unorthodox chords. As a member of a country string band he played a broad repertory of rags, reels, carnival tunes and blues; his *I'm throwin' up my hand* (Melotone 35-10-16, 1935) shows his free-flowing blues technique. In 1933 Davis was ordained as a minister and afterwards played little but religious music. *Lord stand by me* (Melotone 6-05-65, 1935) gives a rare insight into his preaching style and *Twelve gates to the city* (Melotone 7-04-55, 1935), with its rolling rhythms and alternating thumb- and finger-picking, reveals his great speed and fluency. In 1940 Davis moved to New York where he made a living as a street singer in Harlem. *Blow Gab-*

riel and *If I had my way* (Riverside 12.6.11, 1956) demonstrate his guitar technique, his slides, syncopations and rhythms, and the husky, somewhat high-pitched and strained voice interspersed with cries and comments with which he sang his 'holy blues'. In the late 1960s his importance as a religious singer was belatedly recognized.

Of the secularized, guitar-playing Sanctified singers, only one gained a national reputation: 'Sister' Rosetta Tharpe (*b* Cotton Plant, Arkansas, 20 March 1915; *d* Philadelphia, 1973). Raised in Chicago, she sang at the age of six to a congregation of 1000. Her mother was a spiritual singer, but Rosetta was attracted to blues guitar techniques and the ecstatic religion of the Sanctified church. She became known for her electrifying performances and the flow of her compositions at the Holy Roller Church, Harlem. In 1938 she appeared at the 'From Spirituals to Swing' concerts at Carnegie Hall and sang with the swing orchestras of Cab Calloway, Benny Goodman and Count Basie. With Lucky Millinder she recorded a few gospel songs and one or two blues including *I want a tall skinny papa* (Decca 18386, 1942). Her first solo recording, *Rock me* (Decca 2243, 1938), with its surging rhythm and secular title (she also sang it as *Feed me dear Jesus until I want no more*), was followed by many successes, including *I looked down the line and I wondered* (Decca 2328, 1939) and *God don't like it* (Decca 48022, 1943). With a guitar technique closest to that of the blues singer Big Bill Broonzy, she recorded several outstanding vocal duets in the 1940s with Sister Marie Knight and with her mother, Katie

Gospel

Bell Nubin. Subsequently she used choirs and accompanists including the Richmond Harmonizing Four and the Sally Jenkins Singers of the Church of God in Christ, New York, as in *I have good news to bring* (Mercury MMC14057, 1960). Such groups tended to cloud the bright sound of her voice and the brilliance of her guitar playing, though she overcame the latter by using an electric instrument. In the 1960s she toured Europe, recording *Swing low, sweet chariot* (Flame PV1001, 1966) which demonstrated her un-diminished vigour.

Although Tharpe influenced other evangelical singers, of whom Sister O. M. Terrell was among the most compelling, none gained a comparable reputa-tion. Attention was focussed instead on church soloists, of whom the most outstanding, with perhaps the finest gospel voice, was Mahalia Jackson (*b* New Orleans, 26 Oct 1911; *d* Chicago, 27 Jan 1972). She was always a Baptist but she was influenced by the Sanctified church and their spontaneous services as well as the recordings of Bessie Smith. She synthesized her own style, using the long metre of Baptist hymns, the slow melancholy of spirituals, the inflections of blues and the joyous message of the gospel songs. In 1932 she toured the Mid-west with the Johnson Gospel Singers and in 1937 she made four recordings, including *God's gonna separate the wheat from the tares* (Decca 7341, 1937), but they did not sell well. It was her recording of Reverend W. Herbert Brewster's song *Move on up a little higher,* parts 1 and 2 (Apollo 164, 1947), that became the first gospel record to sell a million copies. Against Mildred Falls's steady piano

208

and organ accompaniment Jackson generated impressive power, the song's message interpreted symbolically by her audience. Other successes followed including *In the upper room* (Apollo 272, 1952), carried by the majesty of her singing and the remarkable melisma of the vocal line. Much of this she owed to blues, never more impressively than in *Let the power of the Holy Ghost fall on me* (Apollo 213, 1949). *I'm glad salvation is free* (Apollo 222, 1950) was made at the time Jackson was appointed official soloist of the National Baptist Convention. By the mid-1960s her recordings were becoming cluttered by large choruses and orchestras with sweeping strings. Though she continued to record and her voice was never less than exceptional, it was through her earlier work that she established herself as the greatest female black singer since Bessie Smith.

Among the singers who followed Jackson's lead were Bessie Griffin, who had a good voice but was less charismatic before a congregation, and Marion Williams (*b* Miami, 1927), leader of the Stars of Faith, whose joyous demeanour and freshness of approach won large audiences. But the most popular of the later gospel soloists was James Cleveland (*b* Chicago, 1932). His first professional engagements were with the Thorne Gospel Crusaders and the Beatrix Lux Singers. His voice was strained by singing loudly and his intonation has been compared with Louis Armstrong's. He extended his vocal range with slides, growls and shouts, and in his accompaniments used jazz and blues techniques. Directing choirs in Chicago and Detroit and working with all the leading gospel singers, Cleveland composed prolifically (he is credited with over 300 gospel songs). In the 1960s he had a following comparable with that of the rhythm-and-blues singer Antoine 'Fats' Domino a decade earlier. *There's a brighter day somewhere* (Savoy 4154, 1960), *Sit down servant* (Savoy 4176, 1961) and *Drive the devil 'way* (Savoy 14054, 1962) show the development of his style; later recordings with the Angelic Choir of the First Baptist Church of Nutley, New Jersey, and the Cleveland Singers are often sweet, studied or contrived using 'song sermonettes' and vamping accompaniment. 'King James', as he was nicknamed, drew his enormous following largely from the black middle class.

V Choirs and services

One of the links between pre-war and post-war gospel song was the church choir. Many large churches had substantial choirs, including that of Reverend Adam Clayton Powell's Abyssinian Baptist Church in New York which claimed a congregation of 9000. Like many others of size and reputation it did not record. Thomas Dorsey played a leading part in the organization of gospel choirs, having an important base at his Ebenezer Baptist Church in Chicago where the choir he formed with Theodore Frye was host to many others, inspiring the formation with the singer Sallie Martin (*b* Georgia, 1896) of the National Convention of Gospel Choirs and Choruses, which held annual meetings. Roberta Martin (*b* Helena, Arkansas, 1907; *d* Chicago, 18 Jan 1969) joined the choir as pianist in 1931 and two years later formed a quartet with Theodore Frye; with extra women singers they established a nationwide reputation as the Roberta Martin Singers. Their *Only a look* (Apollo 214, 1948) was a success, but in more mature style is *Where can I go* (Apollo 241, 1950s) and the stimulating *Certainly Lord* (Savoy 140229, 1958).

Another choir with more than 30 years' experience was the Argo Singers, whose performances were smoother and closer in style to spirituals, for example *Jesus is the answer* (Joy Special 5012, *c*1960). Most celebrated of the larger gospel choirs is that of Clara Ward (*b* Philadelphia, 21 April 1924; *d* 1973). Her group became famous when, at the age of 19, she was a success at a National Baptist Convention. In 1947 the Ward Singers were joined by Marion Williams whose impassioned soprano solos and gift for stage performance added to their popularity. But it was Ward herself who inspired and dominated with her powerful voice. Often she used growl effects contrasted with shrill, pure notes, extemporizing to her group's energetic vocal accompaniment, as in the two-part *Happy over there* (Gotham 712, *c*1956) by the Clara Ward Specials. Following a national tour in the Big Gospel Cavalcade (1957) hers was one of the most sought-after choirs. *In that great judgement morning* (Gotham 735, *c*1959) gives some indication of Ward's range, but *Keep me every day* (Roulette R 25233, *c*1965), recorded in the Apollo Theatre, Harlem, demonstrates the power of her performance before a congregation.

Some large choirs were too disciplined to permit

the spontaneity that is such a refreshing feature of the best of them. Reverend Glenn T. Settle's Wings over Jordan of the Gethsemane Baptist Church of Cleveland, Ohio, with some 40 members, was typical; *I'm gonna sit at the welcome table* (King 519, 1953) is among their well-organized recordings. The Back Home Choir of Newark, New Jersey, also with 40 members including the lead singer Joe deLoach, demonstrated how vigorous and exciting a full choir could be in *Thanking him* (Columbia 33CX10112, 1957).

Many large choirs were at their best during church services and concerts, though the three-minute record caught something of the exhilaration of these events, for example Reverend Utah Smith's *I got two wings* (Manor 1051, c1950). Among the most remarkable 78 r.p.m. recordings were those by Reverend Kelsey of the Temple Church of God in Christ, Washington, DC, made with a rudimentary orchestra that used swooping trombone glissandos. The large congregation and choir sang joyous responses to Kelsey's exhortations, with gales of congregational singing to offbeat hand-clapping, as in *I'm a soldier* (MGM (E) 10797, 1948) and *Where is the lion of the tribe of Judea* (Decca 28339, 1951). The full impact of his shouting choir is best conveyed on long-playing record, for instance in the sustained *Did you fall when you come out of the wilderness*, led by Carolima Kirksey and Obezine Lampkin, followed immediately on the disc by Kelsey leading the congregation in *Tell me how long* (Polydor (E) 623.201, 1965).

Among other documentary recordings of services, *Saint Sylvester's Day* (Ducretet-Thomson (F) TKL 93119, 1955), recorded in a small Harlem church, had impassioned preaching and trance-inducing rhythms. Before World War II Elder Charles Beck from Mobile, Alabama, recorded somewhat restrained gospel songs with piano. He was a multi-instrumentalist and at the Way of the Cross Church of God in Christ, Buffalo, he was recorded preaching, singing and playing bongo drums, vibraphone and trumpet on *Drive old Satan away* (Folkways 8901, 1956), leading his congregation in a Holiness shout. If the recordings of the Abyssinian Baptist Gospel Choir (Columbia 1548, 1960), led by the colourful Professor Alex Bradford, may have been overwhelmed by the volume of 120 voices, others, like Reverend Louis Overstreet's *Is anybody there* (Arhoolie 1014, 1962), recorded with electric guitar, drums, tambourine and washboard at the St Luke Powerhouse Church of God in Christ, at Phoenix, Arizona, capture the authentic atmosphere of the black church.

Long-playing records were also issued with black purchasers in mind, incorporating full sermons. *Looking for a bargain* (Peacock PLP 196, 1970) by Reverend W. Leo Daniels, recorded at the Greater Jerusalem Baptist Church of Houston, is typical. Reverend H. W. Marshall's *None of these things move me* (Savoy 14178, 1960s) is almost incoherent in its expressive use of vocal dynamics. The most recorded preacher on long-playing record was Reverend C. L. Franklin (over 70 sermons).

The potential of film to record preachers, con-

213

gregations and singers has been explored. The film
Say Amen Somebody (1982; produced by George and
Karen Nierenberg) included Thomas Dorsey and
Sallie Martin performing one of his most popular
gospel compositions *I was standing by the bedside of a
neighbour* (DRG 12584, 1982). *Black Delta Religion*
(*c*1980; produced by Bill and Josette Ferris) compared
rural Baptist services at Rose Hill, Mississippi, with
an urban Holiness church with its guitars and tambourines. Such documentation is important for there
are signs that the older and more passionate styles of
gospel singing and sermon delivery may be in decline.
During the 1970s the new so-called 'contemporary
gospel' choirs, while often musically more experimental with keys and arrangements, moved closer in
delivery to conventional white choral singing.

VI **Postwar quartets**

After World War II the appearance of small recording
companies released a flood of gospel recordings by
harmonizing quartets who vied with each other, first
in the complexity of their interwoven vocal lines, and
eventually in the extravagance, and even frenzy, of
their performances. Costume and uniform became as
important as performance: gospel choirs dressed in
angels' robes and flowing gowns, or in neat suits with
flowered ties; later, check and coloured suitings
comparable with 'zoot suits' were worn. The quartets
developed dance routines in addition to the spontaneous jerking and 'shouting' dances that had always
been part of Holiness and Sanctified church services.
Groups like the Sensational Nightingales, the Voices

of Victory, the Mighty Clouds of Joy from Los Angeles and the Gospelaires from Dayton, Ohio, produced a steady flow of records, stimulating the formation of gospel groups in every store-front and wayside clapboard church and infiltrating the larger, more orthodox Baptist churches. The opening up of the record industry to independent firms led to a proliferation of recordings.

Early gospel groups were often unaccompanied, relying on vocal dynamics, close harmony and improvised counterpoint for variety, for example the Dixie Hummingbirds' *Ezekiel saw the wheel* (Apollo 155, 1947) and the Bells of Joy in *Stop right now it's praying time* (Peacock 1700, 1955). But some later groups used electric guitars, electric organs and tambourines to create a rhythmic background to their flights of vocal improvisation. With the introduction of instruments, gospel songs tended to become more similar in structure, with reduced content and repetitions of lines or fragments of lines. Such repetitions, sung against each other, were a modern development of the 'call and response' technique.

Though there was continuity in the quartets' repertories, there was a move towards elaborated lines, harsher or more shrill singing and vocal rhythms. The Galilee Singers' *Motherless child when I'm gone* (Decca 7725, 1940), the Selah Jubilee Singers' *Motherless child when mother is gone* (Decca 7905, 1942) and *Motherless child* (Disc 5013, 1946), by the Thrasher Wonders, a family group, show a similar approach, but *When mother's gone* (Peacock 1730, *c*1954) by the Spirit of Memphis has an exaggeratedly

215

high vocal lead that contrasts dramatically with the restrained drum and trombone backing to the vocal group. The gospel song provided a framework for vocal elaboration and original arrangements; hence the structures were often simple but open-ended so that voices could be exchanged or choruses and solo lines alternated with relative freedom.

The singing technique used by gospel singers varies widely, but if 'everything that hath breath' should praise the Lord, every ounce of breath is also used to do so. In gospel music, especially since the 1950s, full-voiced singing is expected, often with shrill sopranos offset by rhythmically chanted vocal accompaniment. Many singers use an artificially rasping or pro-nounced guttural style, especially the male street evangelists and preachers, while women singers fre-quently soar to a shriek using considerable vocal range. Vocal counterpoint and the use of antiphonal leader and chorus techniques are universal. Over the years singing has become more complex and elabor-ate, with extended ornamentation of syllables. Groups like the Sensational Nightingales, the Kings of Harmony, the Famous Davis Sisters or the Soul Stirrers each developed distinctive styles, though fre-quently with the familiar contrast of high tenor and bass against rhythmic vocalizing.

The name Five Blind Boys has been used by two gospel groups, both of which also recorded as the Original Five Blind Boys. Perhaps the better known is the Mississippi group formed in Piney Woods, Mississippi, in 1943 as the Jackson Harmoneers. All the original singers were blind; they included Archie

Brownlee, the lead singer (who died in 1960), Lawrence Abrams, J. T. Clinkscales and Lloyd Woodward, who remained with the group for over 20 years. Many of their early recordings, including *He's my rock* (Peacock 1551, *c*1949), were unaccompanied vocal harmonizing. Others have piano and drums that provide rhythm for the highly antiphonal *Jesus is a rock in a weary land* (Peacock 1723, *c*1950). The rival group, the Five Blind Boys of Alabama, was formed at the same time by students of the Talladega Institute for the Deaf and Blind and led by Velma Taylor. Clarence Fountain (*b* 1927) was the lead singer; other members were Olice Thomas, Johnny Fields and George Scott who also played the guitar. Both groups exploited ecstatic, often shrieking vocals by the leader against harmonized and often repetitive, rhythmic vocal phrases by the rest of the group, as in *When I lost my mother* (Savoy 14044, *c*1957) and *Tell God all about it* (Vee Jay LP 5048, *c*1961). This is typical of the Alabama group, whose extravagant conclusions created an infectious and even hysterical response. Both groups were popular for over 20 years.

Of groups influenced by blues the one most directly linked to the secular tradition was the Staple Singers, led by Roebuck Staples (*b* Winona, Mississippi, 28 Dec 1914), who worked on the same plantation as the blues singer Charley Patton. Though blues remained an influence on his guitar playing he was attracted to his father's Methodist church. He formed the Staples Singers with his son Purvis and daughters Cleotha, Mavis and Yvonne in Chicago in 1948.

Staples claims to have introduced the guitar into Methodist churches, where gospel music was slow to be accepted. His family's well-drilled, carefully harmonized songs do not generate the excitement of some gospel groups and are closer to the spiritual tradition. Early recordings such as *Let me ride* (Vee Jay 846, 1957) are stronger than later ones, but *Everybody will be happy* (Riverside 4518, 1961), with hand-clapping syncopation, has Staples taking a firm lead. Blues influence is pronounced in the structure, tune and inflection of *I've been scorned* (Vee Jay 5014, 1961), while the combination of religious fervour, militancy and blues guitar on *We shall overcome* (Columbia SX6033, 1965), recorded with the choir at Reverend John Hopkins's New Nazareth Church, Chicago, is evidence of their response to the mood of black society. At the same time they recorded one of the finest versions of Dorsey's *Take my hand, precious Lord* (Columbia SX6033, 1965). In the late 1960s the Staple Singers experimented less successfully with a blend of gospel and white country folk forms, gaining a larger audience.

Gospel was the last form of black music to be absorbed by popular music, and when it was assimilated it was, untypically, by black rather than white singers. Many gospel artists found that by secularizing their material while retaining the gospel beat and forms of expression they secured a new audience and their songs entered the rhythm-and-blues lists. Prominent among these artists were Ray Charles (*b* 1932), who began his career as a blind pianist in a gospel group, and James Brown, whose harsh style

owed much to southern preachers. Another was Sam
Cooke, who from 1949 sang with the Soul Stirrers, a
gospel group from Trinity, Texas. Aretha Franklin (*b*
*c*1940), daughter of the much-recorded Reverend C.
L. Franklin, made a number of recordings with him
before finding a new career in rhythm-and-blues.
Some quartets made the transition from sacred to
secular material as freely as the jubilee quartets had
before them: the Southern Jubilee Singers became the
Four Knights, the Royal Sons Quintet recorded
rhythm-and-blues as the Five Royales and Clyde
McPhatter and the Dominoes used gospel-style
singing for their rhythm-and-blues. Its potential to
raise large sums for church and charity (and for
record companies) made gospel a highly commercial,
if not commercialized, music. With the staging of
Black Nativity (1961), a 'gospel-song play' by
Langston Hughes, the cast of which included Marion
Williams, the Stars of Faith and Alex Bradford and
his singers, the potential popularity of gospel music
on the stage was recognized. The amalgam of popular
and gospel music led in the early 1970s to such rock-
gospel shows as *Godspell* and *Jesus Christ, Superstar*.
By the mid-1970s gospel song had become a major
element in the music business.

The power of gospel song to inspire and unite, to
uplift and give strength to the oppressed and under-
privileged was evident during the Civil Rights
movement of the 1960s. James Cleveland's *We are
the soldiers of the army*, made popular by the Gospel
Harmonettes from Alabama, was adapted for the
meetings of Civil Rights campaigners by the

219

Montgomery Trio, one of many songs composed or arranged for this purpose (Smithsonian Collection R023B, 1963). Similarly, Reverend Lawrence Campbell's *Sermon* (Smithsonian Collection R023F, 1963), with which he gained support for the Danville, Virginia, mass meetings, indicates the continuing appeal of the song-sermon. As long as the church is a significant force in black culture, sermons and gospel songs are likely to continue to thrive, even if they change in form and technique.

VII Bibliography

THE BLACK CHURCH

A. H. Fausett: *Black Gods of the Metropolis* (Philadelphia and London, 1944)

St C. Drake and H. Cayton: *Black Metropolis: a Study of Negro Life in a Northern City* (New York, 1945), 600–57

E. F. Frazier: *The Negro Church in America* (New York and Liverpool, 1964)

C. E. Lincoln: *The Black Experience in Religion* (New York, 1974)

COLLECTIONS

W. F. Allen, C. P. Ware and L. McKim Garrison: *Slave Songs of the United States* (New York, 1867/*R*1971)

J. W. and J. R. Johnson: *The Book of American Negro Spirituals* (New York and London, 1925–7)

N. C. Burlin: *Hampton Series: Negro Folk Songs*, iii (New York, 1978), 5f

RECORDINGS

R. A. Waterman: 'Gospel Hymns of a Negro Church in Chicago', *JIFMC*, cxi (1951), 87

Bibliography

A. Bontemps: 'Rock, Church, Rock', *The Book of Negro Folklore*, ed. L. Hughes and A. Bontemps (New York, 1958), 313

S. B. Charters: 'Blind Willie Johnson', Folkways FG 3585 [disc notes]

C. Hayes: 'The Gospel Scene: the Post War Gospel Records', *Blues Unlimited*, nos.3–113 (1963–81)

J. Godrich and R. M. W. Dixon: *Blues and Gospel Records, 1902–1942* (Hatch End, nr. London, 1963, rev. and enlarged 3/1982 as *Blues and Gospel Records, 1902–1943*)

C. Strachwitz: 'Interview with the Staples Family', *American Folk Music Occasional*, i (1964), 13

GOSPEL

J. C. Downey: 'The Gospel Songs and Social Reform', *EM*, ix (1965), 115

M. Jackson and E. M. Wylie: *Movin' on Up: the Mahalia Jackson Story* (New York, 1966)

B. Klatzko: 'In the Spirit', OJL 12–13 [disc notes]

W. Leiser: *Touch Me, Lord Jesus* (Bexhill-on-Sea, 1966)

P. Oliver: *Lo Spiritual* (Milan, 1968)

——: *Mahalia Jackson* (Milan, 1968)

P. Welding: 'Negro Religious Music', BC LP 17–19 [disc notes]

D. Kent: 'An Interview with Reverend F. W. McGee', *American Folk Music Occasional*, ii (1970), 49

T. Heilbut: *The Gospel Sound* (New York, 1971)

T. Bethel: 'Good News, Bad Times', *Jazz Journal*, xxv/5 (1972), 4

J. and A. O'Neal: 'Georgia Tom Dorsey', *Living Blues*, no.20 (1975), 17 [interview]

S. Grossman: 'Reverend Gary Davis 1935–1939', Yazoo L-l023 [disc notes]

R. M. Raichelson: *Black Religious Folksong: a Study in Generic and Social Change* (diss., U. of Pennsylvania, 1975)

D. Evans: 'The Roots of Afro-American Gospel Music', *Jazz Forschung*, viii (Graz, c1977), 119

G. R. Ricks: *Some Aspects of the Religious Music of the United States Negro* (New York, 1977)

D. Seroff: 'Birmingham Quartet Anthology', CL 144 001–002 [disc notes]

W. H. Tallmadge: 'Jubilee to Gospel 1921–1953', JEMF 108 [disc notes]

D. Seroff: 'Biographical Notes', JEMF 108 [disc notes]

K. Lornell: 'Afro-American Gospel Quartets: an Annotated Bibliography and LP Discography of Pre-war Recordings',

JEMF Quarterly, xvii (1981), 19

P. Williams-Jones: *Roberta Martin and the Roberta Martin Singers: the Legacy and the Music* (Washington, DC, 1981) [Smithsonian Institution Catalogue]

H. C. Boyer: 'Contemporary Gospel Music', *Black Perspective in Music*, ii (1982), 5

A. Heilbut: 'The Secularization of Black Gospel Music', *Folk Music and Modern Sound*, ed. W. Ferris and M. Hart (Jackson, Mississippi, 1982), 101

M. Marks: 'You Can't Sing Unless You're Saved: Reliving the Call in Gospel Music', *African Religious Groups and Beliefs: Papers in Honor of William R. Bascom* (Meerut, 1982), 305

H. C. Boyer: 'Charles Albert Tindley: Progenitor of Black-American Gospel Music', *Black Perspective in Music*, xi (1983), 104

P. Oliver: *Songsters and Saints: Vocal Traditions on Race Records* (Cambridge and New York, 1984)

V. Broughton: *Black Gospel: an illustrated history of the Gospel Sound* (Poole, 1985)

D. Seroff: 'On the Battlefield', *Repercussions*, ed. G. Haydon and D. Marks (London, 1985), 30

CHAPTER FIVE

Jazz

I Definition and origins

Attempts at a definition of jazz have always failed, and this reveals something about its mixed origins and later stylistic diversity. Efforts to separate it from other, even related, types of music result in a false primacy of certain aspects, such as improvisation. In fact improvisation is sometimes absent from jazz, lengthy pieces such as Tadd Dameron's *Fontainebleau* (Prestige S7842, 1956) having been fully composed on paper. Another supposed distinguishing feature is the type of rhythmic momentum known as 'swing' (resulting from small departures from the regular pulse). But this, too, is absent from some authentic jazz, early and late.

Further attempts at definition have depended on so-called 'African survivals' in jazz. Over a period of some three centuries about ten million Blacks were shipped from West Africa to the USA. Singing was encouraged on many plantations as an aid to work, but the original forms of such music presumably declined rather quickly: most West African arts were closely related to social usages that were soon destroyed by the policy of many slave owners of dispersing tribal and even family groups. Little is known of this process of decay, still less of the slaves' presumably very slow assimilation of the basic elements of their masters' (European) music. An unaccompanied field holler like Vera Hall's *Trouble so Hard* (L. of C. AAFSL3, 1937) may represent the earliest surviving music of the slaves in the New World, but there is no way of gauging the influences which, by that late recording date, may have changed it. It does not sound African yet its melismatic phrases are not obviously European in shape. It seems to arise only from the singer's immediate circumstances, perhaps symbolizing her people's isolation in an alien land.

The gradual weakening of African elements should not be seen as an entirely negative process. It is possible, for instance, that the prevalence of syncopation first in ragtime and then in jazz was partly the result of an earlier monolinear simplification of African polyrhythms, even if the actual devices of syncopation in extant examples are not very different from those found in European classical music. However, the curiously one-dimensional stylistic purity of Vera Hall's singing, and of similar performances such as Johnny Lee Moore's *Levee Camp Holler* (Atlantic 1348, 1959), suggests that it is misleading to assume jazz to have grown from a single, definitive and equally balanced meeting between African and European characteristics. Nor should one assume that any constituent that does not sound obviously European must be of African provenance.

The original slaves were gathered from large areas of west Africa that still produce many distinct kinds of music. Even in decay, these must be assumed to

have combined with European elements in a variety
of ways though, again, it is impossible to come to a
true understanding of the timing or geographical distribution of this process, or of precisely what African
and European factors were involved. The slaves' new
circumstances may be taken, however, as the main determinant, and in, for example, *Ain't no more cane on
this Brazos* (L. of C. AAFSL3, 1933), recorded by
Ernest Williams and an anonymous group, it is the
rhythm of a collective task (sugar cutting) that shapes
the work song. The sort of antiphony employed here
occurs later in the evolution of jazz in very different
circumstances. The European elements adopted were
extremely simple at first, but a move away from
monody is illustrated by *I be so glad when the sun
goes down* (Atlantic 1346, 1959), recorded by Ed
Lewis and an anonymous group. Here the voices
simultaneously sing a number of versions of a single
melody made up of short pentatonic phrases in strict
metrical patterns that parallel the job of stone breaking. The relation between this kind of vocal heterophony and subsequent instrumental jazz is emphasized by the banjo player Johnny St Cyr's statement
that early New Orleans bands played in 'a sort of
pseudo unison', a point confirmed by such recordings
as Kid Rena's of *Gettysburg March* (Delta 801, 1940).
This piece, audibly of European origin, is played
without marked syncopation, let alone with jazz
phrasing, by trumpet, trombone and two clarinets
with rhythmic accompaniment; each performer, particularly the clarinettists, has his own idea of how the
melody should go.

To what might be termed a post-African musical sensibility, the most foreign aspect of European music would be harmony. In the *Gettysburg March* cited above it was the square-cut melody, not the simple chords it implies, that interested the players; yet it was probably inevitable that in due course they should respond to what was inherent in their chosen material, and this became one of the basic processes in the evolution of jazz. A move in that direction is shown by *The New Burying Ground* (L. of C. AAFSL3, 1936), sung by Willie Williams and an anonymous group. Harmonic combinations are not unknown in some west African music but usually a tribe employs one particular interval (normally the 3rd, 4th, 5th or octave). Although the resulting organum is unrelated to European harmonic usage, a collective memory of it might conceivably have given rise to the sort of harmony found in *The New Burying Ground*. The singers have grasped the idea of 3rds and of putting one above another to form triads; but these chords are used in isolation, as it were, for their immediate sensuous impact, without that concept of functional progression inherent in European tonal harmony. This is prophetic of some aspects of the jazz musician's attitude to harmonic resources.

Even if the Blacks' music was bereft of its original African purposes, it acquired fresh ones in the New World and consequently was not merely changed but renewed. With traditional social ties broken, slaves were probably more open to outside influences and, segregationist attitudes notwithstanding, it is mistaken to think of their music as developing in isolation, however much pain that music might express. The poorest white people were not much better off, and the Blacks' first decisive contact with European harmony might well have come from shape-note hymns, a body of sacred folksong, transmitted in unconventional notations, which won acceptance at the beginning of the 19th century and spread throughout the rural south and midwest, particularly among poor Whites. This music continues to survive, as recordings like *Windham* (Atlantic 1346) and *Calvary* (Atlantic 1349, both 1959) by the Alabama Sacred Harp Singers show, though in performances by Blacks the rhythmic conservatism of such pieces was perhaps gradually modified by more varied accents derived from work songs and field hollers. The newly acquired harmonic feeling is also manifested in spirituals, religious texts set to various types of folk melody, whose origin appears to lie in the white revivalist camp meetings held from 1800 in the south and west, which, surprisingly, Blacks were allowed to attend (see Chapters One and Four). After hearing later recorded performances of such congregational singing one is not surprised to learn that the tendency towards improvisation in American music was first noted (and complained of) in connection with black and white camp-meeting choral singing, as early as 1819.

The banjo and guitar, almost certainly descended from African instruments and the former reported as being used by Jamaican slaves in the 18th century, would also have helped the development of harmonic consciousness. Such recordings as Jimmy Strothers's

227

We are almost down to the shore (L. of C. AAFSL 10, 1936) illustrate the elementary use of the banjo in vocal accompaniment; Vess Ossman began recording ragtime solos on the banjo before the end of the 19th century (e.g. *Eli Green's Cakewalk*, Columbia 3856, 1899). Performances like the Dixieland Jug Blowers' *Banjoreno* (Victor 21473, 1926), a minstrel-style piece featuring three banjos, further suggest the instrument's significance.

Of greater importance must have been the brass bands founded, again unexpectedly, on plantations in Alabama, Louisiana and other states, presumably on the model of pre-revolutionary British army bands. Latter-day brass band recordings such as Bunk Johnson's *Over in Gloryland* (American Music 101, 1945) may give some idea of their music. The existence of such groups as early as 1835 contradicts the widely accepted view that pre-jazz instrumental forms appeared only when the instruments discarded by military bands after the Civil War became available.

In fact the slaves had still earlier non-vocal music, for there are 18th-century reports of groups of Blacks playing various combinations of violin, fife, banjo and assorted percussion in what appeared to contemporary observers to be notably primitive ways. Such pieces as Sonny Terry's *Harmonica Stomp* (Folkways RF202, *c*1939), with harmonica, guitar and washboard, and Ed and Lonnie Young's *Hen Duck* (Atlantic 1346, 1959), played on cane fife and drums, are apparently among the many echoes of this. Performances by jug or juke bands, such as *Ripley Blues*

(Victor 38539, 1928) by Gus Cannon's Jug Stompers and *Barbecue Bust* (ARC 61271, 1936) from the Mississippi Jook Band, may, however, give a better impression of how these groups, and those that accompanied early minstrel troupes, sounded. It seems plausible that such ensembles are the earliest known direct ancestors of the jazz band.

Minstrelsy had its origins in the 18th-century English vogue for plays including black characters and for so-called negro songs performed by comedians with blackened faces. Minstrel entertainers like George Dixon and Thomas 'Daddy' Rice were working in the USA by the late 1820s and the minstrel show crystallized as a form of public entertainment, with some black but predominantly black-faced white performers, during the 1840s. It was apparently through touring minstrel troupes such as Christy's that music derived from that of slaves was first heard outside the plantations – certainly in the north. Its influence on Stephen Foster's *Camptown Races* or *Massa's in de cold, cold ground* (often mistaken for a real spiritual), along with many similar black dialect songs, is obvious, even if the troupes' vocal repertory (items like *Zip Coon* and *Jim Crow*) seems to have sentimentalized and simplified the originals. The troupes' dance music, especially the banjo jigs, was relevant to jazz and survives in such contemporary sources as instruction books for banjo, violin, fife etc, some of which appeared in the 1840s. The origin of these pieces probably lies partly in Scots and Irish folkdances, originally played on the violin or pipes; yet the special rhythmic character of items like *Pea Patch Rag*, first published in an 1845 clarinet tutor, with their emphasis on off-beat accents, may owe something to African music.

A later stage of this music is suggested by solo guitar recordings like Reverend Gary Davis's *Buck Rag* (Transatlantic (E) TRA244, *c*1962), which retains something of a country-dance air; a comparison of this with banjo pieces such as Wade Ward's *Chilly Winds* (Atlantic 1347, 1959) implies that there was no great stylistic distance between black and white music of this sort. As with their singing, all races, particularly in the rural south, appear to have learnt and borrowed from each other, accumulating a common stock of material. An instance is the white hymn-tune called 'The Hebrew Children', which is the same as the black spiritual *Wonder where is good ol' Daniel*. That the types of music that lie behind jazz have a wide racial provenance is indirectly confirmed by the fact that the so-called 'blues scale', with its flattened third and seventh degrees, is not specifically African, still less negro, and least of all exclusively American. Its pentatonic modality is common to folksong of many parts of the world and is found not only in black American folk music but also in white, an example of the latter being the melody *Wayfaring Stranger*.

Similarly, although the microtonal deviations from European tuning that characterize blues singing and playing might have descended from the relation between meaning and pitch inflection in some west African languages, microtones occur in folk music from other parts of the world, for example Moravia. Blues colours much jazz though by no means all; and like 'swing' or the presence of improvisation, this idiom will not serve as a means of defining jazz. Throughout jazz history there have been many significant players (Dizzy Gillespie and Bill Evans, for example) in whose expression blues has had little part.

In sum, the 'African survivals' are difficult to trace decisively either in jazz or in the music that preceded or ran parallel with it, whereas European influences are evident from almost the earliest stages. More important than any one element is the slowly assembled mixture of mutually influential folk and popular styles referred to above, to which all European and several west African races contributed in varying degrees. This may be taken as reflecting the ethnic diversity of the American population. Yet the many, in some cases outwardly incongruous, elements were systematized by the European constituents, these concepts of melody, harmony and rhythm being themselves the fruit of a long tradition in popular and art music.

This accumulation of resources has been subject to sentimentalization and simplification, as noted above with minstrel music; it occurred later with the commercial exploitation of ragtime and has repeatedly happened since with the fashions in popular music, most of them feeding off jazz, which have been generated by the entertainment industry. But this gathering together of resources also resulted in what was in effect a 'matrix' which, perhaps because its broad and composite basis was so different from the single folk traditions from which other forms of art

231

music have arisen, allowed serious artists, principally jazz musicians, to assimilate further, more complex techniques and procedures – again chiefly from European music in the earlier decades – which made possible the growth and stylistic diversity of jazz.

Presumably because of its roots in a wide range of folk and popular styles, the matrix has allowed jazz to retain – indeed, to expand – its central identity through all later acquisitions and refinements in a way that has been impossible for other types of music, such as flamenco, which have kept their links with popular sources but have not developed. A number of American composers used elements of the more accessible contemporary popular music in the early 20th century, and Charles Ives, in such pieces as the second and fourth movements of his Piano Sonata no.1 (1902–8), showed the surest intuitive grasp of this material. Yet jazz represents the fullest and most consistent realization and further development of the matrix's potential.

Among the consequences of the matrix's varied constituents is that similar groupings of stylistic resources have been drawn on at different times. For example, Louis Moreau Gottschalk (1829–69), a widely travelled composer from New Orleans, in pieces like *La bamboula* (sub-titled 'Danse des nègres'), anticipated many features of the piano rag-time of several decades later, including its banjo-derived keyboard figuration. Another example is the so-called 'cool' tendency in phrasing and tone production (see §XIII below), which is assumed to be a unique feature of jazz of the early 1950s. However, as far as one can tell from recordings, it first appeared in the work of the reed players Johnny O'Donnell with the Georgians and Loring McMurray with the California Thumpers, both of whom recorded in 1922. It resurfaced in the 1930s with the work of such men as the alto saxophonist Benny Carter and the pianist Teddy Wilson, then again in the 1950s and 1960s with the music of Lee Konitz and John Tchicai (both alto saxophonists), among others.

A further case is the irregular role taken in jazz expression by vocalized instrumental timbre. A characteristic of folk music in several parts of the world, this is assumed to have lessened as jazz grew more complex. Prominent in jazz of the 1920s, the aggressive vocalization of instrumental sound receded during the 1930s, as the work of such players as the tenor saxophonist Lester Young demonstrates. Yet it returned with considerable emphasis in the following decade with Charlie Parker and bop, weakened in the 1950s as the playing of, among others, Paul Desmond (alto saxophone) and Stan Getz (tenor saxophone) shows, but returned with greater force than ever before in the improvisations of tenor saxophonists like Albert Ayler and Pharoah Sanders in the 1960s. These and other types of recurrence should indicate that the neat sequence of styles proposed in most jazz histories bears little relation to the more complex reality. There has indeed been an evolutionary succession of styles, and this has maintained the continuity, logic and inner necessity that characterize true art. Yet the emergence of a new phase has never rendered others musically less valid, partly because a

233

fresh jazz style involves less real innovation than is usually claimed for it at the time. For instance, many of the supposed new resources of bop in the 1940s, especially its harmonic vocabulary, had been anticipated by advanced players of the 1930s, such as the tenor saxophonist Coleman Hawkins and the pianist Art Tatum, and even earlier, in the 1920s, by the cornettist Bix Beiderbecke and some of his followers like Pee Wee Russell (clarinet).

This process works in both directions. Thus Sidney de Paris, recording *Call of the Blues* in 1944 (Blue Note 40), uses a 'talking' trumpet style perfected over 20 years earlier by King Oliver. *The Funeral* (Polydor (E) 623 235), recorded by the New York Contemporary Five in 1963, clearly echoes the dirges of New Orleans marching bands from a still earlier stage of jazz. And the 5/8, 7/8 and 11/8 over 4/4 of Don Ellis's *Ostinato* (Pacific Jazz PJ55, 1962) exemplify the same polyrhythmic tendency as Lloyd Hunter's *Sensational Mood* (Vocalion 1621) of 1931 with its 3/8 and 3/4 over 4/4, both examples glancing back to the music's pre-history. These relationships across the decades arise out of the underlying matrix of the music's resources and potential, and are, as it were, concurrent as well as chronological. As the end of the 20th century approaches, all jazz styles remain viable, with creative work being done in each. This is partly owing to the speed with which jazz, in response to fast-changing Western culture, has produced stylistic variants. But it should also help to explain how and why certain types of music of the pre-jazz era have survived (in no matter how fragmentary and discontinuous a fashion) and have been recorded, in some cases many decades after their time of origin.

II The earliest jazz

With so much pre-jazz material available it is surprising that so little is known of the earliest real jazz bands. The first name to be identified with jazz (as distinct from transitional forms) is that of the cornettist Buddy Bolden; but information about him is contradictory, suggesting, among other things, that there were at least two men of that name active in New Orleans at that time. In 1931 one of them died in the local lunatic asylum, where he had been since 1907, but there is little to indicate how his music sounded at the turn of the century. Bunk Johnson's discussion of Bolden's style, with whistled illustrations, is inconclusive (American Music 643, 1943), as is the extraordinary vocal imitation of a band of the 1910 period recorded by Louis Keppard (Folkways FA2464, 1957), who claimed to have played with Bolden in 1895. More coherent attempts have been made by survivors from those days to re-create the music of early bands and individual players, among them Dédé Pierce's account of Chris Kelly's trumpet variations on *Careless Love* (Folkways FA2463, 1951) and a version of *Maple Leaf Rag* by a group including Charles Love and Emile Barnes which is allegedly in the manner of a band of the beginning of the century (Folkways FA2464, 1952). As with Punch Miller's demonstration (Folkways FA2465, 1957) of the style of Buddy Petit (c1897–1931), a cornettist of the generation after Bolden's, there is no way of assessing the accuracy of these supposed re-creations. Though highly regarded by their contemporaries, Bolden and many other pioneers were unrecorded; and the exceptions are of little help. Fate Marable's *Pianoflage* and *Frankie and Johnny* (Okeh 40113, 1924), recorded in New Orleans, are so chaotic that it is hard to guess the nature, let alone the quality, of his achievement.

For many years (*c*1907–40) Marable led bands on the Mississippi riverboats, employing numerous players who later became famous, such as Louis Armstrong. Like the early plantation bands and the miscellaneous ensembles that accompanied minstrel troupes, this source of opportunity is a reminder that early attempts at instrumental jazz were not confined to urban centres such as New Orleans. Yet by forcing groups into competition and by allowing better players to move from one band to another, large towns assisted the development of jazz and New Orleans soon became a focal point. Partly as a result of having a musical tradition that reached back well into the 18th century, it provided many outlets for jazz, and this music, or something close to it, was played at parades and funerals, on wagons for advertising and at picnics, as well as in dance halls and cabarets. Many celebrated early jazz musicians were born in or around New Orleans.

In spite of the evident primacy of New Orleans, jazz or something very like it may also have arisen from the widely spread earlier vocal and instrumental forms, particularly those of ragtime, in other centres. Notwithstanding a few recordings such as Jelly Roll Morton's demonstrations of the New Orleans and St

Louis manners of playing *Maple Leaf Rag* (Circle 22, 1938), there is little real knowledge of the geographical distribution of early jazz or of the stylistic consequences of its various locations. But, differently from blues, questions of regional differences of expression and method soon became fairly unimportant. It is symbolic that the first recordings by white New Orleans musicians were made in New York (the Original Dixieland Jazz Band's *Indiana* and *Darktown Strutters' Ball*, Columbia A2297, 1917) and the earliest by New Orleans Creoles and Blacks in Los Angeles (Kid Ory's *Society Blues* and *Ory's Creole Trombone*, Nordskog 3009, 1922).

Yet while the orchestrations of published ragtime pieces by Joplin and others and the ragtime discs (and, earlier still, cylinders) of Sousa's band (which began recording in New York in 1898) and its rivals may have provided some guidelines, performances like those waxed in St Louis as late as 1924–5 by Charlie Creath, another widely praised veteran, are so inconsistent in quality and muddled in their aims as to suggest that in some areas the techniques of playing jazz were hammered out with much uncertainty. Creath's *Won't Don't Blues* (Okeh 8280) and *Cold in Hand* (Okeh 8217, both 1925) exemplify this, and there are many still later recordings, such as Leroy Garnett's *Louisiana Glide* (Paramount 12879, 1929), with its inconclusive mixture of blues and ragtime, which confirm that, for many players, the period of transition to jazz was long and difficult.

The rather formal syncopations of ragtime were especially tenacious, surviving for many years in the

237

output even of a relatively sophisticated band like Bennie Moten's (e.g. *Kansas City Breakdown*, Victor 21693, 1928). Such incongruities were a less happy consequence of the extremely varied contents of the matrix from which jazz arose. Other examples include Fletcher Henderson's *The Chant* (Columbia 817D, 1926), which features a banjo solo clumsily accompanied by an organ, and Duke Ellington's *Black and Tan Fantasy* (Brunswick 3526, 1927) with its two incompatible themes. Meanwhile, clashes between the microtonal inflections of Bessie Smith's blues singing and the fixed pitch of her piano accompaniments (e.g. *You've Been a Good Old Wagon*, Columbia 14079, 1925) indicate the persistence of a different yet not unrelated problem, that of accommodating folk-derived melody within a more recently acquired harmonic language.

III New Orleans

Although it cannot be shown that jazz activities in New York, Kansas City or on the West Coast derived directly from New Orleans jazz, more is understood of the steps taken in that city towards codifying earlier vocal and instrumental heterophony and regularizing the repertory and instrumentation. Thus the earliest coherent jazz ensemble style and method of improvisation of which much is known for certain is associated with New Orleans. It became, and long remained, widely influential (though had it been still more so the kinds of stylistic inconsistency noted above might have been avoided). The size of bands varied, but the melodic lead was usually taken by a cornet (later replaced by a trumpet because of its greater brilliance), an elaborate descant was added by a clarinet (the virtuoso of New Orleans ensembles, drawing on a long tradition of Creole mastery of the instrument) and a melodic bass line was provided by a trombone. A propulsive harmonic–rhythmic accompaniment was provided by a piano (absent on outdoor occasions), banjo or guitar, percussion and tuba (later replaced by string double bass owing to its superior flexibility). Other participants might include an alto or tenor saxophone and, somewhat redundantly, a violin. (The prejudice against saxophones held by most enthusiasts of early jazz has no historical basis, the saxophone family having contributed significantly to almost every phase of jazz.)

This New Orleans style, and in particular the specific role of each wind instrument, presumably arose as the musicians' command of elementary harmony became secure and as, consequently, random heterophony was transformed into counterpoint. The emphasis on independent melodic lines was soon to have further consequences. Meanwhile the earliest recordings in this style had been made by the Original Dixieland Jazz Band (ODJB), starting in 1917. These were widely distributed and promptly imitated, with varied degrees of skill, by groups whose members often had no real understanding of the music. The worst examples are recordings by Earl Fuller's Famous Jazz Band (1917–19), the participants demonstrably having no appreciation of the proper role of each instrument within the ensemble. There entered here, however, a new factor, which has remained of

239

great importance in the growth and evolution of jazz ever since. It was the dissemination of recordings which enabled the music to be known and studied at first throughout the USA and then in other parts of the world, above all in Europe. Far from their point of origin fresh musical developments could quickly be grasped, and records were largely responsible for the almost global interest in jazz that became evident soon after World War I. To this was soon added the influence of radio broadcasts, which were often made from the dance halls where the bands spent much of their time, especially in the 1930s and 1940s.

Although the ODJB had been moderately successful in Chicago in 1916, they were, after a slow start, a sensation in New York. It might be thought that the ragtime craze of the preceding two decades had prepared the way, yet that had not helped Freddy Keppard, the distinguished New Orleans Creole cornettist who in 1916 had taken a band to New York and met with indifference. Perhaps ODJB performances like *Bluing the Blues* (Victor 18483, 1918), full of searing clarinet portamentos and joltingly displaced brass accents, owed more of their character to New York than to New Orleans. And possibly their favourable reception was connected with the violent reaction against Romantic conventions in art that became so marked after World War I. This was already evident in contemporary European works like Satie's *Parade* (1917) and Stravinsky's *Ragtime* for 11 solo instruments (1918).

One consequence of the ODJB's popularity was a vast quantity of uncomprehending press comment which marked the first widespread acknowledgment of the existence of jazz. This, more than their recordings, led to the band becoming the earliest jazz group to perform outside the USA: they played in England for over a year and enjoyed great success. A further result of press attention was that 1917, the year of the ODJB's emergence into fame, has frequently been cited as the date of the 'birth' of jazz. However, quite apart from the evidence of earlier developments rehearsed above, the stylistic consistency of their recordings shows that, like the first published piano rags, this music embodied a sharper focussing – rather than merely a formalization – of preceding, less coherent, endeavours. At this stage the ODJB's repertory demonstrated some of the diverse contents of the matrix that underlies all this music. It was modelled partly on military marches and ragtime, most pieces consisting of several sections, usually of 16 bars each, sometimes with bridge passages, often with an introduction and coda; there would normally be an ensemble improvisation on each theme. The ODJB's recordings usefully reveal the varied origin of this material, as of that played by other early bands. Thus *At the Jass Band Ball* (Aeolian 1205, 1917) and the main section of *Tiger Rag* (Aeolian 1206, 1917) use the harmonic sequences of, respectively, *Shine on, Harvest Moon*, a vaudeville song, and of Sousa's *National Emblem March*. One of the themes of *Livery Stable Blues* (Victor 18255, 1917) derives from the hymn *The Holy City*, while *Fidgety Feet* (Victor 18564, 1918) echoes *At a Georgia Camp Meeting*, a rag of 1897.

241

Elements of march, hymn, rag and blues began to fuse into something more unified, notably with the recordings made in 1922–3 by the New Orleans Rhythm Kings and King Oliver's Creole Jazz Band. Joe Oliver (*b* in or near New Orleans, 11 May 1885; *d* Savannah, 10 April 1938) was one of the cornet and trumpet 'kings' of jazz, a succession of innovatory virtuosos that ran from Buddy Bolden at least to Dizzy Gillespie. After becoming prominent in New Orleans, he went to Chicago in 1919. Oliver led groups well into the 1930s, but made his chief contribution with the Creole Band of 1922–4. The recorded output of this ensemble, and that of the New Orleans Rhythm Kings, a contemporary group likewise consisting of New Orleans musicians active in Chicago, illustrates a move away from the sectional forms borrowed from pre-jazz material – into which improvisation had to be fitted as a series of episodes – towards monothematic pieces that later provided a basis for more continuous extempore playing. Oliver's *Chattanooga Stomp* (Columbia 13003D) represents the former type, his *Krooked Blues* (Gennett 5274, both 1923) the latter. New Orleans Rhythm Kings' performances such as *Discontented Blues* (Gennett 4967, 1922) and *Weary Blues* (Gennett 5102, 1923) have a fluid and melodious sensibility strikingly different from the stately polyphonic density of Oliver's band or the harshness and tension of the ODJB. The fact that these groups were playing such diverse music, despite their overlapping repertories, shows that a wider range of expressive gesture was becoming possible in jazz, and fresh use was soon made of it.

The emphasis by these and other bands on well-developed ensemble counterpoint almost inevitably resulted in the more inventive players making some lines more prominent than others, and then to attempting solo improvisations, whether supported by the rhythm section only or with the other wind instruments adding subdued accompaniment. Solos emerged fugitively at first, as in Doc Behrendson's stop-time clarinet passage in *Hopeless Blues* (Gennett 4886, 1922) by Ladd's Black Aces, then more positively, as with Frank Guarente, an Italian domiciled in the USA and the first noteworthy jazz musician to be born outside America. He led another of the outstanding early bands, the Georgians; his trumpet playing is confidently abrasive in *You Tell Her* (Columbia 3857) yet creates a mood of gentle, pastel-toned melancholy in *Aggravating Papa* (Columbia 3825, both 1923). Another facet of early solo jazz improvising is illustrated by Johnny Dodds's clarinet playing in Oliver's *Room Rent Blues* (Okeh 8148, 1923), and the breaks by Louis Armstrong, then Oliver's second cornettist, in *Tears* (Okeh 40000, 1923) are a decided thrust into the future. Most distinguished of these earliest recorded individual jazz improvisations, however, are Oliver's own poignant cornet solos in *Dippermouth Blues* (two versions, Gennett 5132 and Okeh 4918, both 1923), Leon Roppolo's wayward and introspective clarinet contributions to the New Orleans Rhythm Kings' *Wolverine Blues* (Gennett 5102, 1923) and *Tiger Rag* (Gennett 4968, 1922) and Sidney Bechet's exultantly dominating soprano saxophone playing throughout the Clarence Williams Blue Five's *Wild Cat Blues* and *Kansas City Man Blues* (both Okeh 4925, 1923).

At first jazz had used familiar material to express common sentiments uniting performers and audience. But in music like that cited above one can observe an organic expansion leading to its becoming the vehicle of more individual attitudes. As the writer Ralph Ellison later said (during a symposium at the 1958 Newport Jazz Festival), jazz became 'a discipline of self-discovery. We're trying to discover who we are, and where we are'. The considerable differences between soloists mentioned above underline this diversity of approach; further instances are the opposing tendencies of Johnny Dodds's and Jimmy Noone's clarinet playing in the 1920s, of Henry Allen's and Bobby Hackett's trumpeting in the 1930s and of the piano work of Al Haig and Bud Powell in the 1940s. Even a single recording session by one artist can illustrate this point: Duke Ellington's *Blue Light*, *Slap Happy* (both Brunswick 8297), *Old King Dooji* and *Boy Meets Horn* (both Brunswick 8306), all recorded on 22 December 1938, represent four quite different though related lines of development within his work. This move towards personal expression can be detected even in the relatively small field of piano blues, although it is typical of jazz that more primitive attitudes continued to survive. One may compare the doodling boogie pentatonics of Romeo Nelson's *Head Rag Hop* (Vocalion 1447, 1929) with the clarity and melodic, rhythmic and textural ordering of Montana Taylor's *Indiana Avenue Stomp* (Vocalion 1419, 1929 – later version on Circle 1008, 1946).

244

Jazz, or the most creative part of it, was in the process of becoming a minority art, even if it was some time before the musicians themselves began to think of it as such. With occasional brief accesses of popularity, it has remained so ever since. *Kwela*, the music of South African shanty towns, though influenced by jazz, is nearer to being a true urban folk music than jazz is itself. From the 1920s onwards jazz-flavoured dance music like Abbie Brunies's *Just Pretending* (Columbia 1959D, 1928) was always more popular, even in New Orleans, than the work of true jazz bands like Sam Morgan's (e.g. *Bogalousa Strut*, Columbia 14351D, 1927). Fortunately it was sometimes possible for an uncompromising jazz band to exist within the framework of a larger commercial ensemble, an example being the Georgians, drawn from Paul Specht's dismal orchestra. The necessity of such an arrangement confirms the minority status of jazz.

IV **The jazz solo**

Solo improvisation had by now settled into a form analogous to the Baroque technique of strophic variation on a repeated chord sequence, on the same principle as the chaconne except that it was in 4/4 instead of 3/4. There was a need, however, for a denser harmonic substructure than that provided by the simple material so far used in jazz, to enrich the improvised line. During the 1920s and 1930s this led to a slowly increasing number of substitute harmonies and passing chords, at first implied by the soloist and soon actually stated by the accompani-

245

ment, the result being a considerable speeding-up of harmonic rhythm. This led to an increase in the chordal vocabulary of jazz and to a greater use of dissonance. It might be said that the chains of parallel 7ths in King Oliver's *Froggie Moore Rag* (Gennett 5135, 1923) led to the parallel 9ths of Ellington's *Yellow Dog Blues* (Brunswick 3987, 1928).

A tendency towards – by early jazz standards – advanced harmonic thinking was evident in the cornet improvisations of Bix Beiderbecke (*b* Davenport, Iowa, 10 March 1903; *d* New York, 6 Aug 1931), even on his début recordings of 1922 with the Wolverines. He later worked in large bands led by Jean Goldkette and Paul Whiteman, besides making recordings with small groups under his own name and in partnership with the C-melody saxophonist Frankie Trumbauer. The best of these show a rapid enrichment of his means of expression, and Beiderbecke was among the first, somewhat ahead of Ellington, to explore the effect of upper harmonic extensions, first 9ths, then 11ths and 13ths, not for their developmental potential in terms of functional harmony but for their immediate sensuous impact. No doubt unwittingly, this echoed the non-systematic use of chords in some of the vocal music that long preceded jazz. The growth of jazz's harmonic vocabulary, up to atonality in the late 1950s, followed quite closely, though at a distance of several decades, the development of harmonic resources in European classical music, if in a highly condensed way and without jazz musicians' taking up the larger form-building functions of harmony. In turn this is linked

The jazz solo

with the status of jazz as a peripheral culture, one characterized negatively by its backwardness in relation to more advanced musical idioms elsewhere and positively by its rich variety of styles or dialects.

Within what may be termed the 4/4 chaconne framework individual expression was conveyed through melodic and rhythmic invention, personal qualities of tone and phrasing, and skill in using the harmonic substructure. On the clarinet and particularly the soprano saxophone, Sidney Bechet developed a most striking vein of improvisation with constant melodic invention, impetuous rhythmic freedom and a distinctive sound. In spite of the power and beauty of his playing, however, his choice of chords and passing notes was conventional; a better idea of how great the possibilities were can be gained from Louis Armstrong and Bix Beiderbecke, probably the two most creative jazz musicians active in the 1920s, who used the same resources to produce extremely different results.

Beiderbecke's *Tiger Rag* (HRS 24, 1924) suggests, and the melodic invention and masterly harmonic and rhythmic inflection of *Davenport Blues* (Gennett 5654, 1925) confirm, that he was the first to divine the full potential of the jazz solo. However, the more aggressive brilliance of a long series of recordings made by Armstrong's Hot Five and Hot Seven (1925–8) exerted more widespread influence. The imaginativeness of performances like *Potato Head Blues* (Okeh 8503, 1927) and *Basin Street Blues* (Okeh 8690, 1928; ex.10) uncovered further possibilities for jazz improvisation on all instruments: they led the way to an expansion of melodic, harmonic, rhythmic vocabularies, in particular to increasing freedom in the placing of accents. This is confirmed by Earl Hines's daring keyboard work in the 1928 recordings, particularly *Weatherbird* (Okeh 41454), a duet – almost a duel – for trumpet and piano which fragments the themes of an old King Oliver piece with a remarkable combination of external discontinuity and internal logic. This marks the extreme limits of improvisation technique at the time, and comparison with Oliver's original version (*Weatherbird Rag*, Gennett 5132, 1923) yields a vivid impression of how far this music had travelled during the 1920s.

Ex.10 Opening of Armstrong's solo from *Basin Street Blues* (1928), transcr. M. Harrison

* A brief solo passage occurring during an interruption in the accompaniment, usually lasting 2 or 4 bars and maintaining the underlying harmonies and rhythm of the piece

It might be regretted that Armstrong and others did not continue to use material of this sort. But the process of absorbing into the jazz repertory popular songs of the day, produced by commercial publishing

interests rather than the almost enclosed community
of jazz, had begun some time before. At the start of
the 1920s such bands as the Original Memphis Five
and their many associated groups began to record
jazz versions of numerous popular songs as they
appeared in print. By the end of the decade Armstrong, now working with large bands whose role was
only accompanimental, was following this trend. But
it was Beiderbecke who first showed how decisively
this material could be transmuted into jazz, playing
solos of rare poetic intensity on pieces such as *I'm
coming, Virginia* (Okeh 40843, 1927), admirably
seconded by Bill Challis's sensitive orchestration
(ex.11). Armstrong's accompaniments were inferior,
yet a number of his performances, like *Sweethearts
on Parade* (Columbia 2688D, 1930), attain a similar
level.

Such items contributed to the growing harmonic
sophistication of jazz but their weak melodies led to
problems of style. In some of Art Tatum's early solos,
such as *Cocktails for Two* (Decca 156, 1934), there is
an incongruity between the advanced harmonic and
rhythmic language and complex piano textures and
the naivety of the original tune. Sophisticated harmony was sometimes absorbed only with difficulty.
The pointless modulations of Alphonso Trent's *Black
and Blue Rhapsody* (Gennett 6710, 1928), the lack of
harmonic agreement between piano and banjo in
Armstrong's *Don't Jive me* (Columbia 36376, 1928)
and the selfconscious chromaticisms of Jelly Roll
Morton's *Freakish* (Victor 27565, 1929) reveal
some of these problems.

Ex.11(a) *I'm coming, Virginia:* extract from the original melody

(b) Part of the second chorus of Bix Beiderbecke's solo from *I'm coming, Virginia* (1927), transcr. M. Harrison

Although they have received little credit for it, among the musicians who dealt most effectively with these difficulties were those of the New York school of the late 1920s. Red Nichols (trumpet), the group's moving spirit and frequent organizer, Miff Mole (trombone), Jimmy Dorsey (reeds), Eddie Lang (guitar), Joe Venuti (violin) and others recorded a distinguished and varied body of work. Such pieces as *That's no Bargain* (Brunswick 3407) and *Get a Load of This* (Pathé-Actuelle 11347, both 1926) sensitively use altered 13ths, flattened 5ths, whole-tone scales, heavily syncopated harmonic rhythm and other devices often thought to have been introduced to jazz with bop 20 years later.

Chicago, rather than New York, was, however, the main centre of jazz activities in the 1920s. Numerous musicians from New Orleans settled and were first recorded there, notably King Oliver's Creole Jazz Band, the New Orleans Rhythm Kings, Louis Armstrong's Hot Five and Hot Seven, Jelly Roll Morton, Johnny Dodds and many others. They had an inevitable influence on young local musicians, especially on a circle known as the Austin High School Gang, which included Jimmy McPartland (cornet), Bud Freeman (tenor saxophone), Floyd O'Brien (trombone), Joe Sullivan (piano) and Frank Teschemacher (clarinet). Using the transplanted New Orleans jazz of, particularly, Oliver and Armstrong as a model and adding the strong influence of Bix Beiderbecke, these players, and others irregularly associated with them, such as Muggsy Spanier (cornet), Eddie Condon (banjo) and Gene Krupa (drums), produced a new version of jazz soon identified as the 'Chicago style', which pointed to many later developments.

Typified by such pieces as the Chicago Rhythm Kings' *There'll be Some Changes Made* (Brunswick 4001, 1928), their music was more overtly driving than that of New Orleans, with nervous rhythms and complex textures. Although Freeman (rather than Lester Young) was the first tenor saxophonist to reject Coleman Hawkins's pervasive influence (e.g. *Crazeology*, Okeh 41168, 1928), Teschemacher was

251

the most original Chicagoan. He died young (Chicago, 1 March 1932, aged nearly 26), but an uncompromising sense of identity was evident on even his first recording session (December 1927). He wove spare, angular yet melodically dense lines on his clarinet that were sometimes of almost obsessive intensity. Teschemacher's contributions to Charles Pierce's *Bullfrog Blues* (Paramount 12619, 1928) embody the essense of the laconic, hard-bitten Chicagoan jazz of the late 1920s. The work of the others named above was also significant, however, and most of them remained prominent for many years.

In fact by this stage there were so many excellent musicians involved with jazz, and in so many places, that mention cannot be made of all of them. The trombonist Jack Teagarden (*b* Vernon, Texas, 29 Aug 1905; *d* New Orleans, 15 Jan 1964) was linked with the New York school of Nichols and Mole in many recordings yet was a notably independent figure, the leading jazz musician to come from the south-west, at least until Ornette Coleman's arrival. He had the strong affinity with blues associated with that region, as indicated by *Tailspin Blues* (Victor 38087, 1929), an unusually expressive tone and an ease of movement that enabled him to build on the advances of Miff Mole and to extend considerably the jazz capabilities of the trombone. He possessed a sure ear for recent harmonic innovations and his singing, as in the sombre yet beautiful *Dirty Dog* (Cameo 9174, 1929), added a further dimension to an exceptionally well-rounded style. Teagarden played in various large bands, including Paul Whiteman's for five years, and repeatedly tried to establish big ensembles of his own, usually without success or distinction. The subtle nuances of his improvisations have their full effect only in the countless small groups with which he appeared and recorded, and it is such work – including four years with Louis Armstrong's All-Stars – that secures his place as one of the strongest musical personalities of jazz.

If Teagarden extended the scope of his instrument, Coleman Hawkins (*b* St Joseph, Missouri, 21 Nov 1904; *d* New York, 19 May 1969) may almost be said to have invented, or discovered, the jazz potential of the saxophone family. It was in jazz that these instruments first found an authentic voice of their own. Saxophones had usually participated in New Orleans ensemble jazz, but Hawkins showed the tenor (his own instrument) to be an important solo medium. Bechet had already done this with the soprano saxophone and Adrian Rollini with the bass, yet scarcely anyone else played these instruments, whereas Hawkins won the tenor a permanent central role in jazz. *One Hour* (Victor 38100, 1929), in which he takes a characteristically rhapsodic but disciplined solo, announced the instrument's emancipation from such crudities as slap-tonguing. The differences between the stomping emphasis of his improvisation in Fletcher Henderson's *Sugar Foot Stomp* (Columbia 2513D, 1931) and the romantic flexibility of that in the Chocolate Dandies' *Dee Blues* (Columbia 2543D, 1930) give an idea of Hawkins's range of expression even at this early stage of his career. That career was a long one, spanning several phases of jazz and involving a long stay in Europe during the 1930s and repeated visits later. Hawkins remained interested in the innovations of younger musicians (see §X below), and he was among the dominating figures of jazz for many years.

Sometimes the assertion of a soloist's identity did not depend on innovation or even on improvising. Beiderbecke's *Old Man River* (Okeh 41088, 1928) and Bechet's *Indian Summer* (Bluebird B10623, 1940) are examples of highly personal statements that scarcely depart from their original melodies, individuality being conveyed through tone, phrasing and minute adjustments of timing. Such perform-ances could be enjoyed by listeners with no liking for jazz or demanding music, and different levels of sophistication continued to co-exist. This is illus-trated by the versions of *Bugle Call Rag* recorded by Cannon's Jug Stompers (Victor 38006) and by Duke Ellington's Orchestra (Harmony 577H), both in 1928.

V **Piano jazz**
Among the leading jazz pianists, however, innovation was of prime importance. As with the great 19th-century European composer–pianists, they exploited virtuosity, not merely for display but as a means of absorbing new resources, chiefly rhythmic, harmonic and textural. They also explored tonalities hitherto little used in jazz, for example the sequence of B♭ minor, D♮ and G♮ major in Eubie Blake's *Charleston Rag* of 1921 (Emerson 10434, retitled *Sounds of Africa* on some reissues). Indeed, the pianists, aided by the

autonomy of their instrument, were usually ahead of other players in such matters. Their endeavours gave rise to items like Willie 'the Lion' Smith's *Echoes of Spring* (Commodore 521, 1939), which has an alfresco atmosphere different from that of most jazz, and to large-scale orchestral works such as James P. Johnson's *Harlem Symphony*.

Such undertakings were rooted in the attitude of ragtime composers like Joplin, Lamb and Scott, who, even in the 1890s, a world away from the New Orleans of Buddy Bolden, intended their formal compositions to be considered as art, even if they were in part descended from the sardonic parodies of the cakewalk. A few pianists like Jelly Roll Morton and Earl Hines were independent, but Johnson, Blake and a few other musicians who were insufficiently recorded, for example Luckey Roberts, created out of ragtime the basis of piano jazz. Their influence extends through players like Fats Waller and Art Tatum to post-World War II modernists like Thelonious Monk, who in turn affected Cecil Taylor and other avant-garde figures of the 1960s. They were voracious listeners, often attending to music far removed from jazz, and Johnson in particular, who had a solidly grounded technique in playing and composing, explored the European classics (he mentioned Beethoven and Liszt especially) in search of procedures new to jazz. Such pieces as his *Carolina Shout* (Okeh 4495, 1921) make a more complex and personal impression than Gottschalk's uncomplicatedly triumphant virtuosity or the determined, slightly mechanical, optimism of ragtime (itself the reverse image of the nostalgia and insecurity embodied in Stephen Foster's and other black dialect songs).

Even if Johnson (*b* New Brunswick, NJ, 1 Feb 1894; *d* New York, 17 Nov 1955) and the other pianists of the New York 'stride' school, as it was called, could not play convincing blues (e.g. *Worried and Lonesome Blues*, Columbia A3950, 1923), some music Johnson recorded later (e.g. *Mule Walk*, Blue Note 27, 1943) retained the rural overtones of country dance music. This reconciliation of earthiness and sophistication was necessary to the establishment within jazz of a smoother rhythmic continuity and a more even 4/4 pulse. Johnson's *Keep off the Grass* (Okeh 4495, 1921) has, also, three-beat patterns superimposed on the underlying 4/4 to offset any suggestion of rhythmic squareness. Each aspect of a piece like his *Scouting Around* (Okeh 4937, 1923) is organized in long lines instead of in the tight, repetitive patterns of ragtime.

The first jazz pianist who could be described as a virtuoso, Johnson had, in addition, an extensive career in show business, touring Europe with the musical show *Plantation Days* in the early 1920s and composing the musical *Sugar Hill*, which was produced in Los Angeles, as late as 1949. He wrote a number of standard popular songs, including *If I could be with you one hour* and *Old-fashioned Love*. Johnson also worked, more briefly, in films, and was the music director of Bessie Smith's only film, *St Louis Blues* (1929). He essayed the larger forms of composition, and *Yamekraw* for piano and orchestra was heard at Carnegie Hall in 1928 with W. C. Handy conducting and Fats Waller as soloist;

this piece was also used as the basis of a film of the same name in 1930. Other orchestral works by Johnson include the *Harlem Symphony* (1932), *Jazz-a-mine Concerto* (1934) and *Suite in Sonata Form on St Louis Blues* (1936).

Seemingly free of ragtime influence from the start and displaying a musical sophistication at least equal to that of the New York 'stride' men, was Earl Hines, a pianist from Pennsylvania. He created a great impression in the recordings he made with Armstrong in 1928, when the trumpeter was at his most consciously modernistic. Partly because of Hines's participation, items such as Armstrong's *Skip the Gutter* (Okeh 8631) are shaped with a hard, stinging virtuosity; they include complex ensembles, furious spurts of double-time, much rhythmic jugglery, and some unpredictable harmonic alterations – even glimpses of bitonality from the pianist, as in *Fireworks* (Okeh 8597), a variant of *Tiger Rag*. Hines's solo performances at this time, such as *57 Varieties* (Okeh 8653, also 1928), another *Tiger Rag* variant, jump rather than flow and have an air of indomitable risk-taking. Almost the whole register of the piano is used and the sound is metallic, with every note struck decisively. Textures, like rhythms, are purposefully fragmented, the metre nearly dissolved. Improvisations recorded even a few years later, such as *Down Among the Sheltering Palms* (Brunswick 6403, 1932), with its agitated climax of furiously criss-crossing melodies, show that Hines developed rapidly, and, like Hawkins, Teagarden and his other peers, he remained widely influential.

257

VI **Orchestral jazz**

Another vein of activity led to the emergence of a coherent style of orchestral jazz. The credit for this is normally given to Fletcher Henderson (*b* Cuthbert, Georgia, 18 Dec 1897; *d* New York, 28 Dec 1952), though much of it belongs to Don Redman, his chief arranger in the 1920s. As usual when there is a supposed breakthrough in jazz, there had been many years of preparatory work by others. Apart from the 19th-century plantation brass bands of indeterminate size (see §I above), the roots of orchestral jazz lie in the ragtime recorded by Sousa and his rivals like Charles Prince and Arthur Pryor, all of whom cut recordings in the earliest years of the century. The instrumentation of such items as Prince's *Dixie Girl* (Columbia 1556, 1903), Pryor's *Coon Band Contest* (Victor 4069, 1903; later version on Victor 16079, 1904) or the Columbia Orchestra's *Creole Belles* (Columbia 330, 1901) was three or four cornets, one to three trombones, flute, one or two clarinets, two violins, tuba, percussion, with additions like the piccolo and alto, tenor and baritone horns. Sousa used a larger ensemble, his *At a Georgia Camp Meeting* (Victor 315, 1900), for example, having seven cornets, three flutes and so on.

These bands were followed, especially in New York, by still bigger groups such as Tim Brymn's Forty Black Devils, or the Fifty Merry Moguls, led by Fred Bryan, known as 'the jazz Sousa'. Each used large sections of violins, banjos and mandolins, and even the earliest recording in this genre, Jim Europe's *Too Much Mustard* (Victor 35359, 1913), has five banjos. The music was mostly ragtime in a relentlessly exuberant 2/4, though sometimes with disconcertingly genteel interludes, as in Europe's *Castle House Rag* (Victor 35372, 1914). Essentially a transitional phenomenon, it lacked the textural, indeed contrapuntal, interest of jazz. Yet along with the recordings of Ford Dabney (e.g. *The Jass Lazy Blues*, Aeolian 1218, 1917), the bowdlerization of New Orleans style offered by A. J. Piron's Orchestra (e.g. *Bouncing Around*, Okeh 40021, 1923) and the work of a few other ensembles, this music pointed to Henderson's and Redman's first endeavours. Henderson's earliest bandsmen were much impressed by Piron's group when it played in New York in 1922–3. Their own first recordings were made under the name 'Henderson's Dance Orchestra', which suggests only modest aims, and the instrumentation, for example in *Wang Wang Blues* (Black Swan 2080, 1922), was two cornets, trombone, a three-piece reed section (clarinets and saxophones), piano (played by Henderson himself), banjo (later replaced by guitar), tuba (later replaced by string bass) and percussion. Henderson's model seems to have been Paul Whiteman's ensemble, which used this grouping, for example in *Everybody Step* (Victor 18826, 1921). Whiteman's *Wang Wang Blues* (Victor 18694, 1920) is closely followed by Henderson's recording (as it also was by Duke Ellington's version, Brunswick 6003, 1930).

The balance and approach to scoring that such an instrumentation implies became standard and remained so even when, during the 1930s, in Henderson's and many other bands, the reed section grew to

259

five saxophones (two altos, two tenors, one baritone), the trombones to three, even four, and the trumpets to six and more. Supposedly, one of Redman's most original contributions in his scores for Henderson was the antiphonal duet between brass and reed sections, as in *Houston Blues* (Columbia 164D, 1924), and this simple, often effective, procedure became common in the swing music of the 1930s, for example in Benny Goodman's *King Porter Stomp* (Victor 25090, 1935) arranged by Henderson. But this was a case of jazz again adapting resources from the underlying matrix, the device having derived from the call-and-response patterns of work songs and congregational religious music (see §I above). It had anyway been anticipated by groups like Whiteman's, as in *Anytime, Any Place, Anywhere* (Victor 18694, 1920). Similarly, Redman's excellent use of Henderson's three-piece saxophone section, as in *Naughty Man* (Vocalion 14935, 1924), was foreshadowed in such Whiteman recordings as *Stairway to Paradise* (Victor 18949, 1922), in which the trumpet solo, perhaps by Tommy Gott, is more fluent and expressive than any improvisation in Henderson's records until the arrival of Louis Armstrong in 1924. Armstrong's relaxation of the Henderson band's earlier stiffness is evident in *Go 'long, Mule* (Columbia 228D, 1924).

There is no doubt, however, about Redman's part in establishing the basic method of scoring for large jazz groups, though the Henderson band's contribution was inconsistent and remained so into the 1930s. The rhythmic innovations – within the orchestral field – of *Tozo* (Columbia 970D) and *White-*

man Stomp (Columbia 1059D, both 1927), with their 3/8 and 3/4 over 4/4, have to be set beside the merely decorative approach to dixieland pieces like *Fidgety Feet* (Vocalion 1092, 1927). The effective revision of *Copenhagen* (Vocalion 14926, Oct 1924), based on a version recorded several months before by Bix Beiderbecke's group, the Wolverines (Gennett 5453, May 1924), must be compared with the coarsening and simplification of Oliver's *Dippermouth Blues* under the new title *Sugar Foot Stomp* (Columbia 395D, 1925).

Henderson's contribution was not ultimately an orchestral one; rather, he and his bandsmen showed that improvisation could flourish within the context of written scores, that spontaneity and careful preparation were not incompatible. This discovery was exploited elsewhere, at a higher musical level, and the point about Henderson is confirmed by the fact that his recordings are now valued chiefly for the work of the many gifted improvising soloists he employed during the 1920s and 1930s. Besides Armstrong they included Joe Smith, Tommy Ladnier, Henry Allen and Roy Eldridge (trumpets), Charlie Green, Jimmy Harrison, Benny Morton and Dicky Wells (trombones), Benny Carter and Hilton Jefferson (alto saxophones), and Coleman Hawkins and Chew Berry (tenor saxophones). Redman (*b* Piedmont, West Virginia, 29 July 1900; *d* New York, 30 Nov 1964) continued to lead bands of his own into the 1940s, besides arranging for other leaders. His *Cherry* became a standard popular song, recorded by Armstrong and many others, and *Chant of the Weed* (Brunswick 6211, 1931) is a classic of orchestral jazz.

VII Jazz composition I

Instead of being an adaptation of material from outside jazz, Redman's *Chant of the Weed* is what may be termed a 'composition for band', and a number of such works appeared during the 1920s. A good example is Frankie Trumbauer's *Krazy Kat*, which he recorded with Beiderbecke in 1927 (Okeh 40903). With its unusual and fast-moving chord sequence, this runs counter to the increasing use of popular songs in jazz at that time. Along with other such pieces as *Imagination*, a Fud Livingston score recorded by the Charleston Chasers, one of Miff Mole's groups (Columbia 1260D, 1927), it represented a search for a higher level of structural unity and greater consistency. This aim was pursued more systematically, however, by a few men like Jelly Roll Morton (*b* New Orleans, 20 Oct 1890; *d* Los Angeles, 10 July 1941), the earliest jazz intellectual – the first man to have a coherent general theory of this music and its potential.

It was an unlikely achievement for one who probably engaged in a greater variety of non-musical activities, some of them illegal, than any other major jazz figure. Brothel pianist, pimp, pool shark, Morton was also briefly a boxing promoter and ran a hotel. He began to travel early, but periodically returned to New Orleans and always returned to music. His finest work belongs to 1923–7, when he was based in Chicago, and to the earlier part (1928–30) of his New

York period. In the early 1930s Morton spent several years in obscurity, but recorded a remarkable group of partially autobiographical sessions for the Library of Congress in 1938, followed by commercial recordings in company with such musicians as Sidney Bechet and Henry Allen which attracted the attention of the jazz public just before his death.

The nature of the usual type of jazz band, with each participant making his own creative bid, is such that performances tend to be divided in aim and uneven in quality. A good instance is Armstrong's *Savoy Blues* (Okeh 8535, 1927), in which a superlative cornet solo is followed by a pedestrian one from Kid Ory (trombone), to extremely anticlimactic effect. To counter this Morton, while retaining the immediacy of improvisation, made it submit to a carefully devised structural symmetry in such a way that composed and extemporized elements enhanced each other. Thus he became the first jazz composer – using that term in the special sense applicable to jazz – and his work looks both forward and back. Morton's formal symmetries are not static, like those of ragtime, but developmental, and in such recordings as *Black Bottom Stomp* (Victor 20221, 1926) he brought to a new height the possibilities of the multi-thematic piece with several chord sequences inherited from relevant types of pre-jazz music. Simultaneously, in items like *Doctor Jazz* (Victor 20415, 1926) and *Jungle Blues* (Bluebird B10256, 1927), he demonstrated the potential of 32- and 12-bar monothematic pieces with a single, repeating chord sequence on which progressive jazz musicians would increasingly concentrate. Because they were created by improvising bandsmen yet shaped by a composer, pieces like *Grandpa's Spells* (Victor 20431, 1926) reconcile underlying unity with a degree of variety that long remained uncommon in jazz. The balance between composition and improvisation, contrapuntal and homophonic ensembles, though never the same in any two items, nearly always seems exactly right. The range of colour and texture Morton drew from his small ensembles was also remarkable, but the main point was that his best performances had an integrity and consistency that can only rarely be achieved in jazz organized on more conventional lines.

There are other aspects of Morton's work, such as his brief adaptation, in trio recordings like *Wolverine Blues* (Victor 21064, 1927), of the 'chamber jazz' approach pioneered by Eddie Lang, Joe Venuti and others of the New York school. There is also what he called the 'Spanish tinge', found in piano solos such as *Tia Juana* (Gennett 5632, 1924), a resource earlier drawn from the matrix by Gottschalk in, for example, *Souvenir de Porto Rico* (1857) and again in ragtime pieces like *Spanish Venus* (c1915) by Luckey Roberts. (National colourings appear repeatedly in jazz, further instances being the Gallic refinement of Louis Chauvin's *Heliotrope bouquet*, a 1907 rag, and the seemingly Milhaudian echoes of the Duke Ellington–Billy Strayhorn piano duet *Tonk* (Mercer M1963, 1950).) The conventional description of Morton's output as 'classic New Orleans jazz' is misleading. Rather, its synthesis of improvisation and composition in continuous musical argument points to Ellington's work and beyond that to the music of such later jazz composers as John Lewis and George Russell.

A related, if less obvious, unorthodoxy is apparent in recordings by Tiny Parham, who is thought to have helped Morton with some of his orchestrations. Parham's *Dixieland Doings* (Victor 38111, 1929) has Mortonian zest, and most of his other performances, such as *Blue Island Blues* (Victor 38041, 1929), are finely integrated. The better jazz musicians have always been interested in such endeavours, an instance being the response of the famously spontaneous Armstrong to the simple yet precise formal virtues of Alex Hill's *Beau Koo Jack* (Okeh 8669, 1928), which resulted in one of his best recorded improvisations. Nor was it long before Ellington (*b* Washington, DC, 29 April 1899; *d* New York, 24 May 1974) began to go beyond the limitations imposed by the ten-inch 78 r.p.m. discs on which jazz was then recorded. The first version of his *Creole Rhapsody* (Brunswick 6093, 1931) occupied both sides of a ten-inch record and the expanded, considerably improved, version recorded six months later (Victor 36049, 1931) took up both sides of a 12-inch disc. Indeed, it was Ellington who most decisively followed the line of advance Morton had indicated.

Although the blending of orchestral colours that characterizes Ellington's mature work, for example *Dusk* (Victor 26677, 1940), was anticipated in an elementary way by a few scores such as Don Redman's *Hop Off*, recorded by Henderson (Columbia 35670, 1927), the essence of Ellington's

achievement was that he combined Henderson's preservation of improvising within arrangements for lar-
gish bands with Morton's integration of solo and
ensemble in a unified musical discourse. He began
making records in 1924 and continued to do so prolifically until shortly before his death. His development
is thus well documented. His exceptional originality
had emerged by 1927, yet it came only gradually, and
a piece like *Parlor Social Stomp* (Pathé-Actuelle 7504,
1926) – a confused mixture of theatre music, jazz and
commercial ragtime, using several incompatible types
of rhythm – typifies his early struggles. What focussed
Ellington's powers as a composer were the contributions of the soloists in his band.

The little group Ellington took to New York in
1923 slowly grew to 11 by the end of the decade, to
15 by 1935, 19 in 1946. Each addition, particularly in
the earlier years, was crucial, as each new member
had a distinct musical personality; as the band's later
history showed, changes in personnel at once resulted
in changes in its music. This was one of the factors
that separated Ellington's from the other large bands
of the swing period, and it was only many years later
that a similar situation pertained with Gil Evans.
From the late 1920s onwards and above all during
1932–42, his most creative period, Ellington used the
band as a workshop in which, in the closest collaboration with his musicians, he solved an increasing
range of problems, always involving a reconciliation
of the balanced symmetries of composition with the
spontaneous fire of improvisation. The initial stimulus came from the trumpeter Bubber Miley and the

trombonist Joe Nanton, other important participants including the alto saxophonist Johnny Hodges, the clarinettist Barney Bigard, the baritone saxophonist Harry Carney, the trombonist Lawrence Brown and the trumpeter Cootie Williams who was Miley's replacement. The special skills of these and other men, in particular the highly individual tone-colours they drew from their instruments, were integral parts of Ellington's music.

Yet, once Ellington had sensed his true direction, the ensemble had equal importance. The special atmosphere of the *East St Louis Toodle-oo* theme (Columbia 953D, 1927) depends as much on the slow-moving saxophone and tuba harmonies as on Miley's growling, plunger-muted trumpet line. There were many performances, early and later, such as *Old Man Blues* (Victor 23022, 1930) and *Koko* (Victor 26577, 1940), the impact of which is mainly orchestral. Notwithstanding his collaborative methods, one feels with Ellington, as with all real composers, that melody, harmony, rhythm, colour and texture act together: substance and sonority are indivisible. These relationships slowly grew more subtle and more diversified, resulting in tightly organized pieces like *Buffet Flat* (Brunswick 8231, 1938) and *Harlem Airshaft* (Victor 26731, 1940) in which there are always two things happening at once. In the late 1930s and early 1940s particularly, Ellington and his musicians achieved a variety of expression that was far beyond the reach of other jazz of the time and that has been approached by few since. It is not possible to illustrate all its facets here, but among notable examples are

Saddest Tale (Brunswick 7310, 1934), with its extra-ordinary harmonies, and *Battle of Swing* (Brunswick 8293, 1938), a miniature jazz concerto grosso. Others include the exotic evocations of *Dusk on the Desert* (Brunswick 8029, 1937) and *Bakiff* (Victor 27502, 1941), solo concertos like *Clarinet Lament* (Brunswick 7650, 1936) for Barney Bigard and *Boy Meets Horn* (Brunswick 8306, 1938), parading half-valve and other effects of Rex Stewart's cornet. *Clarinet Lament* derives partly from *Basin Street Blues*, and Ellington undertook several recompositions of this kind, further instances being *Ebony Rhapsody* (Victor 24622, 1934) on Liszt's Hungarian Rhapsody no.2 and *The Sergeant was Shy* (Columbia 35214, 1939) on the New Orleans Rhythm Kings' *Bugle Call Rag*. Also to be noted are the miniature tone-poems that were perhaps the most characteristic of all Ellington's works, though here again the range was wide, from *Daybreak Express* (Victor 24501, 1933) to *Old King Dooji* (Brunswick 8306, 1938). In a few pieces such as *Blue Serge* (Victor 27356, 1941) there is a depth of emotion that has remained rare in orchestral jazz.

There are many pieces like *Jack the Bear* (Victor 26536, 1940) in which Ellington accommodated, say, half a dozen improvising soloists without overcrowd-ing. But there are others, such as *Sepia Panorama* (Victor 26731, 1940), in which excellent themes are left undeveloped. Occasionally another bandleader would exceed the time-limit of the single side of a ten-inch disc – for instance Count Basie on *The World is Mad* (Okeh 5816, 1940) – but never to significant purpose. Ellington, however, was more seriously restricted by what jazz commentators used to commend as 'three-minute form'. In some respects his most remarkable departure, following that of *Creole Rhapsody*, remained *Reminiscing in Tempo* (Brunswick 7546/7) of 1935, which, especially in its structural ambitions, was quite unlike any other American jazz of its period. It was unfortunate that this score had to be recorded in four segments for it is really a continuous whole in which may be detected an exposition, development and modified recapitulation. Here, as in his next work of this kind, *Crescendo and Diminuendo in Blue* (Brunswick 8004, 1937), which occupied both sides of a ten-inch disc, there is scarcely any improvisation. These three pieces mark Ellington's emergence as a fully independent composer, and there is no doubt that he could have gone much farther in the direction that *Reminiscing in Tempo* in particular indicated. That would probably have involved abandoning his orchestra, and he was unwilling to relinquish the pleasure of hearing immediately what he wrote, or of experimenting in close collaboration with musicians who had already given him so much. Thus Ellington may never have realized his full potential as a composer, but at least the intimate relationship between the composer and his creative executants continued for several more years.

VIII **The 1930s: consolidation**

By the close of the 1920s many lines of development for jazz had been initiated and the following decade may appear to have been a period of consolidation. Certainly it was concerned with a further exploration

269

of orchestral resources and with the increasing power and subtlety of solo improvisation. The latter point is confirmed by comparing the understatement of Teddy Wilson's piano playing with the aggressiveness of Earl Hines's on which it is based; or by contrasting the overt romanticism of Coleman Hawkins's tenor saxophone solos with the acutely expressive reticence of those by Lester Young. In each case the effect seems to be of simplification, but really it is a matter of distillation, of a new obliqueness. Such differences suggest how deceptive the apparent conservatism was, and the trumpeting of, say, Henry Allen in Henderson's *Queer Notions* (Vocalion 2583, 1933) is notably more complex, especially in its rhythmic freedom, than that of Louis Armstrong (also from New Orleans); it points, via the work of Frankie Newton, Jonah Jones and Roy Eldridge, to the bop phrasing of Dizzy Gillespie.

Yet it is too simple to nominate growing complexity as the dominant tendency of this period. Rather was it a question, even with the better large bands, of the finest jazz growing less corporeal and celebratory. It had always contained a degree of ambiguity, an example being the contradiction between the sad melodic cadences and the jog-trot rhythm of the New Orleans Rhythm Kings' *Farewell Blues* (Gennett 4965, 1922). But the difference between the simplicity of the Missourians' *Prohibition Blues* (Victor V38120, 1930) and the equivocation between innocence and sophistication of Ellington's *Across the Track Blues* (Victor 27235, 1940) is one measure of what happened to jazz during the 1930s.

The 1930s: consolidation

The latter part of the decade became known as 'the swing era' and jazz, renamed 'swing', enjoyed another few years of popularity. Like the ragtime craze at the turn of the century or the ODJB's sudden fame in 1917, this was largely accidental. The arbitrary nature of success in this sphere is suggested by the fact that in the late 1930s boogie-woogie enjoyed a vogue. This led to some beautiful recordings by Jimmy Yancey, Meade Lux Lewis, Clarence Lofton, Albert Ammons and a few others, yet other closely related aspects of blues piano playing remained unknown to the large public that jazz temporarily had.

It is hard to assess many bands and individuals because of insufficient recorded evidence and the scarcity of reliable contemporary reports. Sometimes a group, such as Walter Page's Blue Devils, made few records yet was acknowledged as a potent influence. Others, like Jesse Stone's Blues Serenaders, could produce a magnificent example of jazz polyphony in *Starvation Blues* (Okeh 8471, 1927) but have no discernible effect on their fellows and make hardly any other records. Some, like the Blue Rhythm Band, showed obvious potential (e.g. *Blue Flame*, Brunswick 6143, 1931) but lacked an arranger good enough to impart a consistent and individual style. Others, such as Harlan Leonard's Rockets, might have excellent scores, like Tadd Dameron's *400 Swing* (Bluebird B10823, 1940), yet fail to make a permanent impression.

Many of these groups were, or started as, what were known as 'territory bands'. Their work took them far away from big cities like New York or Chicago (later

271

Los Angeles) where most recording was done. The geographical distribution of their activities and the quality of their musical achievements are not fully known, yet such groups have always played an essential role in jazz, not least as a training-ground for young musicians. An interesting case, better documented than most, is Bennie Moten, who for over a decade worked at improving his band's music, taking it from the crude beginnings of *Crawdad Blues* (Okeh 8100, 1923) to the individuality of such pieces as *Lafayette* (Victor 24216, 1932), which embodied a substantially different approach to the large ensemble from Henderson's and helped prepare for the jazz of the 1940s.

IX The big band era

It is impossible to place in exact chronological order the events that led to the characteristic orchestral jazz of the later 1930s. Henderson, while as inconsistent as ever, was an influence. Another source, nearly the antithesis of the bucolic early recordings of the territory bands, was the Casa Loma Orchestra. Although this group is energetically misrepresented in most jazz commentary, several more famous bands attempted exact copies of its manner. Among these are the Blue Rhythm Band's *Blue Rhythm* (Brunswick 6143, 1931), Earl Hines's *Sensational Mood* (Brunswick 6379, 1932), Benny Goodman's *Cokey* (Columbia 3011D, 1934), Jimmy Lunceford's *White Heat* (Victor 24568, 1934) and Henderson's *Tidal Wave* (Bluebird B5682, 1934). Even Ellington's *Crescendo and Diminuendo in Blue* (Sept 1937) echoes the Casa

15. *Bessie Smith, 1936*

16. *Louis Armstrong*

17. Duke Ellington

*18. Art Tatum,
early 1940s*

19. Earl Hines, early 1940s

20. Bix Beiderbecke

*21. Lester Young,
early 1940s*

*22. Bud Powell (right) with
Kenny Clark (drums) and
Pierre Michelot (double bass)*

23. *Jimmy Guiffre (left) with Wilfred Middlebrooks (double bass) and Jim Hall*

24. *Charlie Parker*

25. *Ornette Coleman, late 1970s*

26. *Gil Evans*

27. Serge Chaloff

28. Don Ellis

29. Bill Evans, c1976

30. Martial Solal

Loma's use of low-register clarinets in *A Study in Brown* (Decca 1159, Feb 1937). The Casa Loma's own most representative scores, which range from *Casa Loma Stomp* (Okeh 41492, 1930) to the well-sustained two-part *No Name Jive* (Decca 3089, 1940), are terse projections of a singular kind of ensemble virtuosity, concentrating almost to the point of abstraction on line, mass and shape, rather than colour and texture.

A comparable tendency reached its height in the richly inventive scores that Sy Oliver wrote for Lunceford's band. Among many outstanding pieces are *Organ Grinder's Swing* (Decca 908, 1936), full of extreme yet perfectly apposite contrasts, the headlong *Lonesome Road* (Vocalion 4831, 1939), and *Annie Laurie* (Vocalion 1569, 1937), a remarkable translation into jazz. Such performances demonstrated a considerable extension of the large jazz ensemble's capabilities, and Oliver's (rather than Lunceford's) influence extended from conventional swing bands such as Erskine Hawkins's (e.g. *Rocking Rollers' Jubilee*, Bluebird B7826, 1938) to postwar modernism, as in Gil Fuller's work for Dizzy Gillespie's big band (e.g. *Things to Come*, Musicraft 447, 1946).

Another highly accomplished band displaying similar tendencies, for which Oliver later wrote, was led by the trombonist Tommy Dorsey. He had a strong jazz background from the 1920s, as indicated by solos like the one he took in *Milneburg Joys* (Victor 26437, 1939), and good improvisation was always to be heard from his band, for example by the trumpeters Bunny Berigan in *Marie* (Victor 25523, 1937) and

Max Kaminsky in *Davenport Blues* (Victor 26135, 1938), and the tenor saxophonist Bud Freeman in *Stop, Look and Listen* (Victor 36207, 1937). The ensemble achieved a power and tonal balance attained by few of its rivals and scores such as *Song of India* (Victor 25523, 1937) have much finely integrated detail (and one of Berigan's best-argued solos). The varied and well-ordered incident of *Swanee River* (Victor 27233, 1940) should also be compared with the vehement precision of *Loose Lid Special* (Victor 27526, 1941).

More exploratory was the band of Artie Shaw, who was among the first to take up the vexed question of the role of ensemble strings in a more purely jazz context than Paul Whiteman had essayed. Indeed, such pieces as *Streamline* (Brunswick 7852, 1936) contain the most telling use of strings before Robert Graettinger's work for Stan Kenton. Shaw also pioneered the use of the harpsichord in jazz bands, amid the tightly patterned mosaics of his Gramercy Five, a small band within his larger one, typified by the spruce, energetic *Special Delivery Stomp* (Victor 26762, 1940). In performances of more conventional instrumentation, Shaw's clarinet dominates, conveying a fine excitement. Indeed his solos show him to have been one of the most gifted improvisers in jazz, the solo in *Nightmare* (Bluebird B7875, 1938), for example, being fluid, graceful and full of the blues.

Another band led by a great virtuoso was that of Earl Hines (*b* Pittsburgh, 28 Dec 1903; *d* Oakland, Calif., 22 April 1983), who had begun working with large ensembles earlier than most of those associated with 1930s swing. His 1929 orchestral recordings are distinguished only for his own playing, but with them he established the piano as a viable solo instrument in the context of big bands. *Deep Forest*, an interesting score by Reginald Foresythe (Brunswick (E) 01464, 1932), had more character, and by 1934 such items as *Cavernism* (Brunswick 6541) were anticipating the ensemble complexity of the Lunceford band. Brilliant dialogues between piano and orchestra showed Hines's playing to be even more adventurous, above all rhythmically, than in his days with Armstrong in the 1920s, as in *Maple Leaf Rag* (Decca 218, 1934), a revealing jazz commentary on a ragtime piece. Hines's bandleading activities reached their peak in 1939–41, typified by forceful yet sensitively paced interpretations such as *Lightly and Politely* (Bluebird B10727, 1939) and *Number 19* (Bluebird B10674, 1940), scored by Jimmy Mundy and Buster Harding respectively.

There were many other big ensembles active during the 1930s, notably those led by Benny Carter, Andy Kirk, Chick Webb, Cab Calloway, Charlie Barnet and Harry James, but the archetypal large band of the period was that directed by Benny Goodman (*b* Chicago, 30 May 1909; *d* New York, 13 June 1986). Its unacknowledged ancestor was the music recorded by the more sizable Red Nichols groups in the late 1920s, in some of which Goodman took part (e.g. *Indiana*, Brunswick 4373, 1929). Like the titles issued under Goodman's own name in the early 1930s, the Nichols items were performed by ad hoc ensembles brought together only for recording. Until that time he had played with many important Chicago musicians such as the Austin High School Gang, and his early musical training had included lessons with the Chicago Symphony Orchestra clarinettist Franz Schoepp (who also taught Jimmy Noone). Goodman joined Ben Pollack in 1925 and went to New York with that band in 1928. From 1929 to 1934 he was a leading freelance musician in the city, but in the latter year he formed a permanent band. This soon made its reputation with performances like *King Porter Stomp* (Victor 25090, 1935), scored by Fletcher Henderson and including another outstanding trumpet solo from Bunny Berigan. Henderson was responsible for much of Goodman's early library, and (an important factor in the band's success) he applied his method to current popular songs such as *Blue Skies* (Victor 25136, 1935). Other arrangers for the band in the late 1930s included Jimmy Mundy and Edgar Sampson, who had earlier been associated respectively with the Earl Hines and Chick Webb ensembles.

Goodman's band of those years is the best-remembered, yet his most original orchestral work began in 1939 with Eddie Sauter's arrival. Instead of Henderson's nearly mechanical call-and-response patterns between brass and reeds, Sauter's pieces use an almost infinite variety of instrumental blendings, producing a great range of rich and warm colours and textures. In his hands commonplace songs like *Moonlight on the Ganges* (Columbia GL523, 1940) became miniature tone-poems. Goodman's own clarinet solos grew longer and more adventurous than they had usually been with his large band in the late 1930s. Fiery yet shaped with virtuoso precision, they are marked by countless subtle variations of pitch and inflection, an excellent example being *Clarinet à la King* (Okeh 6544, 1941), one of several imaginative miniature concertos that Sauter composed for Goodman and other members of the band. Goodman and several of his musicians, such as the pianist Teddy Wilson, the vibraharpist Lionel Hampton, the guitarist Charlie Christian and the trumpeter Cootie Williams (the last of whom had been in Ellington's orchestra), were heard at their best, however, in small groups (ranging from trio to septet) which he drew from the band. Some of their work represented another development of the 'jazz chamber music' pioneered by Joe Venuti, Eddie Lang and others of the New York school in the late 1920s.

Throughout the 1940s, 1950s and 1960s Goodman went on leading successful big and small groups, which played a continuation of his earlier music without much change. A minor exception to his success was his inconclusive flirtation with bop in the late 1940s, using a large band playing Chico O'Farrill scores. However, Goodman's Septet, with the trumpeter Fats Navarro and tenor saxophonist Wardell Gray, recorded to excellent effect during this period (*Stealing Apples*, Capitol 10173, 1947). Goodman made a number of foreign tours, even as late as the early 1980s, visiting the Far East and Russia among other places. He also continued to appear and record with various classical ensembles.

Complementary, rather than opposed, to the individual and collective virtuosity associated with ensembles like those mentioned above was the massive simplicity of Count Basie's band, a direct descendant of Moten's. Its vein of expression, bounded by, say, the thoughtful *Good Morning, Blues* (Decca 1446, 1937) and the ebullient *One O'Clock Jump* (Decca 1363, 1937), was narrow yet true. The best part of its repertory consisted of 'head arrangements' worked out by the bandsmen themselves rather than notated. Like pieces by Moten such as *Prince of Wails* (Victor 23393, 1932), these often depended on an interplay between ensemble riffs and improvised solos, as in Basie's *Swinging the Blues* (Decca 1880, 1938). The closely interlocking riffs that are so much a feature of pieces like *One O'Clock Jump* were also anticipated elsewhere, as recordings like Goodman's *Bugle Call Rag* (Columbia 36109, 1934) demonstrate. There are a few early Basie items, such as *Evil Blues* (Decca 2922, 1939), which have a haunted, almost outlandish, atmosphere, suggesting that Basie's music had, for a while, more complex undercurrents than were usually apparent. Basie (*b* Red Bank, NJ, 21 Aug 1904; *d* Hollywood, Florida, 26 April 1984) continued to produce fine music until well into the 1940s (e.g. *Stay Cool*, Parlophone (E) R3009, 1946). But from the early 1950s, when the band's popularity began enormously to increase, its output underwent a steep decline of quality, its character determined by arrangers who were mainly hacks, the solos, Basie's own delightful piano contributions aside, stale and cliché-ridden.

X **1930s soloists**

In happier early days, however, the band had in the tenor saxophonist Lester Young (*b* Woodville, Missississippi, 27 Aug 1909; *d* New York, 15 March 1959) the most innovatory jazz improviser between Louis Armstrong and Charlie Parker. His playing with Basie and in accompaniment to Billie Holiday is widely admired, but he, unlike his former employer's ensemble, remained creative for much longer than is even now generally acknowledged. Among numerous fine examples of his later work is the solo on *Taking a Chance on Love* (Verve MGV8205, 1956), which begins with a brilliant restructuring of the melody, followed by two choruses of free, constantly inventive improvisation (ex.12). It was a portent that Young, like the Goodman musicians mentioned above, worked to greatest advantage in small ensembles. Young's *Lester Leaps In* (Vocalion 5118, 1939) is a classic instance, but many recordings illustrate the point, none better than those few which bring Young and Charlie Christian together, such as *Way down yonder in New Orleans* (Vanguard VRS8523, 1939) from one of the New York 'From Spirituals to Swing' concerts. Their playing indicates with striking clarity the direction jazz was to take in the 1940s, as did that of several other prominent soloists at this time. Among them were the trumpeters Henry Allen, Roy Eldridge and Bunny Berigan, the alto saxophonist and arranger Benny Carter, the tenor saxophonist Chew Berry and the pianist Teddy Wilson.

In response to the obliqueness and subtlety of much of this music, the rhythm section acquired greater

Ex.12(a) *Taking a Chance on love*: opening bars of original melody

(b) Opening of Lester Young's solo from *Taking a Chance on love* (1956), transcr. M. Harrison

suppleness in its articulation of the jazz pulse, and Basie was the unexpected innovator. The first prominent pianist to abandon a literal statement of the beat, he preferred to punctuate; this discontinuity was complemented by a stronger interplay of propulsive accents from the drums and cymbals of the percussionist's enlarged kit and by the greater prominence of the string bass. By the turn of the decade almost every aspect of jazz performance had grown more flexible (though it was still being improvised and written, with very few exceptions, in sequences of 12- and 32-bar segments), and so it again turned into

280

something new. The larger public, whose attention had been caught briefly through the sheer impact of the large bands, lost interest and jazz returned to its earlier status as a minority art.

During these shifts of emphasis established musicians had not been idle. Comment on Armstrong (*b* New Orleans, ?4 July ?1900; *d* New York, 6 July 1971) has centred on his conspicuously innovatory work of the 1920s (see §IV above), yet having abandoned small groups and appearing as a star instrumentalist and singer in front of a large band, he continued to develop musically through the 1930s. One could regard 1935–45 as his peak. A comparison of his two accounts of *West End Blues* (Okeh 8597, 1928; Decca 2480, 1939) shows how much more subtly shaded his playing had become, and there is nothing in his early work to stand beside the reconciliation of power and serenity in *Sleepy Time Down South* (Decca 4140, 1941). Besides being a great musician, Armstrong also had capacities as an entertainer (he appeared in many Hollywood films), and this led to aspects of his career that may be regretted. Comparatively late performances like *Back O' Town Blues* (Victor 404006, 1947) find him, though, improvising with electrifying intensity. 1947 was the year he returned to small bands, and he led his All-Stars on world tours almost for the remainder of his life, having long since come, with Ellington, to symbolize jazz in the popular mind.

The personnel of Ellington's orchestra became less stable in the early 1940s as he lost key players such as Cootie Williams in 1940 and in 1942 Barney Bigard (who later became a founder member of Armstrong's All-Stars). Conferences with his musicians were largely replaced by a dialogue with Billy Strayhorn (*b* Dayton, Ohio, 29 Nov 1915; *d* New York, 31 May 1967), a composer, arranger and pianist who had joined his staff in 1939. Strayhorn contributed many sensitive pieces to Ellington's repertory, such as *Chelsea Bridge* (Victor 27740, 1941), which, typically, is based on a motif from Ravel's *Valses nobles et sentimentales*. A major problem concerning Ellington's later production is that of determining what was composed by Ellington and what by Strayhorn. As with Armstrong, much fine music came from Ellington's later years, notably large works in several movements, such as *Such Sweet Thunder* (Columbia JCL1033, 1956–7) and the *Far-Eastern Suite* (RCA LSP3782, 1966), each of which occupies a 12-inch LP.

Despite precedents in Ellington's own work and elsewhere, like *Reminiscing in Tempo*, such large-scale orchestral concepts belonged to a somewhat later period. In the 1930s and beyond soloists were still of the greatest importance to large bands, and ever since the young Bing Crosby appeared with Paul Whiteman in the late 1920s, these ensembles had usually featured singers as well as instrumentalists. Offering jazz interpretations of popular songs of the day and following a lead given by Ethel Waters in the 1920s, they established a tradition quite separate from that of blues singers (though a very few blues vocalists were associated with the bands, as in Jimmy Rushing's alliance with Basie). Noteworthy among them were another Basie singer, Helen Humes, Ivie Anderson with Ellington, Helen Forrest with Goodman, and many others. The most original went on to independent careers, which in some cases lasted far beyond the big band period and into the 1980s, as was the case with Ella Fitzgerald, who began with Chick Webb, and Peggy Lee, who started with Goodman. Other exceptional singers were Mildred Bailey and Lee Wiley, whose careers effectively began with Whiteman; and there were also a few vocal groups which achieved a comparable individuality of expression, in particular the Boswell Sisters.

The most highly regarded jazz singer, though, was Billie Holiday (*b* Baltimore, 7 April 1915; *d* New York, 17 July 1959), who, after working briefly with Lunceford, Henderson, Basie and Shaw, went, like the others, on a path of her own, performing chiefly in small clubs but also at concerts and, in the 1950s, taking some European trips. She recorded extensively almost throughout her career, being accompanied, especially in the earlier years, by small combos of the finest jazz musicians of the time, often led by Teddy Wilson and featuring Lester Young. Although she claimed Bessie Smith and Louis Armstrong as main influences, Holiday shared a close musical and personal affinity with the great tenor saxophonist, as is suggested by recordings like *This Year's Kisses* (Brunswick 7824, 1937).

Many other players with long-established reputations continued to enrich the musical language of jazz, an outstanding instance being Earl Hines. With his days as a leader of large bands behind him, he had returned to small groups and was an early member of

Armstrong's All-Stars. He also toured internationally on his own account and remained one of the great pianists of jazz until the end of his life. An LP Hines made in 1969 called *Quintessential Recording Session* (Chiaroscuro CR101) consists of lengthy improvisations on such themes as *Chicago High Life* and *Just Too Soon* which he had first recorded over 40 years earlier. They use a far more extensive range of resources, a relentlessly purposeful complexity. Similarly Coleman Hawkins's *Body and Soul* (Bluebird B10523, 1939) achieved a balance of motivic relationships and harmonic exploration which resulted in its being regarded as one of the classics of jazz improvisation (ex.13). His sense of musical adventure led him to work with some of the best postwar modernists, employing the composer and pianist Thelonious Monk in his band, recording with Charlie Parker, Fats Navarro, J. J. Johnson and others. Later extended Hawkins solos like *Bird of Prey Blues* (Felsted (E) FAJ7005, 1958) show a remarkable sense of form. A comparable growth is found in both the alto saxophone playing and arranging of Benny Carter, as demonstrated by such LPs as *Further Definitions* (Impulse 512, 1961) and his long, consistently exploratory set of improvisations with Art Tatum (Clef MGC643, Verve MGV8227, 1954).

Although the most singular virtuoso in jazz history, Tatum (*b* Toledo, Ohio, 13 Oct 1909; *d* Los Angeles, 5 Nov 1956) did not have a career fully commensurate with his gifts. He was only twice invited to appear abroad, and, though he regularly gave concerts from 1945 onwards, most of his performances were

Ex.13(a) *Body and Soul*: final bars of original melody

(b) Bars 25-32 of Coleman Hawkins's solo from *Body and Soul* (1939), transcr. L. Porter

in small clubs. However, he was extensively recorded, particularly during the late 1940s and early 1950s, by which time he had developed the richest harmonic and rhythmic vocabularies to be found in this music (ex.14). The tautly disciplined elaboration of Tatum's final work has remained unmatched, except, perhaps, by one other pianist, Cecil Taylor.

The advance in sophistication demonstrated by such music suggests that as the 1940s progressed the outlook of performers was again changing. For most of their listeners, who was playing remained more important than what was being played, and such an attitude, paralleling that of the audiences of 19th-century European virtuosos, was not unreasonable when much improvising was involved. During the 1930s and later, many jazz performers still regarded themselves primarily as entertainers; but as their skill and knowledge improved they moved towards a strictly musical sense of professionalism and an awareness of jazz as an art. Other factors were their visits to Europe, the appreciation they found there, and being written about, chiefly in European publi-

Ex.14 Opening of the third chorus from Art Tatum's *Aunt Hagar's Blues* (Capitol 15520, 1949), based on a 12 bar progression; transcr. M. Harrison

cations. Contact with other music sometimes followed. In 1938, for example, Benny Goodman recorded Mozart's Clarinet Quintet with the Budapest String Quartet (Victor 1884/8) and commissioned Bartók to write *Contrasts* (Columbia 70362/3, 1940). Even ten years earlier such activities would have been inconceivable for a jazz musician. The titles of jazz pieces, too, began to reflect the performers' wider horizons, instances being Ellington's *Smorgasbord and Schnapps* (Brunswick 8380, 1939) and Fats Waller's *London Suite* (HMV (E) B10059/61, 1939), the six movements of which convey his impressions

287

of parts of that city. Jazz might be a minority art, but it was no longer ghetto music.

XI New Orleans II: a continuing tradition

As a complement to this widening of horizons there was growing interest in earlier jazz. These pauses to take stock were to be a recurring phenomenon, but it was towards the end of the 1930s that jazz first became aware that it had a history. One reason for this was the continuing, sometimes increasing, excellence of the work of long-established players. This usefully contradicted the notion that jazz was exclusively a young man's music. Another factor was such events as the 1938–9 'From Spirituals to Swing' concerts in New York; by putting, for example, a blues shouter like Sonny Terry on the same platform as avant-garde figures like Lester Young and Charlie Christian, these concerts gave the audience a perspective on the music that had previously been available only to comparatively few specialist record collectors, most of them in Europe. Partly an additional cause and partly a result of this concern with jazz history were recordings by Bob Crosby and Muggsy Spanier (with large and small groups respectively) which vigorously reinterpreted the 1920s repertory and new pieces composed in that style. Examples are Crosby's *Dogtown Blues* (Decca 15038, 1937) and Spanier's *Bluing the Blues* (Bluebird B10719, 1939). Comparable recordings were made by others, but none was merely a form of revivalism. Thus Crosby's effective compromise between swing orthodoxy and older jazz had been anticipated, as had part of his repertory, by such performances as Tommy Dorsey's of *Weary Blues* (Victor 25159, 1935); a few Jelly Roll Morton items such as *Burning the Iceberg* (Victor V38075, 1929) had still earlier shown that the New Orleans idiom could be adapted to big-band instrumentation. Music like Spanier's and Crosby's met a warmer response than might have been expected in view of the supposed dominance of swing.

This interest in earlier styles led to two related yet musically different movements. The important one was a seeking-out of older musicians, particularly in New Orleans, where jazz had continued following its own path long after the main interest had supposedly moved to Chicago, New York and elsewhere. Typifying this process are Johnny Bayersdorffer's *I wonder where my easy rider's riding now?* (Okeh 40133, 1924), the Original New Orleans Rhythm Kings' *She's Crying for me* (Okeh 40327, 1925), the New Orleans Owls' *Tampeko* (Columbia 688D, 1926), Sam Morgan's *Mobile Stomp* (Columbia 14258D, 1927), Johnny Miller's *Panama* (Columbia 1546D, 1928) and the Lee Collins–David Jones *Tip Easy Blues* (Bluebird B10952, 1929). These were all recorded in New Orleans but no comparable examples are known to have been made there during the 1930s. By that decade, when New Orleans players ventured elsewhere, their music tended to lose its character, an instance being the work of Joseph Robechaux's band recorded in New York (e.g. *King Kong Stomp*, Vocalion 2539, 1933).

By the time records were again made in New Orleans, however, the local jazz idiom had evolved still further on its own lines. This was not grasped until much later, and so the trumpeter Bunk Johnson (*b* New Orleans, 27 Dec 1889; *d* New Iberia, Louis-

iana, 7 July 1949) was, in the 1940s and after, as con-
troversial and misunderstood a figure as Charlie
Parker or Thelonious Monk. It was partly his fault,
because he added ten years to his age in order to
support a claim that he had played with Buddy
Bolden. Pieces like his *827 Blues* (American Music
644, 1945) were assumed to echo the very beginnings
of jazz while actually they represented the most recent
stage in New Orleans music. The ensemble passages
have an unprecedented fluidity, the leading voice
passing from one instrument to another not only in
mid-chorus but almost in mid-phrase; in fact this
music paralleled the increasing flexibility of jazz elsewhere and was strictly a contemporary manifestation.
Performances such as Johnson's *Golden Leaf Strut*
(American Music 644, 1945) have, too, an airy, dancing lightness which in no way lessens the remarkable
expressiveness of the trumpet, clarinet and trombone
lines. Such performances led New Orleans jazz back
into the mainstream of recording activity.

Along with the best of Johnson's work, the most
representative improvisations of the clarinettist
George Lewis (*b* New Orleans, 13 July 1900; *d* New
Orleans, 31 Dec 1968), like *Burgundy Street Blues*
(American Music 254, 1944), and of the trumpeter
and clarinettist Wooden Joe Nicholas, such as *Up
Jumped the Devil* (American Music 640, 1945), have
not been surpassed as examples of latter-day New
Orleans jazz. Lewis had a longer career than most of
these players, leading bands and touring internationally almost until his death. He had increasing
difficulty in finding suitable musicians for his band,
which gradually lost its distinction; but fine record-

ings in the later New Orleans style were made by others. Outstanding among them is Thomas Valentine's *Handy's Boogie* (Jazz Crusade JC2008, 1965), which includes an exceptionally well-sustained 15-chorus alto saxophone improvisation by John Handy.

Handy plays another piece from the same public recording session, *Uptown Bumps*, with a Bechet-like intensity, and in fact the return to full activity of Sidney Bechet (*b* New Orleans, 14 May 1897; *d* Paris, 14 May 1959) was probably the most important single consequence of this renewed interest in New Orleans jazz. He had performed the music since his youth, and early recordings (see §IV above) prove him to have been one of the first great jazz soloists, and almost certainly its earliest saxophone virtuoso. But he travelled widely in Europe, especially in the 1920s, even going as far as Russia, and so it was not until the 1940s that he recorded consistently. Bechet jointly led a band and made some beautiful recordings with Bunk Johnson (e.g. *Days Beyond Recall*, Blue Note 564, 1945). Yet his was always a personal variant of New Orleans jazz and a version of Earl Hines's *Blues in Thirds* (Victor 27204, 1940) with the composer at the piano is more characteristic. So is the fact that Bechet, like Coleman Hawkins, was not afraid of associating with postwar modernists. What he plays in *Klook's Blues* (Vogue (F) V5018, 1949) with the bop drummer Kenny Clarke or *Rose Room* (Vogue (F) LDM3065, 1957) with the French pianist Martial Solal remains rooted in New Orleans but takes account of much of what had happened elsewhere.

A far more widespread though ultimately insignificant movement was the so-called 'New Orleans revival' which for a time ran parallel with, and appeared to grow out of, interest in genuine New Orleans jazz. This arose out of the desire of amateurs (some of whom later became professionals) to emulate the recordings of Spanier, Crosby and the masters of the 1920s. Over several decades this led to the appearance of countless bands playing the repertory of King Oliver, Louis Armstrong and others in what were supposed to be reproductions of their styles (a claim never made by Muggsy Spanier, still less by Bunk Johnson, least of all by Bechet). As early and late examples show (e.g. Lu Watters's *Memphis Blues*, Jazz Man 2, 1941; Steve Lane's *Shreveport Stomp*, Vintage Jazz Music (E) LC325, 1979), such groups have performed with a technical incompetence and lack of imagination that are the negation of jazz. Yet this distorted echo of the true New Orleans jazz, latterly referred to as 'trad' ('traditional jazz'), spread throughout the world and was still active in the 1980s. It has become the longest-lasting movement in jazz but is the only one to have produced no music of value.

XII The 1940s: bop and beyond

Against such a background the new developments of the 1940s appeared revolutionary and were often so called by those who did not understand the previous decade's music. In fact some of the supposed innovations of 'rebop', 'bebop' and 'bop', as the jazz of the immediate postwar period was called, had been pioneered not only by advanced swing players like Coleman Hawkins and Charlie Christian but also by Beiderbecke and the New York school of the late

1920s. The rhythmic subdivisions of bop that frequently turned it from 4/4 into 8/8 – sometimes 12/8
– time had been anticipated by ragtime performances
like Jim Europe's *Down Home Rag* (Victor 35359,
1913), which, though basically in 2/4, take the quaver
as the beat. Even the alleged innovations of executive
technique, particularly with regard to mobility, had
precedents, as may be heard by comparing the
trumpeter Dizzy Gillespie's virtuoso *Be Bop* (Manor
5000, 1945) with the equally accomplished
Heckler's Hop of Roy Eldridge (Vocalion 3577,
1937) and *Till Times Get Better* (Brunswick 7078,
1929) by Jabbo Smith.

Rather than a new departure, bop is best regarded
as a final intensification of swing, and its essentially
traditional nature is underlined by the strong blues
content in the work of its greatest exponent, the alto
saxophonist Charlie Parker (*b* Kansas City, Missouri,
29 Aug 1920; *d* New York, 12 March 1955). There is,
indeed, little in his background of youthful periods in
territory bands such as that of Jay McShann to suggest the origins of the sophistication found at most
levels in his music. He moved on to the bands of Earl
Hines and Billy Eckstine (a popular singer, once with
Hines), and thereafter performed almost entirely in
small groups. The one in the late 1940s that included
Miles Davis (trumpet) and Max Roach (drums) was
of particular importance. With it and the other bands
he led, Parker recorded prolifically, exerting an influence that changed jazz as Armstrong had done earlier
and Ornette Coleman was to later. What bop in general, and Parker especially, did was to increase the
expressive charge of jazz improvisation: they used

293

more chromatic and convoluted melodic lines in which the more complex organization of pitch and rhythm implied a greater number and variety of passing harmonies. More explicit polyrhythms were important, arising between the soloist and the drummer through a constant juggling of shifting accents within small note values. A splendid example is Parker's *Koko* (Savoy 597, 1945) in which he is heard with the drummer Max Roach. (For Parker's solo part see ex.15.)

Ex.15 Bars 17-24 of the second chorus of Charlie Parker's solo from *Koko* (1945), transcr. M. Harrison

Such a piece could almost be described as a *presto lamentoso*, and in spite of its sometimes rapid tempos bop often had a tragic accent which had only been sounded in jazz by a few of the great blues singers of the 1920s like Ma Rainey or Bessie Smith. Instances are the work of the trumpeter Fats Navarro (e.g. *Webb City*, Savoy 900, 1946), with its equivocation between haunting melancholy and virtuoso assertion, and of Bud Powell, the most influential jazz pianist since Art Tatum (e.g. *Hallucinations*, Clef MGC610,

The 1940s: bop and beyond

1951), whose headlong rushes of notes sweep com-
pulsively across the bar-lines, constantly shifting accents (ex.16). As was to be expected of a music with
quite a long tradition, other emotions were conveyed
by bop, for example the grace and urbanity, at whatever tempo, of the piano playing of Al Haig (e.g.
Mighty like a rose, Swing (F) M33325, 1954) and the
work of J. J. Johnson, a trombonist as original and
as influential as Gillespie or Powell were on players
of their instruments or Parker was on everybody.
Typical of Johnson's early work is the very fast *Rif-
fette* (Savoy XP8086, 1947) with its jagged lines and
rapid-fire uninflected notes; a piece like *Blue Mode*

Ex.16 Opening of the third chorus of Bud Powell's *Hallucinations*
(1951), transcr. M. Harrison

295

(New Jazz 814, 1949) showed, however, that, like Parker or Powell, he could improvise impressive blues. Another aspect of bop is demonstrated by Gillespie who, in such items as *Get Happy* (Comet T7, 1945) presents the most apt comic mask to contrast with the darker shades of experience in which Parker dealt.

Comic or tragic, the intensity of these and comparable performances from the 1940s is something that Gillespie (*b* Cheraw, South Carolina, 21 Oct 1917) was unable, or chose not, to maintain. He led small and large bands well into the 1980s, yet despite his continuing virtuosity, his music scarcely ever again displayed the urgency that always marked it in the 1940s. The first wave of postwar jazz had, in any case, its lighter aspects, best represented by vocalists who sustained the tradition of band singers (discussed in §X above) while echoing the later styles of instrumental jazz. Typical was Anita O'Day (*b* Chicago, 18 Oct 1919), who began with the bands of Herman, Kenton and Gene Krupa. But the most distinguished jazz singer of this period was undoubtedly Sarah Vaughan (*b* Newark, 27 March 1924), whose career also lasted well into the 1980s. She started with the bands of Hines and Eckstine, then spent considerable time with the boppers, recording a superb *Loverman* with Parker and Gillespie (Guild 1002, 1945). Again it is probable that, from the jazz viewpoint, she never surpassed her early work.

Bop, in any case, was something of a private music and, following on from the swing players' growing awareness in the 1930s of jazz as being more than entertainment, the situation of its proponents was comparable with that of 19th-century artists who felt an increasing alienation from society. As noted, many of the outstanding performers of their generation had first congregated in large bands led by Hines, Eckstine and others, but they had little sympathy with such ensembles. The decline of conventional swing bands has been much lamented, but it was musically inevitable as much of the scoring for such groups had become increasingly unrelated to soloists' subtilization of the idiom. As early as Basie's *Taxi War Dance* (Vocalion 4748, 1940) there is an unpleasant contradiction between the almost vocal inflection of Lester Young's beautifully structured tenor saxophone phrases and the mechanical repetitions of the band. Gillespie, together with such composers and arrangers as Tadd Dameron (who went on to exceptional achievements of his own) and Gil Fuller, tried to adapt bop to the big band and inevitably failed. A piece such as Dameron's *Good Bait* (Victor 20-2878, 1947) juxtaposes forward-looking bop solos with backward-looking swing ensembles. It is significant that the few entirely satisfying performances by the large band that Gillespie led for several years, like George Russell's *Cubana Be/Bop* (Victor 20-3145, 1947), went in quite another stylistic direction. The orchestral resources of jazz had grown extensively over the previous 20 years and their next most constructive applications were to come from unpredictable sources.

Links with tradition were nonetheless sometimes plain, as in Woody Herman's group, for example, which began in the 1930s as 'The band that plays the blues'. In 1944–5, however, new personnel turned it into a modernistic ensemble, with the trumpeter Sonny Berman, the trumpeters and arrangers Shorty Rogers and Neal Hefti, the trombonist Bill Harris, the saxophonists Flip Phillips and John LaPorta, the composer, arranger and pianist Ralph Burns, the bass player Chubby Jackson and the drummer Don Lamond. Besides great solo strength the band also developed exceptional virtuosity, so much so that Stravinsky was persuaded to compose his *Ebony Concerto* for it (Columbia 7479M, 1946). More characteristic, though, were pieces like *Apple Honey* (Columbia 36803) and *Blowing Up a Storm* (Columbia 37059, both 1945) which retained strong orchestral impact while reflecting recent developments in jazz. This group was known as Herman's First Herd. Further changes of personnel, bringing in the saxophonists Stan Getz, Zoot Sims, Herbie Steward and Serge Chaloff in particular, led to the Second Herd. It presented jazz that was a degree cooler in items such as Rogers's *Keen and Peachy* (Columbia 38213, 1947) and Jimmy Giuffre's *Four Brothers* (Columbia 38304, 1947) as well as successful extended pieces like Burns's four-part *Summer Sequence* (Columbia 38366/7, 1946–7).

Again, the music of Stan Kenton could almost be said to begin where that of Jimmy Lunceford left off, and the former's *Intermission Riff* (Capitol 298, 1946) uses the same theme as the latter's *Yard Dog Mazurka* (Decca 4032, 1941). Kenton's organization also spanned decades but was at its best in its early years.

The 1940s: bop and beyond

Such pieces as Pete Rugolo's *Fugue for Rhythm Section* (Capitol 10127), *Chorale for Brass, Piano and Bongos* (Capitol 10183) and the eventful *Monotony* (Capitol 10124, all 1947) exemplify a genuinely modern orchestral manner avoiding, even more than Herman, the compromises with swing practice that Gillespie made. This vein was continued with later pieces such as Bill Russo's *Egdon Heath* (Capitol T598, 1954). But there were many versions of Kenton's band. The most jazz-orientated in the conventional sense was the one that recorded pieces like Shorty Rogers's *Jolly Roger* (Capitol 1043, 1950) and Gerry Mulligan's *Young Blood* (Capitol H383, 1952). The most original was the large ensemble with strings that recorded, most notably, the music of Robert Graettinger. His abrupt, incandescent *House of Strings* (Capitol 28009, 1950) puts ensemble strings to their most apt use in jazz. Graettinger's main achievement, however, is his *City of Glass* (Capitol 28062/3, 1951); each of its four movements is fairly brief yet dense with activity, the many strands of the textures being all different but all essential. Nowhere is the powerful imagination that informs this music more apparent than in its sheer compressed force.

Boyd Raeburn's was a short-lived band similar to Kenton's, equally modernistic, as titles like *Boyd Meets Stravinsky* (Jewel GN10002, 1946) rather too overtly suggest. This explosive piece by Ed Finckel has merits, however, as do George Handy's pastel-toned *Yerxa* (Jewel GN10001, 1945) and *Dalvatore Sally* (Jewel D1-1, 1946) with its sharply contrasting moods and tempos. The band also has distinguished soloists like the pianist Dodo Marmarosa and the tenor saxophonist Lucky Thompson.

Of these large ensembles the one that made the most radical departure was that led by Claude Thornhill playing scores by Gil Evans. The addition of french horns and such woodwind as piccolo and bass clarinet to the conventional jazz resources and the reintroduction of the tuba with a more melodic role than it had in the 1920s yielded a strikingly fresh sound. More significant were the climates of feeling, largely new to jazz, which Evans's writing explored. There were a few precedents in scores Eddie Sauter had made for Red Norvo's large band a decade before, such as *Remember* (Brunswick 7896, 1937). Yet Evans handled his material in such a drastic way that it amounted to recomposition in such cases as *Arab Dance* (Columbia 55041, 1946) and *Robbins' Nest* (Columbia 38136, 1947). The extreme individuality of Evans's sense of colour and texture, and his unusually personal harmonic style and skill in variation, are even more apparent in three of Charlie Parker's singular themes: *Anthropology* (Columbia 38224), *Yardbird Suite* (Columbia 39122) and *Donna Lee* (Harmony HL7088, all 1947). The big bands had, in fact, survived by transforming themselves into something different; and later they were to do so again.

XIII The 1950s: cool jazz
Especially in such pieces as *La Paloma* (Columbia 55041, 1947), where what Jelly Roll Morton called 'the Spanish tinge' again emerges from the matrix,

The 1950s: cool jazz

Evans and the Thornhill musicians seem to distance themselves from the emotion expressed, and this was a natural enough reaction to the unselfconscious intensity of bop. This tendency was also apparent in the work of such reed players as Lee Konitz (alto saxophone), Stan Getz (tenor saxophone) and others. But some of the most significant developments in this new 'cool' manner were made by ensembles, and this was a portent for the future.

The most direct consequence of Evans's initiatives was a dozen 1949–50 recordings made by Miles Davis (*b* Alton, Ill., 25 March 1926) with a nonet which reduced the Thornhill instrumentation to its essentials. Items like *Boplicity* (Capitol 60011, 1949) and *Moondreams* (Capitol EAP1-459, 1950), both scored by Evans, made more concentrated use of the recent discoveries. The repertory consisted largely of 'compositions for band' of the type first found in the late 1920s, the composer and arranger having become one, in the manner of Ellington. There are many indications of how jazz would move in future, an instance being the modality of *Israel* (Capitol 60011, 1949). This memorable reinterpretation of the blues by John Carisi is in the Dorian mode. These strikingly original performances include fine improvised solos from Davis's trumpet, from Gerry Mulligan (baritone saxophone), Lee Konitz and others who were to shape the jazz of the next few years. But it was the scores by Evans, Carisi, Mulligan and John Lewis that broke new ground. Several years later Davis and Evans further explored the worlds of sound and expression discovered with these short pieces. In *Miles Ahead*

(Columbia CL1041, 1957) and *Porgy and Bess* (Columbia CL1274, 1958) a number of items are linked in continuous musical frescos, using the double-sided 12-inch LP to dictate form, just as earlier musicians had used the ten-inch 78 r.p.m. disc which was then the norm. Complementing the passionate intensity of Davis's improvisations on trumpet and flugelhorn, Evans contributes the most original jazz orchestral writing since Ellington's of 1938–42, and the latter record offers a singular instrumental reinterpretation of Gershwin's opera. Also relevant is the Evans–Davis *Sketches of Spain* (Columbia CL1480, 1959–60), which includes a thoroughgoing recomposition of Rodrigo's *Concierto de Aranjuez*. Also using a large ensemble like the Davis–Evans collaborations, yet achieving comparable intimacy, John Carisi's *Moon taj* and *Angkor Wat* (Impulse A9, 1961) traverse similar territory by a different route. Here themes and conventional structure dissolve, and these pieces, vibrant with shifting lines and colours, are at once precise and elusive. Carisi described them as 'tonal and serial'.

Such comments raise interesting points (to be taken up again below, see §XIV), but unfortunately little more was heard from Carisi himself. Gil Evans (*b* Toronto, 13 May 1913) went on to a major, if intermittent, career as a bandleader, gaining international recognition in the 1960s and 1970s as the most original writer for large jazz ensembles since Ellington (e.g. *Gil Evans at the Montreux Jazz Festival*, Philips (J) RL6043, 1974).

Earlier work of related aesthetic intent was that of

the highly literate West Coast group of the 1950s, centred on Los Angeles. This was comparable with the New York group of the late 1920s in that although it included some excellent improvisers – for example the alto saxophonists Art Pepper, Herb Geller and Bud Shank and the pianists Carl Perkins, Russ Freeman and Lou Levy – it was concerned largely with technical sophistication and the extension of the musical language of jazz. An impressive variety of improvisational and compositional procedures was tellingly used, mainly with small ensembles. Examples are Jimmy Giuffre's densely contrapuntal treatment of *My Funny Valentine* (Atlantic 1238, 1956), the 4th-chord harmony of Lyle Murphy's *Fourth Dimension*, the polytonality of his *Poly-doodle* (both Contemporary C3506, 1955) and of Duane Tatro's *Easy Terms*, the modality of the latter's *Backlash* and the counterpoint of his *Outpost*, pursued in clashing streams of independent triads (all Contemporary C3514, 1955). These are mostly in the 'composition for band' genre, as are Jack Montrose's carefully developed *Etude de concert* and Shorty Rogers's *Shapes, Motions, Colours* (both Contemporary C2511, 1953–4). The less formal side of the school's activities may be represented by Rogers's *Sam and the Lady* (Capitol T2025, 1951), the playing of Herb Geller in *Jazz Studio 2* (Decca DL8079, 1954) and performances by the Gerry Mulligan Quartet like *Nights at the Turntable* (Pacific Jazz 602, 1952).

Apart from Mulligan's commercially successful group, this music received little attention. It ought to have broadened the horizons of jazz but is one of a number of examples in the music's history of initiatives not being taken up. The same could be said of the work of Lennie Tristano and the musicians associated with him, though two of his recordings, *Intuition* and *Digression* (both Capitol EAP1-491, 1949), were belatedly recognized as having anticipated the 'free jazz' of the 1960s and after. (This is also true of a fairly similar West Coast collective improvisation, the Rogers–Giuffre–Shelly Manne *Abstract no.1*, Contemporary C3584, 1954.) At least until George Russell established a comparable position some years later, Tristano was the sole jazz musician of standing who was regarded in the jazz world as a distinguished teacher, and his pupils included Lee Konitz (alto saxophone), Warne Marsh (tenor saxophone) and Billy Bauer (guitar). Though appearing rarely in public, he made some fine recordings with certain of his pupils, such as *Crosscurrent* (Capitol 57-60003, 1949), marked by a supple linear astringency. Tristano's best music, however, is in his piano solos, both early and late, instances being *Reiteration* (Prestige 7250, 1949) and *G Minor Complex* (Atlantic 1357, 1962). These demonstrate his ability to develop ideas with spontaneous fire yet to play them immaculately, to reconcile musical sophistication with an essentially intuitive approach to improvisation.

XIV Jazz composition II

Such paradoxes recall the skills of Morton and Ellington in fusing improvisation with composition, and this practice was continued after World War II not only by Ellington himself but by several others besides Gil Evans, most of them pianists. Thelonious Monk (*b* Rocky Mount, North Carolina, 10 Oct 1917; *d* Englewood, NJ, 17 Feb 1982) was an uncommonly original pianist with regard to the sounds he drew from the instrument, the technique he used for doing so and the way he employed them in the textures of small ensembles. Despite the more obviously radical departures of wind players, there is no better instance of the extent to which jazz musicians can develop an independent approach to an instrument. The best of Monk's early recordings contain his finest work. He later re-recorded many of his themes too frequently but the initial versions of *Evidence* (Blue Note 549), *Mysterioso* (Blue Note 560), *Epistrophy* (Blue Note 548, all 1948), *Criss Cross* and *Eronel* (both Blue Note 1590, both 1951) and a few other pieces convey the essence of what he had to offer: an unusually acute awareness of the expressive weight of melodic, rhythmic and harmonic relationships pursued, with a rigour uncommon in jazz, in forceful yet curiously abstract studies of specific musical ideas. Some appear to be almost excessively simple, as in his blues, *Straight, No Chaser* (Blue Note 1589, 1951), which has to do with fluctuations between major and minor ('blue') thirds. A more elaborate case is *Skippy* (Blue Note 1602, 1952), which puts flattened fifths to different but related uses. It follows that an exceptional level of thematic, or motivic, consciousness was demanded of Monk's musicians, and only a few achieved organic improvisations on – or rather in – his compositions; they included Milt Jackson (vibra-

305

harp) and Art Blakey (drums) in all but the last of the items mentioned above, and Lucky Thompson (tenor saxophone) in *Skippy*.

Unusually for a jazz musician, Monk did not begin recording until he was 30, by which time he had a sizable body of mature compositions ready. Their uncompromising character led to his being neglected for many years, though eventually he won considerable popularity, and toured the world. In his early, and most creative, years Monk was thought to be linked with the boppers, although, as both a composer and improviser, his was always an independent line of endeavour. This was also true of Tadd Dameron (*b* Cleveland, 21 Feb 1917; *d* New York, 8 March 1965). If Monk in the 1960s became less adventurous, Dameron was conservative in the better sense from the start – a rarity in jazz. He wrote several memorable though scarcely boppish scores for Gillespie's large band, such as *Our Delight* (Musicraft 399, 1946), yet he achieved his best results independently with more intimate groups. Examples are *Casbah* (Capitol 57-60006, 1949) and *Fontainebleau* (Prestige S7842, 1956) which tend, with their careful developments and contrasts, towards the Ellingtonian tone-poem for band. Monk and, even more, Dameron were thwarted in the realization of their gifts through being prevented during their most productive years from maintaining a regular ensemble. A jazz composer must do this if he is to profit from collaboration with a group of improvisers sufficiently familiar with his work to contribute to it creatively. Like Monk, however, Dameron produced good work early in his career, particularly with a group that included Fats

Navarro, the trumpeter, who was his most perceptive interpreter; a notable example is the extended version of *Good Bait* (Manor (E) M503, 1948).

John Lewis (*b* Le Grange, Ill., 3 May 1920) was more fortunate with the Modern Jazz Quartet (MJQ), which became one of the longest-lasting ensembles in jazz history, with only one personnel change in 21 years until 1974; it broke up, re-formed, and was still active in the 1980s. This band, too, was stylistically conservative but in its earlier years was adventurous with form. Milt Jackson's vibraharp playing was always the most immediate attraction and was heard to greatest advantage within the sort of framework provided by a Monk or a Lewis. More original, though, was the MJQ's integration of all elements, both in collective improvisation and in pieces that adapt Baroque procedures such as the triple fugue *Three Windows* (Atlantic 1284, 1957). The fullest realization of the MJQ's powers, standing with the best work of Morton, Ellington or George Russell, is *The Comedy* (Atlantic S1390, 1960–62), an LP-length composition in several movements. Other aspects of Lewis's gifts as a composer have been neglected because of the long life of the MJQ. They are exemplified by such lucidly argued pieces as *Sketch 1*, recorded by J. J. Johnson (Blue Note BLP5028, 1953), and *Three Little Feelings* (Columbia CL941, 1956) for brass ensemble.

Less well known is the large and exceptionally consistent body of music produced by George Russell (*b* Cincinnati, 23 June 1923). The carefully ordered and densely packed detail of *The Bird in Igor's Yard* (Capitol (H) 5C052.80853, 1949) confirmed the independence suggested by *Cubana Be/Bop*, written for Gillespie. More singular than these orchestral pieces, however, were *Odjenar* (Prestige 753) and *Ezz-thetic* (Prestige 843, both 1951), probing compositions for small ensemble recorded by Miles Davis and Lee Konitz. Russell went on to develop a system of harmonic relationships, based on modality, which he called the 'Lydian Chromatic Concept of Tonal Organization'; this was described by John Lewis as the first contribution made by jazz to the theory of music. Russell's work in the 1950s and later maintained a strong personal identity not only in its harmonic tissue but also in its melodic and rhythmic configurations and in the unusual challenges it set for improvisers – challenges fully met by such players as Art Farmer (trumpet), Bill Evans (piano) and Barry Galbraith (guitar). Examples include *Lydian M-1*, recorded by the vibraharpist Teddy Charles (Atlantic 1229), *Knights of the Steamtable* (Victor LPM2534, both 1956) and *The Day John Brown was Hanged*, an impressively sustained piece, yet as tersely astringent as the rest, recorded by the alto saxophonist Hal McKusick (Victor LPM1336, 1957).

As with the MJQ, collective improvisation within carefully devised frameworks was one of the two main aims, if not often the achievement, of Charles Mingus's Jazz Workshop, the other being an attempt at breaking the boundaries of repeating 12- and 32-bar chord sequences. The latter were becoming ever more constricting as bases for improvisation in view of the sheer density of musical incident that characterized the best jazz performances of the 1950s. Before Mingus, there were a few attempts at getting away from the *AABA* pattern of four 8-bar phrases of popular song form, and some of these should be mentioned. They include the 12 + 8 + 12 structure of Ellington's *Hip Chick* (Brunswick 8221, 1938) and, considerably later, John Lewis's *S'il vous plaît*, recorded by Miles Davis's 'Capitol' band (Cicala (I) BLJ8003, 1950), which has 12 + 12 + 8 + 12, and Duane Tatro's *Dollar Day* (Contemporary C3514, 1955), which has 12 + 12 + 12 + 4 + 12. More enterprising is Teddy Charles's *Wailing Dervish* (Prestige 164, 1953), in which the rondo-like 64-bar chorus is in the pattern *ABACADA*. In all such cases, however, the principle of a repeating chord sequence is retained. More indicative of later developments was Charles's *Variations on a Motive by Bud [Powell]* (Prestige 164, 1953) in which there is no recurring harmonic substructure and improvisations are based on an irregular fluctuation between two key-centres a semitone apart. Other performances, apparently following Lennie Tristano's initiatives of 1949 noted above, drew close to free collective improvisation, among them Teo Macero's *Explorations* (Debut DLP6, 1953).

Mingus (*b* Nogales, Arizona, 22 April 1922; *d* Cuernavaca, Mexico, 8 Jan 1979) was the bass player on that item and Macero (tenor saxophone) in turn participated in Mingus's *Minor Intrusion* (Bethlehem BCP65, 1954), which is a more systematic attempt at devising a structure not founded on a constantly repeating chord sequence. It is based on the opposition

of two different moods or atmospheres which sometimes interrupt and sometimes interact with each
other; at one point there is interesting use of quarter-
tones. Further significant pieces by Mingus include
Love Chant, with its conventional yet greatly slowed-
down and extended chord sequence, and the incanta-
tory, partly onomatopoeic *Pithecanthropus erectus*
(both Atlantic 1237, 1956), one of a number of large,
often programmatic works, sometimes of LP length,
that he undertook. Usually the improvisers had considerable freedom, in solos and ensembles, but
Mingus, a virtuoso bass player, sought to control the
music's shape and direction from the centre of the
ensemble. A man of unstable temperament, however,
he rarely held a band together long enough for his
musicians to become a fully integrated team, although
inspired moments were not infrequent. Perhaps the
group which made the LP *East Coasting* (Bethlehem
BCPS6019, 1957), with Clarence Shaw (trumpet),
Jimmy Knepper (trombone), Bill Evans (piano) and
others, was the only completely satisfying band with
which Mingus ever recorded. It is unfortunate that
some of the initiatives in Mingus's work in the early
1950s were never specifically taken up by others. He
himself went in other directions and one may regard
his later output with diminishing enthusiasm.

Meanwhile the high dissonance level of such pieces
as Cecil Taylor's *Tune 2* (Transition 19, 1957)
bordered on atonality and implied, despite the elaborate 88-bar chorus that underlies it, that the hurried,
restricted excursion jazz had made into European
harmonic and other borrowings was nearing an end.

Jazz composition II

The potentially productive dialogue between residual tonal logic and that suggested by atonality (hinted at in such Taylor performances as *Of What*, Contemporary C3652, 1958) was, again, never coherently exploited, least of all by Taylor himself. By this time, however, there had been several attempts at using serial technique, or at least in some way adapting it to jazz. As the music approached chromatic saturation, this was predictable, but the matter had been raised much earlier, at least from outside. Ernst Krenek had incorporated jazz and ragtime elements in the atonal fabric of his opera *Der Sprung über den Schatten* (1923). Serial technique appears in Mátyás Seiber's *Jazzolettes* (1929–32), in the second of which the trumpet leads off with a complete 12-note row which is promptly inverted by the trombone. More elaborate and much less impressive is Rolf Liebermann's Concerto for Jazzband and Symphony Orchestra (1954). At this date jazz musicians became involved. Both Shorty Rogers's *Three on a Row* (Contemporary C3584) and Duane Tatro's *Turbulence* (Contemporary C3514, both 1954) deploy serial procedures in simple but effective ways, Teo Macero's *24+ 18+* (Columbia CL842, 1955) with greater elaboration. The Mátyás Seiber–John Dankworth Improvisations for Jazzband and Symphony Orchestra of 1959 (Saga (E) X1P 7006) succeeded where Liebermann had failed, for this substantial yet forgotten piece fuses jazz improvisation with a highly accomplished use of serial composition: there is here a true meeting of minds, and musics. Also lengthy, Don Ellis's Improvisational Suite no.1 (Candid 8004, 1960) significantly tilts the balance in favour of improvisation while responding to certain of Stockhausen's ideas about time and tempo. An uncommonly percipient explorer, Ellis (*b* Los Angeles, 25 July 1934; *d* Hollywood, 17 Dec 1978) also worked with George Russell and was soon to be involved with fruitful alliances between jazz and Indian musical methods (see §XV below).

In Bill Evans's *Twelve-tone Tune* (Columbia C30855, 1971) a note-row is harmonized tonally though with much chromatic alteration, 4th-chords etc, and this is typical of the way such musicians continued to expand traditional resources (ex.17). Evans (*b* Plainsfield, NJ, 16 Aug 1929; *d* New York, 15 Sept 1980) was the most influential jazz pianist since Bud Powell and one of the most widely capable of any period. He worked mainly in a trio format with bass and drums, these ensembles tending towards a degree of collective improvisation. But he was able to meet the demands of the Miles Davis sextet that made *Kind of Blue* (Columbia CL1355, 1959) and of such composers as George Russell, Charles Mingus and Milton Babbitt. Evans's own manner was usually introspective, with a wider range of touch and greater use of the sustaining pedal than had been customary with jazz pianists. The resulting diversity of tone-colour was allied to an unusually free vein of melodic invention and to a subtle harmonic idiom often conveyed with highly syncopated left-hand chords. Even in his trio performances the effect was to weaken the conventional feeling of metre. *Kind of Blue* also made a radical move away from harmony as a structural determinant of jazz improvisation. The themes of the

Jazz composition II

Ex.17(a) Original note row

(b) Opening of Bill Evans's *Twelve-tone Tune* (1971), transcr. M. Harrison

five tracks and all the solos derive from various scales instead of from chord sequences. *So What*, for example, uses the Dorian mode. Its 32-bar chorus follows a conventional *AABA* pattern and the same eight-bar melodic phrase is heard in all four sections; the *A* sections, though, are in the Dorian mode on D, the *B* section in the same but on E♭, providing an

313

element of contrast without harmonic implications. Modality was often used to obscure the harmony without denying the presence, or the gravitational effect, of a tonal centre. An advantage was that the soloist, released from the syntax and timing of tonal harmony, no longer had to keep to a precise chordal timetable. This had been partly anticipated by a few players like Lester Young, who were oblique in their approach to chord changes and phrase-lengths. *Kind of Blue* was another in the long series of LPs (also including the Capitol *Birth of the Cool* recordings and the Gil Evans initiatives, see §XIII above) that Davis continued to issue into the 1980s and which were highly influential in the character of their music and the methods it embodied and because they introduced many young players who went on to notable careers of their own. Two further examples are *ESP* (Columbia CL2350, 1965) with Wayne Shorter (tenor saxophone), Herbie Hancock (piano), Tony Williams (drums) and others, and *In a Silent Way* (Columbia CS9875, 1969) with Chick Corea and Joe Zawinul (electric pianos), John McLaughlin (guitar) and others.

A musician earlier brought forward by Davis was John Coltrane (*b* Hamlet, North Carolina, 23 Sept 1926; *d* New York, 17 July 1967), who had already done notable work under Monk's leadership. Following on the departures of *Kind of Blue*, Coltrane, a virtuoso on tenor and soprano saxophones, in pieces such as *Mr Knight* (Atlantic 1382, 1960), retained links with traditional blues playing while allowing harmony little influence on the melodic line. In his

314

version of *My Favourite Things* (Atlantic 1361, 1960)
more drastically irregular phrase-lengths obscure the
four- and eight-bar divisions of the substructure and
notes not belonging to the prevailing mode are used.
This is taken further in *India* (Impulse A542, 1961),
resulting in a sort of modal chromaticism. Such performances were the work of Coltrane's celebrated
quartet, in which, over ostinatos on piano and bass,
the leader and the drummer (Elvin Jones) conducted
long, often furious, dialogues. This, again, was a
highly influential group. In fact the use of modal
devices became widespread not only in pure improvisation but also in more formal situations, even
penetrating the relatively enclosed world of Duke
Ellington. The theme of the 'Blue Pepper' movement
of his *Far-Eastern Suite* (RCA LSP3782, 1966), for
example, is built on three different eight-note scales
over a pedal point, a version of this procedure having already appeared in John Graas's *Id* (Decca
DL8677, 1957).

Harmony played only a small part, too, in shaping
the music produced by hard bop groups like Art
Blakey's Jazz Messengers (*Buhaina's Delight*, Blue
Note BLP4104, 1961) and Horace Silver's Quintet
(*Finger Popping*, Blue Note BLP4008, 1959). A few
earlier ventures such as Coleman Hawkins's unaccompanied tenor saxophone solo *Picasso* (based on
the chords of *A Prisoner of Love*, Clef MGC674,
1948) suggested a desire to escape conventional
accompaniments. Relevant too are Art Tatum's *Mr
Freddy Blues* (20th Century-Fox 3033, 1950), in which
dissonant tone-clusters reinforce the cross-rhythms

but are harmonically non-functional, and Cecil Taylor's *Nona's Blues* (Verve 8238, 1957) which uses sophisticated, virtually atonal harmony yet creates a prophetically un-European sound and feeling strengthened by the tárogato-like tone of Steve Lacy's soprano saxophone.

XV The 1960s: freedom and exoticism

It seemed as if jazz were about to enact its own 'decline of the West' and the virtual abandonment of harmony by the alto saxophonist Ornette Coleman (*b* Fort Worth, 19 March 1930) was less surprising than it appeared in the early 1960s. The underlying chaconne principle of jazz had produced increasingly top-heavy results as the music's resources had continued to expand on all except the structural level. The best of Coleman's efforts, such as his long *Cross Breeding* solo (Atlantic 1394, 1961), one of the great recorded jazz improvisations, showed that it was at last possible for an improviser (as distinct from a composer like Ellington) to alter the time-scale of this music to produce larger organic wholes. Another, still more remarkable case was his *Free Jazz* (Atlantic 1364, 1960), a seamless LP-length collective improvisation by eight players. The freely roving melodies of these and other performances of Coleman's such as *Congeniality* (Atlantic 1317, 1959; ex. 18) looked back beyond jazz, beyond the blues and other related music, to the folklike innocence of Vera Hall's *Trouble so Hard* (see §I above). It already seemed to promise a new beginning for jazz as an independent music

purged of its European borrowings. The freedom
jazz had apparently won began to look as if it were
part of the movement, in science and philosophy as
well as the arts, that tended to consider and express
the world in terms of possibility rather than necessity.

Ex.18 Opening of Ornette Coleman's solo from *Congeniality* (1959),
transcr. M. Harrison

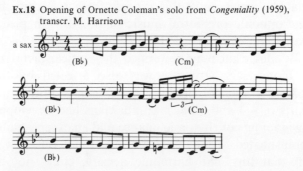

This separation was seemingly confirmed by the
tenor saxophonist Albert Ayler. Though its extremely
simple thematic bases had been anticipated by Coltrane (e.g. *Blues to Bechet*, Atlantic 1382, 1960),
Ayler's work, with its melismatic lines, harsh vocalization of timbre and use of registral extremes,
rejected European procedures even more fiercely than
Coleman's. Such pieces as *Ghosts* (Debut (D) DEB
144, 1964) and *Spirits Rejoice* (ESP 1020, 1965)
are typical in that they demonstrate a break-up of the
structural background of jazz. Repeating harmonic
cycles had already gone; now steady pulse and metre
disappear, as does equal-temperament tuning. Groups
like the New York Contemporary Five (e.g. *When
Will the Blues Leave?*, Polydor (E) 623234, 1963) and
the New York Art Quartet (e.g. *No.6*, ESP 1004,

317

1964) were working out methods of ensemble structure dependent on contrapuntal motivic development. Following the initiative of Coleman's *Free Jazz*, further tightly-knit LP-length collective improvisations such as Don Cherry's *Complete Communion* (Blue Note BLP4226, 1965), using several carefully related themes, took this process further, as did the heterophonic orchestral music of Sun Ra, in pieces like *Other Worlds* (ESP 1014, 1965).

Besides what may be termed the vertical factor of harmony, jazz structure was also affected by the horizontal ones of rhythm, metre, tempo. Within the limits of 4/4 and 12/8, jazz musicians had developed a wide range of rhythmic nuance and an exceptionally sophisticated approach to musical time. But it was felt that this, like harmonic density, could not be taken further without radical changes, the first affecting what had hitherto been one of the most prominent features of jazz in all styles: its constant tempos. 'Free' tempos (rubato, accelerandos, ritardandos) became factors virtually for the first time and are found in, for example, Don Ellis's *How Time Passes* (Candid 8004, 1960) and Charles Mingus's *Black Saint and Sinner Lady* (Impulse AS35, 1963). Of particular interest is Coleman's *Lonely Woman* (Atlantic 1317, 1959), in which only the drums keep a strict tempo while the alto saxophone, trumpet (Don Cherry) and double bass not only play at different tempos but do so with considerable rubato.

Another factor was what might be called 'melodic' drumming. It had begun in bop with, say, the poly-

The 1960s: freedom and exoticism

rhythmic interlocking of Charlie Parker's alto saxophone lines and Max Roach's elaborate drumming.
The role of percussion was further enhanced in hard
bop, especially by Art Blakey, and this was extended
in free jazz by percussionists like Sunny Murray and
Milford Graves. In such music the traditional rhythm
section almost disappeared: the double bass's part
was now melodic, the piano, because of its equal-
temperament tuning, had gone.

In the sphere of metre, there had been isolated early
ventures into 3/4 time, such as James P. Johnson's
1918 piano roll *Eccentricity* (Biograph BLP1001Q)
and Benny Carter's *Waltzing the Blues* (Vocalion (E)
S19, 1936). Later ventures, such as Dave Brubeck's
highly publicized records *Time Out* (Columbia
CS8192, 1960) and *Time Further Out* (CS8490, 1961),
if more systematic, were notable mainly for the
beautiful alto saxophone improvisations of Paul
Desmond. More relevant to the growth of jazz resources were Don Ellis's subsequent *Barnum's Re-
venge* in 7/4, *Upstart* in 11/8 (both Pacific Jazz
PJ10123, 1967) and *Indian Lady* in 5/4 (Columbia
CS9585, 1968). Several features of this music, among
them its intricate recurring patterns of stress, were a
consequence of Ellis's involvement with Indian music.
The situation was now comparable with that reached
earlier in European art music. While a universal
system of tonality prevails, folk and similar material
can provide little more than touches of colour, but
when tonality weakens it becomes possible for
hitherto extraneous elements to affect the musical
language and furnish the basis for new styles. And

319

this is what happened: jazz went through a period of exoticism.

For example John Coltrane's group, with changes in personnel such as the addition of Eric Dolphy (flute, bass clarinet, alto saxophone), and Rashied Ali to supplement then replace Elvin Jones, began to try various supposedly African and vaguely 'eastern' devices. Usually this was only at a superficial level, as in the LP *Meditations* (Impulse AS9110, 1966), in which the teaming of Jones and Ali is supposed to approximate to African rhythmic complexity. Elsewhere there was much talk of affinities with African music, mostly without anything specific being said as to which African music. Jazz musicians had little contact with the real thing and no evident awareness of increased activity in ethnomusicology, in spite of Eric Dolphy implausibly claiming the influence of African pygmies on his work. A few meetings did take place, but these resulted in crude juxtapositions rather than fusion, an instance being Jean-Luc Ponty and Sahib Shihab's *Jazz Meets Arabia: Noon in Tunisia* (BASF/MPS (G) ST20640, 1966), which presents jazz improvisation over a dense and unrelated foundation of north African rhythms. More convincing is the incorporation of Bantu and Zulu elements into Chris McGregor's *Brotherhood of the Breath* (RCA (E) STNE2, 1971), played by British and expatriate South African musicians. A related case is the partnership between cool Swedish jazz and Turkish folk music in the Sevda ensemble's *Maffy Faly* (Caprice Riks (Sd) LP31, 1971).

The other distant culture that seemed most relevant

was that of India, and here the matter went beyond a mere romantic attraction because the long tradition of improvisation on ragas did have parallels with free jazz. As in the African flirtations, most jazz musicians had little understanding of the procedures of Indian music, but Ravi Shankar performed effectively with such jazz players as Paul Horn (*Portrait of a Genius*, World Pacific WPS1432, 1965). Horn was involved in other fruitful partnerships of this kind, notably *Paul Horn in India* (World Pacific WPS1447, 1967) and *Paul Horn in Kashmir* (WPS1445, 1967), the former with pupils of Shankar, the latter with Kashmiri musicians. In all cases the pieces are identified by the ragas used. Another associate of Shankar's, Hari Har Rao, formed the Hindustani Jazz Sextet, which flourished in the mid-1960s, with the trumpeter Don Ellis. As well as trumpet and sitar, the instrumentation included alto and tenor saxophones, tabla, dholaka and so on. Besides this group's work, note should be taken of Ellis's unrecorded *Synthesis*, performed in 1966 by the Hindustani Jazz Sextet and the Los Angeles Neophonic Orchestra, which successfully employed two contrasting ragas as sources of thematic material and bases for improvisation; Ellis's *New Nine* (Pacific Jazz 20112, 1965) used melodic material derived from a raga and a blues. Surprisingly, however, the most fully integrated results were obtained in Britain, by the Joe Harriott–John Mayer Double Quintet. Harriott was a jazz alto saxophonist from Jamaica, Mayer an Indian violinist with a command of European compositional techniques. They used a larger team

321

of Indian and jazz musicians than Ellis and Hari Har Rao, and in such works as Mayer's lengthy *Partita* (Columbia (E) SCX6122, 1967) fused unconstrained Indian and jazz improvisations within frameworks shaped by the composer from both Indian and European musical elements.

The bossa nova (Portuguese slang for 'new touch') was a milder exotic element. Rather like South African *kwela*, this is an example of a partly folk and partly popular music being influenced by jazz, mainly through recordings, and jazz borrowing back from the result. It is also related to the 'Spanish tinge', which had surfaced in such pieces as Morton's piano solo *Tia Juana* (1924) and at several later stages in jazz history. A good example of bossa nova music is João Gilberto's *Chega de Saudade* (Odeon (Ar) MOFB3073, 1959) which presents romantic melodies with light accompaniments using modifications of one of the three basic samba rhythms. The infusion of jazz lent this music greater substance, as was first demonstrated by *Holiday in Brazil* (World Pacific WP1259, 1959) by the West Coast alto saxophonist Bud Shank and the Brazilian guitarist Laurindo Almeida, who had begun exploring jazz and Brazilian fusions as early as 1953 (before the bossa nova existed in Brazil). The definitive jazz and bossa nova alliances, however, are associated with the tenor saxophonist Stan Getz. These are *Jazz Samba* by Getz and Charlie Byrd (Verve 8432, 1962) and *Getz-Gilberto* by Getz, João and Astrud Gilberto (Verve 8545, 1964). Also noteworthy is Paul Desmond's *Bossa Antigua* (RCA LPM3320, 1965).

XVI **New resources**

Within the context of these African, Indian and Brazilian adventures some aspects of European music almost seemed like another exotic resource. There was more extensive use of such instruments as flute, oboe, french horn etc, this having started not with the West Coast school of the 1950s but in the 1920s with Paul Whiteman, a more influential figure than is usually admitted. At this earlier period contact with European classical music sometimes led gifted musicians to leave jazz or at least feel dissatisfied with it. The Spanish composer and pianist Federico Elizalde, whose bandleading exerted an important influence on the development of jazz in Britain during the late 1920s and early 1930s, wrote large-scale jazz pieces such as *The Heart of a Nigger* (Decca (E) K686/7, 1933) and *Bataclan*, but finally devoted himself to symphonic composition and conducting. Mel Powell, a brilliant pianist, after working extensively in jazz (particularly with Benny Goodman) went on to study with Hindemith at Yale and to compose music untouched by jazz.

Some of the finest early jazz musicians seemed to be aware of the limitations of their music, Bix Beiderbecke probably being the first to sense them and the first to take an interest, during his short life (1903–31), in modern European music. Relevant too are Charlie Parker's remarks when, a generation later, he applied to Edgard Varèse for composition lessons: 'Take me as you would a baby, and teach me music. I only write in one voice. I want to have structure. I want to write orchestral scores.' Especially in view of

323

what Ornette Coleman was to do a generation later, it is striking that Parker, one of the most creative musicians in jazz, should have felt this need for a fresh start. More remarkable is that he should have had the insight to approach Varèse who, among other things, pioneered the breakdown between stylized 'musical' sound and 'noise'. However, Beiderbecke, Parker and others seem never to have doubted that solutions to the formal problems of jazz could be found within the resources of the European tradition.

One reason the situation looked so different by the 1960s was that there were now musicians, only a few initially, who were at ease in both jazz and classical music. Among them were the pianists Bill Evans from jazz and Friedrich Gulda from classical music. This was among the factors leading to the concept of 'third-stream' music, a term coined by Gunther Schuller which originally referred to works that synthesized the essential characteristics and techniques of Western art music with those of jazz. In one sense all jazz can be described as third-stream music, yet the movement so specified gave rise to outstanding pieces, among them the Dankworth–Seiber Improvisations for Jazzband and Symphony Orchestra (see §XIV above). Other examples were Harold Shapero's *On Green Mountain*, a kind of jazz chaconne on Monteverdi's *Zefiro torna*, Milton Babbitt's *All Set*, in which all parameters are serialized in what sounds like a particularly intense collective improvisation (both Columbia WL127, 1956), and most of the items on the Teo Macero–Bob Prince *What's New?* disc (Columbia CL842, 1955–6). Several of Gulda's large-scale ventures have retained their interest, among them his *Music for Four Soloists and Band* (Polydor (G) 583.709, 1965), a sort of jazz concerto grosso in which a large band of conventional instrumentation acts as ripieno to the concertino of Freddy Hubbard, J. J. Johnson, Sahib Shihab and the composer himself. The most valuable works from this earlier phase of third stream, however, are Schuller's own *Variants on a Theme of John Lewis*, *Abstraction* and *Variants on a Theme of Thelonious Monk* (all Atlantic 1365, 1960), in the last two of which Ornette Coleman takes part. Here, above all in the palindromic *Abstraction*, advanced deployments of serial techniques fuse with jazz improvisation, particularly from Coleman. All these pieces seek out common ground between the various idioms with impressive perception.

The next stage, associated especially with the pianist and teacher Ran Blake, involved the combination of jazz with ethnic music from many different parts of the world. This recalls Stockhausen's integration, with much electronic modification, of recordings of many different kinds of folk and traditional music in his *Telemusik* (1966) and the emergence of the concept of 'world music' – all musics finally being parts of a single entity. This attitude is perhaps best represented in jazz by Don Cherry's trio, Codona (three records, all titled *Codona*, ECM (G) 1132, 1177, 1243, 1979–82), which improvises on a wide range of ethnic music with a considerable diversity of instruments including the trumpet, sitar and berimbau.

325

Expansion of resources in another direction took place in orchestral jazz. At the most obvious level it was a matter of increased instrumental doublings by the players. For example, the five-man reed section of Don Ellis's 1968 band, as in *Electric Bath* (Columbia CS9585), had one piccolo, five flutes, two clarinets, one bass clarinet, two each of soprano, alto and tenor saxophones and one baritone saxophone. With added electronic modification this is a long way from the five-piece saxophone sections, with an occasional doubling on clarinet, of the typical big band of the 1940s, let alone the smaller sections of earlier decades.

Ellis's large ensemble and those led by Sun Ra, Gil Evans and others confirmed, despite continued talk in jazz commentary about the 'death' of big bands, that such groups retained a capacity for transforming themselves. They did so most importantly, so far as the musical language of jazz is concerned, in terms of colour, which gradually became a function of structure. The Chicago AACM (Association for the Advancement of Creative Musicians) used a vast range of instruments and 'sound makers' to give new dimensions to their type of free jazz. Here sound masses were subject only to gradual changes of pitch content, dynamic and colour. Lacking attack, this music was marked by the absence of motion, articulation and sometimes of intensity. A good instance is Muhal Richard Abrams's *Levels and Degrees of Light* (Delmark 413, 1968).

Such music approximates to the effects obtainable through electronics, used extensively in a band such as Ellis's, a feature not inherent in the music but one that entered, as it were, from outside. Inevitably there were isolated precedents for this impact of technology, such as the electric-guitar playing of Charlie Christian with Benny Goodman's large and small groups. But that was an elementary enhancement. Now available were such devices as the multivider, which doubles the pitch of a line of notes an octave lower, the varitone, which provides automatic harmonization of melodies at chosen intervals, reverberation units, wa-wa pedals, fuzz-tone pedals, phrase-shifters and sound filters. There were also several types of synthesizer, a fine example of their use in jazz being the LP *Homage to Charlie Parker* (Black Saint (I) BSR0029, 1979) by George Lewis and Richard Teitelbaum. There were several devices like the echoplex, which enabled a soloist to superimpose new material on an electronically produced echo of what has gone before, creating the sort of contrapuntal texture heard in Don Ellis's trumpet solo in *Open Beauty* (Columbia CS9585, 1968). The use of electronics resulted in an equalization of the strength of different instrumental parts, thus intensifying and rendering more complex the impact of collective improvisation. It also noticeably increased the volume level of jazz groups, particularly small ones. An idea of the greater textural density may be gained by comparing the instrumentation of Miles Davis's *Kind of Blue* (1959) – trumpet, alto and tenor saxophones, piano, double bass and drums – with that of his *Big Fun* (CBS PG32866, 1969–72) – trumpet, soprano saxophone, flute, bass clarinet,

327

piano, electric piano, electric organ, electric guitar, electric bass, drums, 'African' percussion, sitar, electric sitar, tambura and tabla.

The use of such resources and the wholesale employment of electronics were closely related to jazz musicians' hesitant affiliations with rock, which by the 1960s had engulfed Western popular music. This was a *mélange* of rhythm-and-blues and country-and-western music, themselves commercial dilutions of forms of folk expression. The prime characteristics of rock music were repetition and the squareness of its heavy rhythms. Its international success led to a crisis of confidence for jazz musicians, who particularly in the 1960s found their own audiences, especially among the young, much reduced. Rock had made elementary borrowings from jazz, and it was in order for jazz (as in the case of the bossa nova) to borrow back. It is impossible to determine to what extent this was inspired by musical curiosity or by the desire of certain well-established jazz musicians to experience success as widespread as that enjoyed by the worst rock bands. They may also have been affected by the grotesquely pretentious claims made for rock by numerous pseudo-intellectuals during the 1960s.

As at several other points in jazz history, the lead was taken by Miles Davis, who completely transformed whatever appropriations he made from rock. This is demonstrated by the highly influential LPs *Bitches' Brew* (Columbia 2-GP26, 1969) and *A Tribute to Jack Johnson* (Columbia CSKC30455, 1970). The essential point was Davis's use of electrified instruments and devices leading to multilayered ostinatos on keyboards, percussion etc; and these were not necessarily fixed, but could gradually change. To these were added high-quality solo and collective improvisation, modality and open-ended structures. Such music was an abstraction of rock and seemed to have considerable further possibilities, these being taken up by former members of Davis's bands.

Thus Herbie Hancock's *Sextant* (Columbia KC32212, 1973) is of interest for its counterpoint of long, asymmetric rhythmic patterns, while in Chick Corea's *Return to Forever* (ECM (G) ST1022, 1972) echoes of rock are combined with the sort of exoticism discussed above, here in the form of Brazilian and Yoruba elements. Further instances are John McLaughlin's Mahavishnu Orchestra (e.g. *Birds of Fire*, Columbia KC31996, 1973) and Wayne Shorter and Joe Zawinul's Weather Report (e.g. *I Sing the Body Electric*, Columbia PC31352, 1971–2). However, Shorter's work immediately before Weather Report is of more lasting interest, an example being *The Odyssey of Iska* (Blue Note 84363, 1970). Following the initiatives of Ellington, Dameron and others, this is a tone poem for jazz band portraying a mythical journey by the Nigerian Ulysses. Its superiority to any of the jazz-rock amalgams noted here is a reminder that although the latter embodied the most readily accepted jazz style since swing in the 1930s its popularity was short-lived.

There were several reactions, one of them, almost inevitably, being a return to 'acoustic jazz'. In its most extreme form, and taking a cue from Coleman Haw-

329

kins's *Picasso*, this led to unaccompanied playing by wind instrumentalists and others. Despite a few exceptional pieces like John Lewis's *Harlequin* piano solo (Atlantic 1272, 1957), jazz had always been poor in silence and this new solo music made a refreshing change. The movement had begun some years before with isolated instances such as Sonny Rollins's *Body and Soul* (MGM C776, 1958) and Jimmy Giuffre's *Propulsion* (Columbia CL1964, 1962), but now whole LPs (and an occasional whole concert) were devoted to unaccompanied jazz improvisations. A late example is Steve Lacy's *Eronel* (Horo (I) HZ11, 1979), which is filled with soprano saxophone solos on Thelonious Monk themes. Somewhat different are the trombonist Roswell Rudd's *The Definitive Roswell Rudd* (Horo (I) HZ12, 1979) and the particularly beautiful *Upon Reflection* (ECM (G) 1148, 1979) by the English saxophonist John Surman, which both involve multi-recording. Such performances are sometimes introverted but they led to extensions of instrumental technique. A good instance is the work of Evan Parker (e.g. *Monoceros*, Incus (E) 27, 1978), who discovered and brought under control a considerable variety of new effects on the soprano and tenor saxophones.

Though not a reaction against the electronic avant garde, another tendency that ran counter to it was that of jazz musicians popularizing jazz. The music industry (publishers, record companies etc) had always offered dilutions of ragtime, blues and jazz, some of which led to rock. That was popularization from the outside. But as early as the late 1940s the

George Shearing Quintet had presented a musicianly watering-down of bop. There were similar ventures later, for example by the alto saxophonist 'Cannonball' Adderley, a simplifier of Charlie Parker's music. Little of permanent worth was produced on these occasions, yet because it was popularization from inside jazz the resulting music had at least a degree of integrity, and may have led listeners towards more substantial fare.

Another development, which though again not exactly a reaction against the avant garde took a different direction, was what became known as the jazz repertory movement. This was also related to the tendency of jazz to take stock, and even look backwards, whenever the future seemed more than usually uncertain. Earlier, such bands as those led by Muggsy Spanier and Bob Crosby had not attempted a literal re-creation of past music, but that is precisely what the jazz repertory ensembles did. The best were, indeed, remarkably accurate and in tune with the spirit of the original recorded performances – and far removed from the amateurishness of the New Orleans revival (see §XI above). Fine examples are Dave Wilborn's *The New McKinney's Cotton Pickers* (Bountiful B38000, 1972), Dick Hyman's *Ferdinand 'Jelly Roll' Morton* (CBS (E) 61666, 1974) and *Running Wild* by Alan Cohen's New Paul Whiteman Orchestra (Argo (E) ZDA167, 1975). Public appearances by such groups made some of the best early jazz familiar in live performances again, and in some cases at a higher level of musicianship than obtained in the originals. Further, the movement recovered

331

music that might otherwise have been lost, an example being the New Orleans Ragtime Orchestra performing rags in early orchestrations which had been forgotten for several decades (Arhoolie 1058, 1971). More important, and the most welcome single result of the jazz repertory movement, was the rescue of Ellington's *Black, Brown and Beige*. The composer made studio recordings of only a few extracts from this, but working from a poor-quality on-location recording of a complete performance by the Ellington band in 1943 and an incomplete published score, Alan Cohen and Brian Priestley constructed a complete score for performance by Cohen's band (Argo (E) ZDA159, 1972).

Another aspect of such ventures is their concern for the craft of playing jazz, and this may be seen in part as a reaction against the licence that some of the lesser free jazz improvisers allowed themselves. There also appeared a number of soloists whose stylistic conservatism was unexpected for the late 1970s, such as the tenor saxophonist Scott Hamilton and the trumpeter Warren Vaché (*Skyscrapers*, Concord CJ111, 1979). The resulting music was too often bland, but that was never true of the work of the trumpeter Wynton Marsalis, an exceptional player who was equally at home in the classical repertory and in jazz. The essentially conservative cast of his music was never in doubt, however, and the same is true, within different terms of reference, of the tenor saxophonist David Murray. Here was a continuation, some might say a revival, of Albert Ayler's music (*3D Family*, Hat Hut (I) U/V, 1978). There was no sense of progress, and this was also true of the admired World Saxophone Quartet, of which Murray became part (*Live in Zürich*, Black Saint (I) BSR0077, 1981).

In the work of countless musicians, in Europe as much as the USA, free jazz consolidated its position. By the mid-1980s one felt that most such American and many European ensembles were recycling the music of the past 20 years rather too easily; hard bop had declined in a comparable way in the 1960s. Then, too, much turned on the role of Ornette Coleman. There was a certain parallel between Coleman's position in jazz and that of Schoenberg in European music earlier in the century. Having relinquished tonality, Schoenberg composed a series of freely atonal scores that contain much of the greatest music he produced, but the demands they made on even his imagination were exorbitant. The result was a period of silence, followed by his resorting to the serial method. Coleman's concept of jazz similarly required true improvisation all the time, which is why he said that he always tried 'to play without memory'. Again, the stress on the inventive capacity was too great. He evidently became unwilling to take a leading part in jazz and did not appear in public for long periods.

This was disturbingly reminiscent of the reluctance of Louis Armstrong after about 1930 and of Charlie Parker after about 1950 to play a leading innovatory role – which is not to say that these men did not produce their finest music after these dates. Parker's best recordings in the years just before his death, such as *Chi Chi* (Verve MGV8005, 1953), suggest a growth in his own powers as an improviser and an extension

333

of the bop idiom itself. But this music, like Armstrong's 1935–45 work, had less influence than what he had done before. The other similarity between the situations of Schoenberg and Coleman is perhaps even more significant than the first. At one time it was assumed widely that the former's serial method would be the main highway of future classical composition. Certainly it has been widely influential, but many other methods of writing music persist. Similarly it appeared at one stage that Coleman had made possible for jazz a completely new and independent beginning, yet although free jazz is unquestionably a most important part of contemporary jazz, many other paths are followed, some of them, as already noted, of a distinctly conservative sort.

The fact is that jazz is no longer dominated by a master innovator as it was by Armstrong, Parker and Coleman in turn. Albert Ayler was the last musician who might have taken that role and he died (apparently murdered) in 1970. Jazz skills underwent a clearly perceptible growth over several generations and it has become much harder to detect a pattern, a single line of development. Changes in skill and changes in style remain intimately related, but, despite attempts at a new synthesis by a few musicians like Anthony Braxton (e.g. *Four Compositions*, Black Saint (I) BSR0066, 1983), jazz no longer has a *lingua franca*. There is instead an extreme diversity of styles and methods and this situation is international. Like classical music and the other arts, notably painting, jazz has entered a post-modernist phase: all styles, the music of all periods, are, it seems, valid.

In the mid-1980s a few short lines of descent could be traced. For example, Ornette Coleman's Prime Time band (e.g. *Of Human Feelings*, Antilles 2001, 1979) led to such groups as Defunkt (e.g. *Defunkt*, Ariola (G) 203.274, 1980) and the Decoding Society (e.g. *Nasty*, Moers Music (G) 01086, 1981). But it has increasingly been a question of bands and individuals finding their own way; jazz has become more of an individual, less of a collective endeavour. It is as if the entire contents of the initial matrix are at last available at the same time. This is suggested by some of Jimmy Giuffre's distillations, such as his *Dragonfly* (Soul Note (I) SN1058, 1983), which reconciles the blues with the Orient, and much else. Another characteristic venture of the period is Charlie Haden's rather sombre *Ballad of the Fallen* (ECM (G) 1248, 1982), an LP-length work in several movements which conjures jazz out of folk music from Spain and Chile, El Salvador and Portugal. The large, elaborately organized work, still fundamentally a European model, continues to exert a powerful attraction. Carla Bley's *Escalator over the Hill* (three unnumbered LPs on the Jazz Composers label, 1970–71), a kind of opera incorporating many styles of jazz and musical techniques with folksongs from many parts of the world, remains a landmark even though weakened by including several 1960s pop idioms. The pioneering George Russell achieved in the orchestral version of his *Electronic Sonata* one of the largest wholly convincing structures produced by jazz. Though issued in 1983 (Soul Note (I) SN1044/45), this hour-long piece was recorded in 1966–7. The instrumental parts are accompanied by a tape that gathers together music from many parts of the world, so that a geographical and cultural, as well as musical, polyphony results.

XVII Europe

It should be noted that the solutions to formal and other problems embodied in such works pertain only to the individuals concerned, and sometimes only to the single piece. Bley's, Giuffre's, Haden's or Russell's way cannot be anyone else's, any more than it has proved that Coleman's can (his many would-be disciples notwithstanding). There are several reasons for considering these matters from a European angle. The first is that the response from the other side of the Atlantic to jazz and related American music was so prompt; indeed, it began almost certainly before jazz existed as a separate entity.

Dvořák was the first significant European composer to respond to some of the elements in the matrix of American music that contributed to jazz. However, the pentatonic melodic shapes of, for example, his String Quartet op.96 (1893), known as the 'American', are as characteristic of his native Czech folksongs as of those of American Blacks or Indians; at most his contact with the latter emphasized an inherent proclivity in the works he wrote in the USA. Delius's *Appalachia* (1902), sub-titled 'Variations on an Old Slave Song', makes a strikingly perceptive response to the spirit of black song, of which the composer had considerable experience in Florida during 1884–5. Such receptivity is less surprising if one remembers Chopin's and Berlioz's praise of Gottschalk's earliest negro-influenced piano works in Paris during the 1840s, or the enthusiasm with which Sousa's ragtime performances were greeted in that same city in 1900. Satie's *Jack-in-the-Box* (1899) already shows an understanding of ragtime, an idiom that recurs in his ballet *Parade* (1917) and *La grande excentrique* (1919). It was extensive experience of ragtime that prepared European musicians and their audiences for jazz.

The French in particular welcomed both types of music as antidotes to Teutonic solemnity, a point confirmed in reverse by the ironic quotation from *Tristan und Isolde*, to be played 'avec une grande émotion', in Debussy's *Golliwogg's Cake-walk* (1906–8). Sympathy with idioms derived from popular music led Debussy to write further such pieces. It in turn accorded with the enthusiasm for *bal musette*, circus and cabaret preached by Jean Cocteau and others in such aesthetic manifestos as *Le coq et l'harlequin* (1921), and with the interest in African sculpture of artists like Picasso and Epstein, following Derain and Vlaminck. The cultural ambience was such that the terseness of gesture and hard, clear, unromantic outline of the music of Louis Mitchell's Jazz Kings and the ODJB received a warm welcome in Paris and London respectively soon after World War I.

These and other early jazz missionaries had a double impact on European musical activity, their most immediately productive influence being on classical composers. Milhaud became interested in jazz after hearing Billy Arnold's band in London in 1920, and the impression was confirmed by a visit to New York in 1922. He wrote several pieces affected by these experiences, foremost among them *La création du monde* (1923), a ballet that remained the most vital and sensitive of all early European compositions influenced by jazz. Comparable, however, were several pieces by Martinů and Ravel. Indeed, the influence was pervasive, though one may object to the use of jazz as a symbol of moral depravity in two operas, Weill's *Aufstieg und Fall der Stadt Mahagonny* (1927) and Berg's *Lulu* (1929–35). Later pieces such as Stravinsky's *Ebony Concerto* (1945) and Wolpe's Quartet for trumpet, tenor saxophone, piano and percussion (1950) signify that the influence was no mere passing fashion. It continues to the present day, as in several of Tippett's works, notably his Symphony no.3 (1970–72).

Mitchell's Jazz Kings, the ODJB and others soon had imitators in most European countries. As early as 1919 the Farres Dansorkester recorded *Dill Pickles Rag* in Stockholm (Pathéfon (Sd) 53911) and the Original Eccentric Band recorded *Tiger Rag* in Berlin (Homokord (G) 15983). Only in the 1980s has the microgroove reissue of many hitherto exceedingly rare early recordings begun to yield an outline of how widespread such activities were, even in countries like Finland, Spain and Hungary. Jazz survived against all odds under the Communists in Russia and the Nazis in Germany.

For about two generations European jazz was necessarily imitative, but its first outstanding figure had emerged by the early 1930s. This was Django

Reinhardt (*b* Liberchies, 23 Jan 1910; *d* Fontaine-bleau, 16 May 1953), a Belgian gypsy domiciled in France who was the equal of the best Americans and altogether a leading personality in the jazz of his time. He won international celebrity not only through his recordings with American musicians visiting Europe, such as Benny Carter and Coleman Hawkins, but also with the Quintet of the Hot Club de France, founded in 1934. An all-string group in which he was part-nered by the violinist Stephane Grappelli and backed with two further guitars and bass, this provided an improbable yet wholly apt setting for some of Rein-hardt's most brilliant improvisations. His pre-emi-nence led to an underrating of some other early jazz musicians, among them the French trumpeter Philippe Brun and the English composer Reginald Foresythe. It was only after World War II, however, that Euro-pean jazz began to take a direction – eventually a number of directions – wholly its own. The first post-war European jazz player of international stature was unquestionably the Swedish baritone saxophonist Lars Gullin, like Reinhardt a leading exponent of his instrument and a masterly improviser. Also note-worthy were the West German trombonist Albert Mangelsdorff (*Trombirds*, MPS (G) 68.069, 1972) and the French pianist Martial Solal (*Bluesine*, Soul Note (I) SN1060, 1983). There are many others, among them the Norwegian saxophonist Jan Garbarek (*Eventyr*, ECM (G) 1200, 1977), the Hungarian guitar-ist Attila Zoller (*Conjunction*, Enja (G) 3051, 1979), the Polish violinist Zbigniew Seifert (*Man of the Light*, Pausa 7077, 1976), and the English guitarist John

339

McLaughlin (*Extrapolation*, Polydor (E) 2310 018, 1969). Intelligent adaptations of serial technique to jazz composition and improvisation were made by the Czech Pavel Blatný (*Third Stream Compositions*, Supraphon (Cz) 015 0528, 1968) and by the English musician David Mack (*New Directions*, Columbia (E) 33SX1670, 1964). New ground was broken by European free jazz, which developed into a particularly independent movement. It seems unfortunate that, with a few exceptions like the composer and multi-instrumentalist Anthony Braxton and the trombonist George Lewis, most American musicians have chosen to ignore its many discoveries, especially considering that free jazz in the USA has made few real advances since the early 1970s.

Beginning in the 1920s, what might be termed the 'jazz appreciation movement' spread throughout Europe and eventually to many other parts of the world, finally to the USA. Musicians were quick to notice that their reception abroad was different from that at home; Europe became a haven for American jazz players and has remained so. In the USA jazz was for a long time thought of as at best a form of entertainment, whereas elsewhere it was almost from the first recognized as a significant strand in contemporary music. Foreign audiences, again in Europe especially, were less transitory.

The first serious book on the subject, E. F. Burian's *Jazz*, appeared in Prague in 1928, a decade before anything comparable (Winthrop Sargeant's *Jazz Hot and Hybrid*, New York, 1938) came out in the USA. And a further ten years were to pass before anything else of similar quality was published in America, Sydney Finkelstein's *Jazz: a People's Music* (New York, 1948). The efforts of a few isolated pioneer American writers such as Robert Donaldson Darrell notwithstanding, opposition to jazz in its country of origin was, aside from its lowly status as part of the entertainment business, a result of the conservative nature of 'official' American art. The interests that ridiculed Ives or Ruggles were unlikely to unbend to jazz. So it was in Europe that the systematic study of jazz began, the comprehensive tracing, documentation and reissue of recordings, the publication of many books and periodicals in several languages.

One result of such scholarly activity is that there is greater awareness of more of the past. In fact past and present in jazz have for a considerable time been drawing closer together. As early as 1957 it was no longer incongruous for Bob Brookmeyer and Jimmy Giuffre in new versions of *Some Sweet Day* and *Sweet Like This* for their LP *Traditionalism Revisited* (Pacific Jazz PJ1233) to quote complete King Oliver, Louis Armstrong and Dave Nelson solos from the original 1920s recordings. It is as if, paradoxically, all the main elements of jazz were drawing closer despite the increasingly separate nature of individual musicians' paths within it, and despite there no longer being a *lingua franca*. This suggests a growing inner unity behind the advancing outward diversity. The investigations of scholars as much as the improvisations of musicians imply that jazz can neither repeat its past nor escape it; it constantly adds to, and thereby modifies, everything that has previously happened.

Hence the impossibility, noted at the start, of framing a definition, of finding an image that can stand as an adequate symbol of its true nature.

XVIII Bibliography

GENERAL REFERENCE WORKS

G. Poole: *Enciclopedia de swing* (Buenos Aires, 1939)

N. Ortiz Oderigo: *Panorama de la música afroamericana* (Buenos Aires, 1944)

W. Laade, W. Ziefle and D. Zimmerle: *Jazz-Lexikon* (Stuttgart, 1953)

G. Testoni and others, ed.: *Enciclopedia del jazz* (Milan, 1953, rev. and enlarged 2/1954)

A. M. Dauer and S. Longstreet: *Knaur's Jazz Lexikon* (Munich, 1957)

J. Jörgensen and E. Wiedemann, eds.: *Jazzens hvem-hvad-hvor* (Copenhagen, 1962; rev. Ger. trans. as *Mosaik Jazzlexikon*, 1966)

F. Ténot and P. Carls: *Dictionnaire du jazz* (Paris, 1967)

C. Schreiner: *Jazz Aktuell* (Mainz, 1968)

C. Bohländer and K. H. Holler: *Reclams Jazzführer* (Stuttgart, 1970)

BIOGRAPHICAL DICTIONARIES

F. Usinger: *Kleine Biographie des Jazz* (Offenbach am Main, 1953)

L. Feather: *The Encyclopedia of Jazz* (New York, 1955, rev. and enlarged 2/1960)

S. B. Charters: *Jazz – New Orleans 1885–1963* (New York, 1958, rev. 2/1963)

L. Feather: *The Encyclopedia of Jazz in the Sixties* (New York, 1967)

J. Chilton: *Who's Who of Jazz* (London and Philadelphia, 1970, rev. and enlarged 4/1985)

L. Feather and I. Gitler: *The Encyclopedia of Jazz in the Seventies* (New York, 1976)

Bibliography

M. Hayes, R. Scribner and P. Magee: *Encyclopedia of Australian Jazz* (Eight Mile Plains, 1976)

GENERAL DISCOGRAPHIES

C. Delaunay: *Hot Discography* (Paris, 1936, rev. 4/1943 as *Hot discographie*, rev. and enlarged 5/1948 as *New Hot Discographie*, part rev. 6/1951 by Delaunay and K. Mohr as *Hot discographie encyclopédique*)

H. Schleman: *Rhythm on Record ... 1906 to 36* (London, 1936)

O. Blackstone: *Index to Jazz* (Fairfax, Virginia, 1945–8)

K. Mohr: *Discographie du jazz* (Geneva, 1945)

B. Møller: *Dansk jazz discography* (Copenhagen, 1945)

A. Schwaninger and A. Gurwitsch: *Swing discographie* (Geneva, 1945)

D. Carey and A. J. McCarthy: *Jazz Directory* (Fordingbridge, later London, 1949–57, ii–iv rev. 2/1955–7)

B. Semeonoff: *Record Collecting: a Guide for Beginners* (Chislehurst, 1949, rev. 2/1951)

H. Nicolausson: *Svensk jazzdiskografi* (Stockholm, 1953)

H. H. Lange: *Die deutsche Jazz-Discographie ... von 1902 bis 1955* (Berlin, 1955)

J. Grunnet Jepsen: *Jazz Records, 1942 – [1969]: a Discography* (Holte and Copenhagen, 1963–70)

B. Rust: *Jazz Records*, i: *1897–1931* (Hatch End, nr. London, 1961, 2/1961 with index by R. Grandorge); ii: *1932–1942* (Hatch End, 1965); i, ii, as *Jazz Records: A–Z, 1897–1942* (London, rev. [3]/1969, rev. and enlarged 4/1978, 5/1983)

H. H. Lange: *Die deutsche '78er': Discographie der Jazz- und Hot-Dance-Musik, 1903–1958* (Berlin, 1966)

D. Langridge: *Your Jazz Collection* (London, 1970)

W. C. Allen: *Studies in Jazz Discography* (New Brunswick, NJ, 1971)

T. Stagg and C. Crump: *New Orleans Revival* (Dublin, 1973)

W. Bruyninckx: *60 Years of Recorded Jazz: 1917–77* (n.p. [Mechelen], n.d. [1978–81])

R. D. Laing and C. Sheridan: *Jazz Records: the Specialist Labels* (Copenhagen, 1981)

J. Litchfield: *The Canadian Jazz Discography, 1916–1980* (Toronto, 1982)

CRITICAL DISCOGRAPHIES

F. Ramsey jr and C. E. Smith: *Jazz Record Book* (New York, 1942)

343

F. Ramsey jr: *A Guide to Longplay Jazz Records* (New York, 1954/*R*1977)

A. McCarthy and others: *Jazz on Record: a Critical Guide to the First Fifty Years: 1917–67* (London, 1968)

M. Harrison and others: *Modern Jazz: the Essential Records (1945–1970)* (London, 1975)

M. Harrison, C. Fox and E. Thacker: *The Essential Jazz Records*, i: *Ragtime to Swing* (London, 1984)

BIBLIOGRAPHIES

J. Ganfield: *Books and Periodical Articles on Jazz in America from 1926–1932* (New York, 1933)

A. P. Merriam and R. J. Benford: *A Bibliography of Jazz* (Philadelphia, 1954/*R*1970)

R. Reisner: *The Literature of Jazz* (New York, 1954, rev. and enlarged 2/1959)

J. Chaumier: *La littérature du jazz* (Le Mans, 1963)

L. Kleberg: *Svensk jazzbibliografi* (Stockholm, 1964)

A. Elings: *Bibliografie van de nederlandse jazz* (Nijmegen, 1966)

C. Herzog zu Mecklenburg: *International Jazz Bibliography: Jazz Books from 1919 to 1968* (Strasbourg, 1969, suppls. 1971, 1975)

D. Kennington: *The Literature of Jazz* (London, 1970, rev. with D. L. Read 2/1980)

S. Winick: *Rhythm: an Annotated Bibliography* (Metuchen, NJ, 1974)

J. Voigt and R. Kane: *Jazz Music in Print* (Winthrop, Mass., 1975, rev. 3/1982 as *Jazz Music in Print and Jazz Books in Print*)

D. Horn: *The Literature of American Music in Books and Folk Music Collections: a Fully Annotated Bibliography* (Metuchen, 1977)

N. Rücker: *Jazz Index: Bibliographie unselbständiger Jazzliteratur* (Frankfurt am Main, 1977–80)

D. Allen: *Bibliography of Discographies,* ii: *Jazz* (New York and London, 1981)

E. S. Meadows: *Jazz Reference and Research Materials* (New York and London, 1981)

B. Hefele: *Jazz Bibliographie/Jazz Bibliography* (Munich, 1981)

C. Clark: *Jazz Readers' Guide* (London, 1982)

GENERAL HISTORIES

M. Howe: *Blue Jazz* (Bristol, 1934)

V. Skaarup and M. Goldstein: *Jazz* (Copenhagen, 1934)

A. Caraceni: *Il jazz delle origini ad oggi* (Milan, 1937, rev. 2/1945)

Bibliography

S. M. Kristensen: *Hvad jazz* (Copenhagen, 1938)

W. Hobson: *American Jazz Music* (New York, 1939, rev. 2/1941/*R*1976)

F. Ramsey jr and C. E. Smith, eds.: *Jazzmen* (New York, 1939/ *R*1977)

N. Hellström, ed.: *Jazz: historia, teknik, utövare* (Stockholm, 1940)

A. Coeuroy: *Histoire générale du jazz* (Paris, 1942)

R. Goffin: *Jazz: from the Congo to the Metropolitan* (Garden City, NY, 1944/*R*1975, rev [2]/1946 as *Jazz: from Congo to Swing* [in Eng. trans.]; Fr. orig. pubd as *Histoire du jazz*, Montreal, 1945, rev. [2]/1948 as *Nouvelle histoire du jazz: du Congo au bebop*)

A. Niemoeller: *Story of Jazz* (Kansas City, 1946)

I. Laing: *Jazz in Perspective: the Background of the Blues* (London, 1947/*R*1976)

L. Cerri: *Jazz: musica d'oggi* (Milan, 1948)

B. Heuvelmans: *De la bamboula au be-bop: esquisse de l'évolution de la musique de jazz* (Paris, 1951)

M. Bouvier-Ajam: *Connaissance du jazz* (Paris, 1952)

N. Ortiz Oderigo: *Historia del jazz* (Buenos Aires, 1952)

B. Ulanov: *History of Jazz in America* (New York, 1952/*R*1972)

S. Porto: *Pequena história do jazz* (Rio de Janeiro, 1953)

J.-E. Berendt: *Das neue Jazzbuch: Entwicklung und Bedeutung der Jazzmusik* (Frankfurt am Main, 1953, rev. and enlarged 5/1981 as *Das grosse Jazzbuch: von New Orleans bis Jazz Rock*; Eng. trans., 1962, rev. 1982, as *The Jazz Book: from New Orleans to Fusion and Beyond*)

N. Shapiro and N. Hentoff, eds.: *Hear me Talkin' to ya* (New York and London, 1955/*R*1966)

A. Francis: *Jazz* (Paris, 1958; rev. Eng. trans. by M. Williams, 1960/*R*1976)

M. W. Stearns: *The Story of Jazz* (New York, 1956, rev. and enlarged 2/1958/*R*1970)

J. S. Roberts: *Black Music of Two Worlds* (New York, 1972)

D. Morgenstern: *Jazz People* (New York, 1976)

SPECIALIST HISTORIES

F. Ramsey jr.: *Chicago Documentary* (London, 1944)

R. Goffin: *La Nouvelle Orléans: capitale du jazz* (New York, 1946)

N. Griffin: *To Bop or Not to Bop?* (New York, 1948)

L. Feather: *Inside Be-bop* (New York, 1949/*R*1977 as *Inside Jazz*)

S. B. Charters and L. Kunstadt: *Jazz: a History of the New York Scene* (Garden City, NY, 1962/*R*1981)

I. Gitler: *Jazz Masters of the Forties* (New York, 1966/*R*1983 with discography)

H. Kmen: *Music in New Orleans: the Formative Years 1791–1841* (Baton Rouge, 1966)

H. Lange: *Jazz in Deutschland: die deutsche Jazz-Chronik, 1900–1960* (Berlin, 1966)

R. Pernet: *Jazz in Little Belgium 1881–1966* (Brussels, 1967)

M. Williams: *Jazz Masters of New Orleans* (New York and London, 1967)

M. Dorigné: *Jazz*, i: *Les origines du jazz: le style Nouvelle Orléans et ses prolongements* (Paris, 1968)

R. Russell: *Jazz Style in Kansas City and the South West* (Berkeley, 1971, rev. 2/1973)

A. Wilder: *American Popular Song: the Great Innovators, 1900–1950* (London and New York, 1972)

I. Carr: *Music Outside: Contemporary Jazz in Britain* (London, 1973)

E. Jost: *Free Jazz* (Graz, 1974)

D. Schiedt: *The Jazz State of Indiana* (Pittsboro, 1977)

W. J. Schafer and R. B. Allen: *Brass Bands and New Orleans Jazz* (Baton Rouge, 1977)

M. J. Budds: *Jazz in the Sixties: the Expansion of Musical Resources and Techniques* (Iowa City, 1978)

J. S. Roberts: *The Latin Tinge: the Impact of Latin American Music on the United States* (New York, 1979)

M. Luzzi: *Uomini e avantguardie jazz* (Milan, 1980)

T. Stoddard: *Jazz on the Barbary Coast* (Chigwell, Essex, 1982)

M. Miller: *Jazz in Canada* (Toronto, 1982)

B. Taylor: *Jazz Piano: History and Development* (Dubuque, 1982)

F. Starr: *Red and Hot: the Fate of Jazz in the Soviet Union, 1917–1980* (New York and Oxford, 1983)

J. Godbolt: *A History of Jazz in Britain, 1919–50* (London, 1984)

J. Litweiler: *The Freedom Principle: Jazz after 1958* (New York, 1984)

I. Gitler: *Swing to Bop* (New York, 1985)

J. Godbolt and A. Morgan: *A History of Jazz in Britain, 1950–70* (London, 1986)

SOCIOLOGICAL AND RELATED WORKS

F. W. Koebner: *Jazz und Shimmy* (Berlin, 1921)

A. Frankenstein: *Syncopating Saxophones* (Chicago, 1925)

A. Baresel: *Das Jazz-Buch* (Leipzig, 1926, rev. ?2/1929)

L. Arntzenius: *Amerikaansche kunstindrukken* (Amsterdam, 1927)

Bibliography

P. Bernhard: *Jazz: eine musikalische Zeitfrage* (Munich, 1927)

R. Mendl: *The Appeal of Jazz* (London, 1927)

I. Schwerké: *Kings Jazz and David* (Paris, 1927, 3/1936 as *Views and Interviews*)

A. G. Bragaglia: *Jazz Band* (Milan, 1929)

R. Sonner: *Musik und Tanz: vom Kulttanz zum Jazz* (Leipzig, 1930)

C. Vica: *Classicisme au jazz* (Paris, 1933)

O. Soby: *Jazz kontra europaeisk musikkultur* (Copenhagen, 1935)

H. Asbury: *The French Quarter: an Informal History of the New Orleans Underworld* (New York, 1937)

A. Bettonville: *Paranoia du jazz* (Brussels, 1939)

W. G. Gilbert and C. Poustochkine: *Jazzmuziek: inleiding tot de volksmuziek der noord-amerikaansche negers* (The Hague, 1939, rev. 2/1948)

H. Vémane: *Swing et moeurs* (Lille, 1943)

E. Bernhard and J. de Vergnies: *Apologie du jazz* (Brussels, 1945)

P. Edwards: *Notions élémentaires sur le jazz* (Liège, 1945)

E. Willems: *Le jazz et l'oreille musicale: étude psychologique* (Geneva, 1945)

I. David: *Jazz et les hommes d'aujourd'hui* (Brussels, 1946)

S. M. Kristensen: *Jazzen og dens problemer* (Copenhagen, 1946)

E. Walles: *Jazzen anfaller* (Stockholm, 1946)

W. G. Gilbert: *Rumbamuziek: volksmuziek van de midden-amerikaansche negers* (The Hague, n.d. [1947])

M. Dorigné: *La guerre du jazz* (Paris, 1948)

J. Slawe: *Einführung in die Jazzmusik* (Basle, 1948)

W. Twittenhoff: *Jugend und Jazz* (Mainz, 1953)

C. Bohländer: *Das Wesen der Jazzmusik* (Frankfurt am Main, 1954)

E. Bartsch: *Neger, Jazz und tiefer Süden* (Leipzig, 1956)

W. L. Grossman and J. W. Farrel: *Jazz and Western Culture* (New York, 1956)

A. Dauer: *Der Jazz: seine Ursprünge und seine Entwicklung* (Kassel, 1958)

F. Newton: *The Jazz Scene* (London, 1959, New York, 1960/R1975)

N. Hentoff: *The Jazz Life* (New York, 1961/R1975)

N. Leonard: *Jazz and the White Americans: the Acceptance of a New Art Form* (Chicago and London, 1962)

R. Ellison: *Shadow and Act* (New York, 1964)

R. Gold: *A Jazz Lexicon* (New York, 1964, rev. 2/1975 as *Jazz Talk*)

347

Jazz

E. Routley: *Is Jazz Music Christian?* (London, 1964)

P. Krähenbühl: *Der Jazz und seine Menschen: eine soziologische Studie* (Berne and Munich, 1968)

M. Stearns and J. Stearns: *The Jazz Dance: the Story of American Vernacular Dance* (New York, 1968)

C. Major: *Dictionary of Afro-American Slang* (New York, 1970)

R. Denisoff and R. Peterson, eds.: *The Sounds of Social Change* (Chicago, 1972)

O. M. Walton: *Music: Black, White and Blue: a Sociological Survey of the Use and Misuse of Afro-American Music* (New York, 1972)

C. Nanry, ed.: *American Music: from Storyville to Woodstock* (New Brunswick, 1972)

J. V. Buerkle and D. Barker: *Bourbon Street Black: the New Orleans Black Jazzman* (New York, 1973)

A. Rose: *Storyville, New Orleans* (University, Alabama, 1974)

C. Hamm, B. Nettl and R. Byrnside: *Contemporary Music and Music Cultures* (Englewood Cliffs, 1975)

J. Haskins: *The Creoles of Colour in New Orleans* (New York, 1975)

R. Backus: *A Political History of Jazz* (Chicago, 1977)

A. Hodes and C. Hansen, eds.: *Selections from the Gutter* (Berkeley, 1977)

G. McCue, ed.: *Music in American Society, 1776–1976* (New Brunswick, 1977)

L. Ostransky: *Jazz City: the Impact of our Cities on the Development of Jazz* (Englewood Cliffs, 1978)

C. Nanry and E. Berger: *The Jazz Text* (New York, 1979)

R. Morris: *Wait until Dark: Jazz and the Underworld, 1880–1940* (Bowling Green, 1980)

M. McKee and F. Chisenhall: *Beale Street Black and Blue* (Baton Rouge, 1981)

E. Jost: *Eine Sozialgeschichte des Jazz in den USA* (Frankfurt am Main, 1982)

HISTORY, ANALYSIS

A. Ferro: *A idade do Jazz-Band* (Lisbon, 1924)

A. Coeuroy and A. Schaeffner: *Le jazz* (Paris, 1926)

H. Osgood: *So This is Jazz!* (Boston, 1926/R1978)

E. F. Burian: *Jazz* (Prague, 1928)

R. Goffin: *Aux frontières du jazz* (Paris, 1932)

E. Ferand: *Die Improvisation in der Jazzmusik* (Zurich, 1938)

W. Sargeant: *Jazz Hot & Hybrid* (New York, 1938, enlarged 3/1964/R1975)

Bibliography

C. Cosmetto: *La vraie musique de jazz* (Lausanne, 1945)

S. W. Finkelstein: *Jazz: a People's Music* (New York, 1948/ *R*1975)

J. E. Berendt: *Der Jazz: eine zeitkritische Studie* (Stuttgart, 1950)

N. Ortiz Oderigo: *Estetica del jazz* (Buenos Aires, 1951)

L. Malson: *Les maîtres du jazz* (Paris, 1952, rev. 6/1972)

J. Guinle: *Jazz panorama* (Rio de Janeiro, 1953)

G. Legrand: *Puissance du jazz* (Paris, n.d. [1953])

J. E. Berendt: *Variationen über Jazz* (Munich, 1956)

L. Tyrmand: *U brzegów Jazzu* (Kraków, 1957)

J. Mehegan: *Jazz Improvisation* (New York, 1959–65)

L. Ostransky: *The Anatomy of Jazz* (Seattle, 1960)

A. M. Dauer: *Jazz, die magische Musik* (Bremen, 1961)

J. Coker: *Improvising Jazz* (Englewood Cliffs, 1964)

W. Mellers: *Music in a New Found Land* (London, 1964)

A. Asriel: *Jazz: Analysen und Aspekte* (Berlin, 1966, rev. 2/1977)

J. Gonda: *Jazz* (Budapest, 1967, rev. 2/1981)

W. Russo: *Jazz Composition and Orchestration* (Chicago and London, 1968)

G. Schuller: *Early Jazz: its Roots and Musical Development* (New York, 1968)

C. Fox: *Jazz in Perspective* (London, 1969)

J. Coker: *The Jazz Idiom* (Englewood Cliffs, 1975)

A. Polillo: *Jazz: la vicenda e i protagonisti della musica afroamericana* (Milan, 1975, rev. and enlarged 2/1983)

M. Gridley: *Jazz Styles* (Englewood Cliffs, 1978, rev. 2/1985 as *Jazz Styles: History and Analysis*)

J. L. Collier: *The Making of Jazz: a Comprehensive History* (New York and London, 1978)

J. Chilton: *Jazz* (Sevenoaks, 1979)

G. Endress: *Jazz Podium: Musiker über sich selbst* (Stuttgart, 1980)

P. Tanner and M. Gerow: *A Study of Jazz* (Dubuque, 1981)

E. Jost: *Jazzmusiker* (Frankfurt am Main, 1982)

G. Sales: *Jazz: America's Classical Music* (Englewood Cliffs, 1984)

CRITICISM

L. Thoorens: *Essai sur le jazz* (Liège, 1942)

R. de Toledano, ed.: *Frontiers of Jazz* (New York, 1947 rev. 2/ 1962)

A. Hodeir: *Hommes et problèmes du jazz* (Paris, 1954; Eng. trans., 1956/*R*1975, as *Jazz: its Evolution and Essence*)

349

L. Cerri: *Antologia del jazz* (Pisa, 1955)

N. Ortiz Oderigo: *Perfiles del jazz* (Buenos Aires, 1955)

H. Ray: *Les grandes figures du jazz* (Brussels, 1955)

N. Hentoff and A. J. McCarthy, eds.: *Jazz: New Perspectives* (New York, 1959/R1974)

M. Williams, ed.: *The Art of Jazz: Essays on the Nature and Development of Jazz* (New York, 1959/R1975)

M. James: *Ten Modern Jazzmen* (London, 1960)

B. James: *Essays on Jazz* (London, 1961/R1985)

B. Green: *The Reluctant Art: Five Studies in the Growth of Jazz* (London, 1962)

A. Hodeir: *Toward Jazz* (New York, 1962/R1976)

M. Williams, ed.: *Jazz Panorama* (New York and London, 1962/R1979)

R. Hadlock: *Jazz Masters of the Twenties* (New York, 1965/R1985)

M. Williams: *The Jazz Tradition* (New York, 1970, rev. 2/1983)

A. Hodeir: *The Worlds of Jazz* (New York, 1972)

M. Harrison: *A Jazz Retrospect* (Newton Abbot, 1976, rev. 2/1977)

J. E. Berendt: *Ein Fenster aus Jazz: Essays, Portraits, Reflexionen* (Frankfurt am Main, 1977)

H. Lyttelton: *The Best of Jazz*, i: *Basin Street to Harlem* (London, 1978); ii, *Enter the Giants* (New York, 1982)

G. Giddins: *Riding on a Blue Note: Jazz and American Pop* (New York and Oxford, 1981)

——: *Rhythm-a-ning* (New York, 1985)

M. Williams: *The Jazz Heritage* (New York, 1986)

BIOGRAPHIES, CRITICAL STUDIES

R. D. Darrell: *Black Beauty* (Philadelphia, 1933) [Duke Ellington]

J. de Trazegnies: *Duke Ellington* (Brussels, 1946)

B. Ulanov: *Duke Ellington* (New York, 1946/R1975)

A. Lomax: *Mister Jelly Roll: the Fortunes of Jelly Roll Morton* (London, 1950, 2/1973)

W. C. Allen and B. A. L. Rust: *King Joe Oliver* (Belleville, NJ, 1955)

B. James: *Bix Beiderbecke* (London, 1959); repr. in *Kings of Jazz*, ed. S. Green (New York, 1978)

M. James: *Dizzy Gillespie* (London, 1959); repr. in *Kings of Jazz*, ed. S. Green (New York, 1978)

H. Brun: *The Story of the Original Dixieland Jazz Band* (Baton Rouge, 1960)

Bibliography

C. Fox: *Fats Waller* (London, 1960); repr. in *Kings of Jazz*, ed. S. Green (New York, 1978)

M. Harrison: *Charlie Parker* (London, 1960); repr. in *Kings of Jazz*, ed. S. Green (New York, 1978)

H. Walters jr.: *Jack Teagarden's Music* (Stanhope, NJ, 1960)

M. Williams: *King Oliver* (London, 1960); repr. in *Kings of Jazz*, ed. S. Green (New York, 1978)

C. Delaunay: *Django Reinhardt* (London, 1961/R1981)

M. James: *Miles Davis* (London, 1961); repr. in *Kings of Jazz*, ed. S. Green (New York, 1978)

R. Reisner: *Bird: the Legend of Charlie Parker* (New York, 1961, 2/1962)

M. Williams: *Jelly Roll Morton* (London, 1962); repr. in *Kings of Jazz*, ed. S. Green (New York, 1978)

D. Connor and W. Hicks: *BG on the Record: a Bio-discography of Benny Goodman* (New Rochelle, NY, 1969)

M. Jones and J. Chilton: *Louis: the Louis Armstrong Story, 1900–1971* (London, 1971)

M. Abrams: *The Book of Django* (Los Angeles, 1973)

W. Allen: *Hendersonia: the Music of Fletcher Henderson and his Musicians* (Highland Park, NJ, 1973)

R. Russell: *Bird Lives: the High Life and Hard Times of Charlie (Yardbird) Parker* (New York, 1973)

R. Berton: *Remembering Bix* (New York, 1974)

V. Simosko and B. Tepperman: *Eric Dolphy: a Musical Biography and Discography* (Washington, DC, 1974/R1979)

R. M. Sudhalter, P. R. Evans and W. Dean Myatt: *Bix: Man & Legend* (New Rochelle, NY and London, 1974)

J. Chilton: *Billie's Blues: a Survey of Billie Holiday's Career 1933–59* (London, 1975) [with bibliography]

T. Lord: *Clarence Williams* (Chigwell, London, 1976)

T. Bethell: *George Lewis: a Jazzman from New Orleans* (Berkeley, Calif., 1977)

D. Jewell: *Duke: a Portrait of Duke Ellington* (London, 1977)

J. Chilton: *McKinney's Music: a Bio-discography of McKinney's Cotton Pickers* (London, 1978)

S. Green, ed.: *Kings of Jazz* (London, 1978)

D. Marquis: *In Search of Buddy Bolden, First Man of Jazz* (Baton Rouge, 1978)

H. Westerberg: *Boy from New Orleans: Louis 'Satchmo' Armstrong: on Records, Films, Radio and Television* (Copenhagen, 1981)

M. and E. Berger: *Benny Carter: a Life in American Music* (Metuchen, NJ, 1982)

351

I. Carr: *Miles Davis* (London, 1982)

B. Priestley: *Mingus: a Critical Biography* (London, 1982)

J. Chambers: *Milestones,* i: *Miles Davis, 1945–60* (Toronto, 1983)

J. L. Collier: *Louis Armstrong: an American Genius* (New York, 1983)

D. Gelly: *Lester Young* (Tunbridge Wells, 1984)

B. James: *Coleman Hawkins* (Tunbridge Wells, 1984)

——: *Billie Holiday* (Tunbridge Wells, 1984)

A. Morgan: *Count Basie* (Tunbridge Wells, 1984)

B. Priestley: *Charlie Parker* (Tunbridge Wells, 1984)

J. Chambers: *Milestones*, ii: *Miles Davis since 1960* (Toronto, 1985)

P. S. Machlin: *Stride: the Music of Fats Waller* (London, 1985)

L. Porter: *Lester Young* (London, 1985)

MEMOIRS

P. Whiteman and M. M. McBride: *Jazz* (New York, 1926)

M. Mezzrow and B. Wolfe: *Really the Blues* (New York, 1946)

E. Condon and T. Sugrue: *We Called it Music* (New York, 1947/ *R*1985)

W. Manone and P. Vandervoort: *Trumpet on the Wing* (New York, 1948)

S. Hughes: *Second Movement* (London, 1951)

E. Waters and C. Samuels: *His Eye is on the Sparrow* (New York, 1951)

A. Shaw: *The Trouble with Cinderella* (New York, 1952)

L. Armstrong: *Satchmo: my Life in New Orleans* (New York, 1954)

B. Dodds and L. Gara: *The Baby Dodds Story* (Los Angeles, 1959)

S. Bechet: *Treat it Gentle*, ed. D. Flower (London, 1960)

M. Kaminsky and V. E. Hughes: *My Life in Jazz* (New York, 1963)

W. Smith and G. Hoefer: *Music on my Mind* (New York, 1964)

[G. M.] Foster, T. Stoddard and R. Russell: *Pops Foster: the Autobiography of a New Orleans Jazzman* (Berkeley, 1971)

R. Stewart: *Jazz Masters of the 30s* (New York, 1972)

H. Hawes: *Raise up off Me* (New York, 1973)

L. Collins: *Oh, Didn't he Ramble?*, ed. F. J. Gillis and J. W. Miner (Urbana, 1974)

C. Calloway and B. Rollins: *Of Minnie the Moocher and me* (New York, 1976)

D. Gillespie and A. Fraser: *To be, or not . . . to Bop* (Garden City, NY, 1979)

Bibliography

A. Pepper and L. Pepper: *Straight Life* (New York and London, 1979)

A. O'Day and G. Eells: *High Times, Hard Times* (New York, 1981)

B. Bigard: *With Louis and the Duke*, ed. B. Martyn (London, 1985)

ICONOGRAPHIES

C. Delaunay: *Hot iconographie* (Paris, 1939)

T. Rosenkrantz: *Swing Photo Album* (Copenhagen and London, 1939 rev. 2/1964)

M. Jones: *Jazz Photo Album* (London, 1947)

W. Claxton: *Jazz West Coast* (Hollywood, 1955)

O. Keepnews and B. Grauer: *A Pictorial History of Jazz* (New York, 1955, rev. 4/1968)

A. Heerkens: *Jazz* (Alkmaar, n.d. [1956])

F. Ramsey jr.: *Been Here and Gone* (New Brunswick, 1960)

D. Stock and N. Hentoff: *Jazz Street* (Garden City, NY, 1960)

L. Gillenson, ed.: *'Esquire's' World of Jazz* (New York, 1962)

J. Oliver: *Jazz Classic* (London, 1962)

A. Rose and E. Souchon: *New Orleans Jazz: a Family Album* (Baton Rouge, 1967)

W. Rockmore: *Preservation Hall Portraits* (Baton Rouge, 1968)

G. Fernett: *Swing Out* (Midland, Mich., 1970)

L. Huber: *New Orleans: a Pictorial History* (New York, 1971)

R. Martinez: *Portraits of New Orleans Jazz* (New Orleans, 1971)

C. Fox and V. Wilmer: *The Jazz Scene* (London, 1972)

J. E. Berendt: *Jazz: a Photo History* (New York, 1979)

W. Gottlieb: *The Golden Age of Jazz* (New York, 1979)

D. Spitzer: *Jazzshots* (Miami, 1980)

C. Parker and F. Paudras: *To Bird with Love* (Poitiers, 1981)

F. Driggs and H. Lewine: *Black Beauty, White Heat* (New York, 1982)

JAZZ ON FILM

P. Whannel: *Jazz on Film* (London, 1966)

D. Meeker: *Jazz in the Movies* (London, 1972, rev. 2/1981)

J. R. Hippenmeyer: *Jazz sur films* (Yverdon, 1973)

H. Gautier: *Jazz au cinéma* (Lyons, n.d.)

PERIODICALS

Argentina: *Jazz Magazine* (1945–6); *Jazzomania* (1939–); *Jazz Up* (1957–72); *Sincopa y ritmo* (1946–)

353

Australia: *Australian Jazz Quarterly* (1946–57); *Jazz Down Under* (1975–7)

Austria: *Jazzforschung* (1969–)

Belgium: *Music* (1924–39); *Point du jazz* (1969–); *Sweet and Hot* (1960–); *Swing Time* (1950–56)

Canada: *Coda* (1958–)

Chile: *Anuario de jazz* (1967–)

Denmark: *Jazzrevy* (1953–); *Musik revue* (1967–)

Finland: *Rytmi* (1934–)

France: *Cahiers du jazz* (1959–); *Jazz, Blues & co.* (1975–); *Jazz-hot*: 1st ser. (1935–40), 2nd ser. as *Jazz hot* (1945–); *Jazz magazine* (1954–); *Revue du jazz* (1948–)

Germany: *Hot Jazz Info* (1973–); *Jazzbrief* (1960–); *Jazzfreund* (1956–); *Jazz Katalog* (1959–); *Jazz Musik* (1957–); *Jazz Podium* (1952–)

Great Britain: *Discographical Forum* (1960–); *Discography* (1942–6); *Discophile* (1948–58); *Hot News* (1935–6); *Jazz Express* (1979–); *Jazz Forum* (1946–7); *Jazz Journal* (1948–); *Jazz Monthly* (1955–73); *Jazz Music* (1943–60); *Jazz News* (1956–64); *Jazzology* (1944–7); *Jazz Record* (1943–4); *Jazz Studies* (1964–71); *Jazz Tempo* (1943–4); *Matrix* (1954–75); *Pick-up* (1946–7); *Rhythm* (1926–39); *Storyville* (1965–); *Swing Music* (1935–6); *The Funker* (1959–61); *The Wire* (1982–)

Greece: *Tzaz* (1974–)

Iceland: *Jazz bladid* (1953–9)

Italy: *Collezione di musica jazz* (1960–); *Discoteca* (1959–); *Jazz di iere e di oggi* (1959–); *Jazzland* (1948–); *Musica jazz* (1945–)

Japan: *Jazz Hot Club Bulletin* (1948–); *Swing Journal* (1947–)

Netherlands: *Doctor Jazz* (1972–); *Jazz wereld* (1965–); *Micrography* (1968–); *Rhythme* (1937–9)

Norway: *Jazzbladet* (1961–); *Norsk jazz* (1955–7)

Poland: *Jazz* (1956–); *Jazz forum* (1967–)

Spain: *Aria jazz* (1934–6); *Ritmo y melodia* (1943–)

Sweden: *Estrad* (1929–); *Jazz-disco* (1960); *Orkesterjournalen* (1933–); *Swingtime* (?1960–)

Switzerland: *Jazz Bulletin* (1952–); *Jazz Statistics* (1956–63)

USA: *Afterbeat* (1970–); *Billboard* (1894–); *Clef* (1946–); *Climax* (1955–); *Different Drummer* (1973–5); *Down Beat* (1934–); *Jazzfinder* (1948–9); *Jazz Information* (1939–41); *Jazzletter* (1981–); *Jazz Quarterly* (1958–60); *Jazz Record* (1943–7); *Jazz Review* (1958–61); *Jazz Times* (1980–); *Journal of Jazz Studies* (1973–9); *Journal of the International Association of Jazz Record Collectors* (1968–); *Metronome* (1885–1961); *Record Changer* (1942–58); *Record Research* (1955–); *Tempo* (1933–40)

General index

Abrams, Lawrence, 217
Abrams, Muhal Richard, 326
Abyssinian Baptist Gospel Choir, 213
Acadians ('Cajuns'), 139–41
Ace, Johnny [Alexander, John Marshall, jr.], 109
Adderley, Cannonball [Julian Edwin], 331
Adins, Georges, 125
Africa, 2, 6, 40, 92–3, 159, 223–5
Alabama, 18, 65, 70, 71, 100, 124, 127, 192, 194, 196, 198, 201, 202, 213, 217, 219, 228
Alabama Sacred Harp Singers, 227
Albright, William Hugh, 31
Alexander, Texas [Alger(non)], 57, 61, 95, 124, 133
Alexander, John Marshall, jr.: see Ace, Johnny
Alexandria (Louisiana), 103
Algiers (Louisiana), 71
Ali, Rashied [Patterson, Robert], 320
Allen, Austin, 130
Allen, Ed, 55
Allen, Fulton: see Fuller, Blind Boy
Allen, Henry [James; Red], 244, 261, 263, 270, 279
——, New York Orchestra, 58
Allen, Lee, 130
Allen, William Francis, 5, 6, 10
Allison, Luther S., 112
Almeida, Laurindo, 322
Alphabetical Four, 203
Altheimer, Joshua, 74
America: see South America; USA
American Decca, 51

American Record Corporation, 51
Amerson, Rich [Richard Manuel], 18, 124
Ammons, Albert (C.), 76, 90, 91, 271
Anderson, Ivie [Ivy Marie], 282
Angola (Louisiana), 119, 125, 149
——, State prison, 119, 125
Anniston (Alabama), 73
Anthony, Eddie, 67
Archive of Folksong of the Library of Congress, 17, 18, 118, 121
Ardoin, Amadé, 140
Ardoin, Black [Lawrence], 142
Ardoin, Bois Sec [Alphonse], 140, 142
Argo Singers, 211
Ariola, 335
Arizona, 213
Arkansas, 65, 87, 100, 104, 164, 196
Armstrong, Louis, 52, 53, 54, 55, 57, 132, 209, 236, 243, 247, 248, 249, 251, 253, 257, 260, 261, 263, 265, 270, 275, 279, 281, 282, 283, 292, 293, 333, 334, 341; pl.16
——, All-Stars, 253, 281, 282, 284
——, Hot Five, 247, 251
——, Hot Seven, 247, 251
Arnold, Billy, 337
Arnold, Jerome, 137
Arnold, Kokomo [James; Gitfiddle Jim], 82–3, 86, 136, 164
Arvanitas, Georges, 112
Atlanta (Georgia), 17, 53, 65, 66, 67, 73, 79, 89, 100, 117, 121
——, Mount Calvary Church, 195
——, Tidwell's Barbecue Place, 65
Atlantic City, 28

357

General index

Blackwell, Scrapper [Francis], 80–81, 87, 136
Blake, Blind [Arthur], 46, 47, 79, 83, 117
Blake, Eubie [James Hubert], 24, 29, 31n, 32n, 254, 255
Blake, Ran, 325
Blakey, Art [Buhaina, Abdullah Ibn], 306, 319
——, Jazz Messengers, 315
Bland, Bobby [Robert Calvin; Bobbie Blue], 108–9, 113, 115
Blank, Les, 126, 142
Blatný, Pavel, 340
Blesh, Rudi [Rudolph], and Janis, Harriet: *They All Played Ragtime*, 30
Bley (née Borg), Carla, 335, 336
Bliggen, Dora ['The Blackberry Woman'], 41
Blind Willie Dunn's Gin Bottle Four, 57
Bliss, Philip [Paul], 190
Bloomfield, Mike [Michael], 137
Bluebird, 51
Blue Rhythm Band, 271, 272
Blues Boy: *see* King, B. B.
Blues Unlimited (periodical), 126–7
Blues World (periodical), 127
Bobbie Blue: *see* Bland, Bobby
Bo Diddley [McDaniel, Ellas], 98, 146
Bogan, Lucille [Jackson, Bessie], 71, 144
Bolcom, William, 31, 32n
Bolden, Buddy [Charles Joseph], 235, 236, 242, 255, 290
Bolton (Mississippi), 62, 68
Bonds, Brownsville Son, 83
Bonner, Juke Boy [Weldon H. Philip], 171
Boogie Woogie Trio, 90
Boone, Blind [John William], 74
Boswell Sisters [Connee, Martha and Helvetia], 283
Bouchillon, Chris, 132

Bowman, Euday [Louis], 29, 49
Boyd, Eddie [Edward Riley], 90, 101, 111, 138
Boyer, Horace C., 203, 216
Bracey, Ishmon [Ishman], 64–5, 88
Bradford, Professor Alex, 213, 219
Bradford, [John Henry] Perry, 50, 51, 146
Bradley, Will [Schwichtenberg, Wilbur], 91
Bradshaw, Tiny [Myron], 94, 110
Brand, Eastman, 19
Braxton, Anthony, 334, 340
Brazil, 322
Brazoria (Texas): Clemens State Farm, 120
Brazos plantation, 126
Brazos river, 151
Brewster, Reverend William Herbert, 193, 208
Brim, John, 157
Broadway Rastus: *see* Melrose, Frank
Brockman, Polk, 117
Brookmeyer, Bob [Robert], 341
Brooks, Hadda, 95
Broonzy, Big Bill [Conley, William Lee], 77, 79, 80, 87, 88, 89, 101, 122, 123, 126, 133, 134, 144, 145, 146, 157, 163, 207
Brother George and his Sanctified Singers, 206
Broven, John, 127
Brown, Charles, 94, 95, 109
Brown, Clarence Gatemouth, 97
Brown, Gabriel, 100, 120
Brown, Henry, 125
Brown, James, 218
Brown, Joe Washington, 18, 139
Brown, Lawrence, 267
Brown, Milton, 134
——, Musical Brownies, 134
Brown, Robert: *see* Washboard Sam
Brown, Roy, 97, 135
Brown, Ruth, 97

359

361

General index

364

General index

Gitfiddle Jim: *see* Arnold, Kokomo
Giuffre, Jimmy [James Peter], 298, 303, 304, 330, 335, 336, 341; pl.23
Glendora (Mississippi), 105
Glenn, Lloyd, 95
Glinn, Lillian, 53
Glosson, Lonnie, 132
Glover, Mae, 132
Golden Eagle Gospel Singers, 203
Golden Gate Jubilee Quartet, 202, 203
Goldkette, Jean, 246
Goodman, Benny [Benjamin David], 207, 260, 272, 275–7, 278, 279, 283, 287, 323, 327
——, Septet, 277
Gordon, Jimmie, 146, 157
Gordon, Richard, 118
Gordon, Roscoe, 109
Gospelaires, 215
Gospel Harmonettes, 219
Gott, Tommy, 260
Gottschalk, Louis Moreau, 23, 24, 232, 255, 264, 337
Graas, John, 315
Graettinger, Robert [Bob], 274, 299
Grainger, Sister Ethel, 194
Grainger, Porter, 146
Grant (née Pettigrew), Coot [Leola B.], 58, 133
Grappelli [Grappelly], Stephane, 339
Grateful Dead, The, 138
Graves, Blind Roosevelt, 205–6
——, Mississippi Jook Band, 206
Graves, Milford [Robert], 319
Graves, Uaroy, 205–6
——, Mississippi Jook Band, 206
Gray, Wardell, 277
Green, Charlie, 261
Green, Cornelius: *see* Lonesome Sundown
Green, Lee [Porkchops], 77, 175
Green, Silas, 58
Greensboro (Georgia), 84
Greenville (South Carolina), 117, 122

Greenwood (Mississippi), 85
Griffin, Bessie, 209
Griffin, John, 19
Griffin, Lovie, 19
Griffin, Ollie, 67
Guarente, Frank [Francesco Saverio], 243
Gulda, Friedrich, 324, 325
Gullin, Lars [Gunnar Victor], 339
Guthrie, Woody [Woodrow Wilson], 123, 133
Guy, Buddy [George], 113–14

Hackett, Bobby [Robert Leo], 244
Haden, Charlie [Charles Edward], 335, 336
Haig, Al [Alan Warren], 244, 295
Hall, B., 174
Hall, Vera, 18, 224, 316
Hallelujah! (film), 58
Hamilton, Scott, 332
Hamlet (North Carolina), 314
Hammond, John, 90, 122
Hampton, Lionel, 277
Hampton Institute, Virginia, 14, 15
Hampton Singers, 14
Hampton University, Virginia, 191–2
Hancock, Herbie [Herbert Jeffrey], 314, 329
Handy [Hendleman], George [Joseph], 299
Handy, John, 291
Handy, W. C. [William Christopher], 48–9, 126, 164, 192, 256
Harding, Buster [Lavere], 275
Harlem Hamfats, 85, 87–8
Harney, Ben [Benjamin Robertson], 24, 25, 43
Harriott, Joe [Arthurlin], 321
Harris, Bill [Willard Palmer], 298
Harris, Charles K., 152
Harris, Hi Tide, 120
Harris, Pete, 120
Harris, Wynonie, 93, 135
Harrison, Jimmy [James Henry], 261

365

General index

Howard and Emerson (publishers), 29
Howell, Joshua Barnes 'Peg Leg', 67
Howling Wolf [Burnett, Chester Arthur], 63, 104–5, 146, 175
Hubbard, Freddy [Frederick Dewayne], 325
Hughes, [James Mercer] Langston, 219
Humes, Helen, 282
Hungary, 338
Hunter, Alberta [Beatty, Josephine], 50, 52
Hunter, Lloyd, 234
Hurston, Zora Neale, 118, 120
Hurt, Mississippi John, 46, 47, 128
Hutchinson, Frank, 130
Hutto, J. B., 108
Hyman, Dick [Richard Roven], 31n, 331

India, 321
Indiana, 79
Indianapolis, 80
Indianola (Mississippi), 62, 109
Ink Spots, 29, 94, 202
Interstate Grocer Company, 106
Italy, 127
Ives, Charles, 232, 341

Jackson (Mississippi), 99, 106, 117, 127
Jackson, Bessie: see Bogan, Lucille
Jackson, Bo Weevil, 63
Jackson, Bull Moose [Benjamin Clarence], 94
Jackson, Chubby [Greig Stewart], 298
Jackson, George Pullen, 7, 8, 9
Jackson, Jim, 46, 50
Jackson, Lil Son [Melvin], 98, 125
Jackson, Mahalia, 200, 208–9; pl.14
Jackson, Milt [Milton], 305, 307
Jackson, Monroe [Moe], 135
Jackson, Sister Odette, 194

Jackson, Papa Charlie, 46, 60
Jackson, Willie, 57
Jackson Harmoneers, 216–17
Jacksonville (Florida), 47, 191
Jacobs, Walter: see Little Walter
Jamaica, 321
James, Elmore, 86, 104, 105, 108, 145, 165
James, Harry [Hagg], 275
James, Skip [Nehemiah], 63–4, 72, 86, 128
Janis, Harriet, and Blesh, Rudi: *They All Played Ragtime*, 30
Japan, 114, 127
Jefferson (magazine), 127
Jefferson, Blind Lemon, 60, 62, 96, 118, 119, 124, 130–31, 134, 143, 144, 153, 166, 167
Jefferson, Hilton, 261
Jefferson Airplane, 138
Jenkins, Bobo [John Pickens], 100, 157
Jennings (Alabama), 18
Jennings (Louisiana), 139
Jesus Christ, 1, 11
Jewett (Texas), 61
Joe Harriott–John Mayer Double Quintet, 321
Johnson, Angeline, 205
Johnson, Blind Willie, 205
Johnson, Bunk [William Geary; Johnson, Willie], 228, 235, 289–90, 291, 292
Johnson, Edith, 77
Johnson, Guy B., 7
Johnson, J. J. [James Louis; Jay Jay], 284, 295, 307, 325
Johnson, James [Stump], 144
Johnson, James P. [Price], 29, 32n, 56, 255–7, 319
Johnson, James Weldon, 15, 191
——, brother of, 191
Johnson, Lonnie [Alonzo], 57, 58, 61, 86, 101, 133, 143, 164
Johnson, Mary, 77
Johnson, Merline, 134

367

General index

Lynn Virginia: State Farm, 120

McAbee, Palmer, 171
McClennan, Tommy, 85, 143
McCollum, Robert: *see* Nighthawk, Robert
McCormick, Mack, 125
McCoy, Charlie [Charles], 64, 88, 133
McCoy, Joe, 72, 85, 88
McCoy (née Douglas), Minnie: *see* Memphis Minnie
McCoy, Viola, 51
McDaniel, Ellas: *see* Bo Diddley
McDowell, Fred, 124
Macero, Teo [Attilio Joseph], 309, 311, 324
McFadden, Charlie, 144
McFarland, Buck, 74
McGee, Dennis, 140
McGee, Reverend (later Bishop) Ford Washington, 17, 198
McGhee, Brownie [Walter Brown], 84–5, 99, 123, 133, 206
McGranahan, James, 190
McGregor, Chris, 320
Mack, David, 340
McKim, Lucy: *see* Garrison, Lucy McKim
McKusick, Hal [Harold Wilfred], 308
McLaughlin, John, 314, 339–40
——, Mahavishnu Orchestra, 329
McMurray, Loring, 233
Macon (Georgia), 121
McPartland, Jimmy [James Donald], 251
McPhatter, Clyde, 219
McShann, Jay [James Columbus], 293
McTell, Blind Willie [William Samuel], 66, 100, 121
Maghett, Samuel [Magic Sam], 113, 145
Malcolm, Horace, 88
Mamou (Louisiana), 140

Mangelsdorff, Albert, 339
Manhasset (New York), 122
Manne, Shelly [Sheldon], 304
Marable, Fate, 57, 236
Marlin (Texas), 205
Marmarosa, Dodo [Michael], 300
Marsalis, Wynton, 332
Marsh, Warne (Marion), 304
Marshall, Arthur, 27
Marshall, Reverend H. W., 213
Martin, C. F. (instrument makers), 165
Martin, Fiddlin' Joe, 121
Martin, Roberta, 200, 210–11
——, Singers, 211
Martin, Sallie, 210, 214
Martin, Sarah, 52
Martinů, Bohuslav, 338
Maryland, 190
Mason, C. H., 196
Massaro, Salvatore: *see* Lang, Eddie
Matthews, Artie, 28, 32n, 49, 74
Mayall, John, 137
——, Blues Breakers, 137
Mayer, John, 321, 322
Mayfield, Percy, 114
Melrose, Frank [Broadway Rastus; Kansas City Frank], 133
Memphis (Tennessee), 45, 61, 62, 68, 69, 70, 71, 82, 92, 99, 100, 104, 105, 109, 115, 125, 135, 166
Memphis Jug Band, 69, 151
Memphis Minnie [McCoy (née Douglas), Minnie: Kid Douglas], 71–2, 101; pl.7
——, Blues Monday parties, 72
Memphis Slim, 90, 101, 138
Meridian (Mississippi), 131
Merriweather, Major: *see* Big Maceo
Mexico, 54
Miami, 211
Michigan, 66
Mickle, Elmon: *see* Drifting Slim
Middle Georgia Singing Convention No.1, 17

370

General index

General index

Oklahoma, 95
Oklahoma City, 198–9
Oklahoma Ridge Runners [Buster and Jack], 130
Oliver, King [Joe], 57, 79, 234, 243, 246, 248, 251, 261, 292, 341
——, Creole Jazz Band, 79, 242, 251
Oliver, Paul, 125
Oliver, Sy [Melvin James], 273
Olmsted, Frederick Law, 40
Olsson, Bengt, 127
Opelousas (Louisiana), 141
Original Dixieland Jazz Band (ODJB), 237, 239, 240, 241, 242, 271, 337, 338
Original Eccentric Band, 338
Original Five Blind Boys, 216
Original Memphis Five, 249
Original New Orleans Rhythm Kings, 289
Ory, Kid [Edward], 237, 263
Osceola (Arkansas), 115
Ossman, Vess L. [Sylvester Louis], 32n, 228
Oster, Harry, 124, 148–9
Overstreet, Reverend Louis, 213
Owsley, Bill, 88

Page, Walter [Sylvester]: Blue Devils, 271
Paramount, 51, 54, 79; pl.12
Paramount All Stars, 136
Parham, Tiny [Hartzell Strathdene], 265
Paris, 112, 291, 337
Paris, Sidney de, 234
Parker, Charlie [Charles, jr.], 233, 279, 284, 290, 293–4, 295, 296, 300, 319, 323–4, 331, 333, 334; pl.24
Parker, Evan, 330
Parker, Herman [Little Junior], 109
——, Blues Consolidated, 109
Parks, Gordon, 120
Parrish, Lydia, 17
Patton, Charley, 62–3, 64, 85, 104, 105, 153, 217

Paul, Les [Polfus, Lester], 96
Paul, St: Epistle to the Colossians, 1
Peer, Ralph, 51
Peerless Four Quartette, 202
Pelicans, 94
Penniman, Richard: see Little Richard
Pennsylvania, 257
Penny, Hank, 93
Pepper, Art [Arthur Edward, jr.], 303
Perkins, Carl, 136, 303
Perrow, E. C., 48
Perry County (Alabama), 19
Perryman, Rufus: see Speckled Red
Petit, Buddy [Crawford, Joseph], 235
Petway, Robert, 85
Philadelphia (Mississippi), 112
Philadelphia (Pennsylvania), 207, 211
——, East Calvary Methodist Episcopal Church, 190
Phillips, Flip [Filipelli, Joseph Edward], 298
Phillips, Washington, 204
Phoenix (Arizona): St Luke Powerhouse Church of God in Christ, 213
Picasso, Pablo, 337
Pickens, Buster [Edwin Goodwin], 174
Piedmont (West Virginia), 261
Pierce, Charles, 252
Pierce, Dédé [De De; La Croix, Joseph], 235
Pilgrim Jubilee Singers, 201
Pinewood Tom: see White, Josh
Piney Woods (Mississippi), 216
Piron, Armand [John], 259
——, Orchestra, 259
Pitre, Wild Bill, 142
Pittman, Sampson, 120
Pittsburgh, 274
Plainsfield (New Jersey), 312
Platters, 94

373

376

General index

377

General Index

Walnut Grove (Georgia), 65
Wand, Hart, 49
Ward, Clara, 211
Ward, Wade, 240
Ward Singers, 211
Wardlow, Gayle Dean, 127
Ware, Charles Pickard, 5–6, 10
Washboard Sam [Brown, Robert], 71, 74, 88, 134, 146, 157
Washboard Trio, 71
Washington (DC), 265
——, Archive of Folksong, Library of Congress, 17, 18, 118, 121
——, Temple Church of God in Christ, 212
Washington, Booker T., 69
Washington, George: *see* Bull City Red
Waterford, Crown Prince [Charles], 97
Waters (née Howard), Ethel, 52, 126, 282
Watson, D. R., 160–61
Watson, J. F., 9
Watters, Lu [Lucious], 292
Watts, Isaac, 2, 7, 16, 19
WDIA (radio station), 109, 110
Weaver, Sylvester, 134
Weaver, Curley [James], 65, 66
Webb, Chick [William Henry], 275, 276, 283
Weill, Kurt, 338
Welch, Nolan, 74
Weldon, Will: *see* Casey Bill
Wells, Dicky [William], 261
Wells, Junior [Blackmore, Amos, jr.; Wells, Amos, jr.], 114
Welsh, Joe, 110
Wenner-Gren Foundation, 124
Wesley, Charles, 2, 19
Wesley, John, 2
West Point (Mississippi), 104
Wheatstraw, Peetie [Bunch, William; Devil's Son-in-law; High Sheriff from Hell], 74, 81–2, 143, 156, 173
White, Bukka [Booker T. Wash-

ington], 63, 74, 85, 109, 120, 128
White, Clarence Cameron, 14
White, Josh [Joshua David; Pinewood Tom], 83, 122–3, 164, 204
——, Carolinians, 123
White, Leroy [Lasses], 49
White, Newman I., 7
Whitefield, George, 2, 193
Whiteman, Paul, 246, 252, 259, 260, 274, 282, 283, 323
Whittacker, Hudson: *see* Tampa Red
Whittle, Daniel Webster, 190
Who, The, 137
Wilborn, Dave [David Buckley], 331
Wilborn, Nelson: *see* Nelson, Red
Wiley, Lee, 283
Wilkins, Robert, 206
Williams, Bert [Egbert Austin], 43
Williams, Big Joe [Joseph Lee], 85, 99, 129
Williams, Clarence, 50, 52, 54, 69, 146, 244
——, Blues Five, 52, 244
Williams, Cootie [Charles Melvin], 267, 277, 281
Williams, Douglas, 49
Williams, Eddie [Edward], 95
Williams, Ernest, 225
Williams, George, 57
Williams, Henry, 67
Williams, Marion, 209, 211, 219
Williams, Poor Joe, 125
Williams, Robert Pete, 125, 143, 148–9; pl.10
Williams, Spencer, 50
Williams, Tony [Anthony], 314
Williams, Willie, 226
Williamson (i), Sonny Boy [Miller, Rice; Miller, Alex], 104, 105–6, 109, 114, 170
Williamson (ii), Sonny Boy [John Lee], 89, 101, 102, 103, 145
Willis, Ralph, 100
Wills, Bob [James Robert], 134

379

Music index

Music and recordings discussed in this volume are listed by title or first line only; titles of other works mentioned are followed by the composer's name in parentheses. Composers and performers are listed in the General index.

Music index

Music index

385

Music index

Music index

389

Music index

Music index

Music index